A WOMAN LIVING
IN THE SHADOW
OF THE
SECOND WORLD WAR

Dedication

This book is dedicated to a wartime generation
who showed courage and stoicism
in the face of unprecedented difficulties.

In particular we should remember
the men of both Lindfield parishes
who lost their lives in the 1939–1945 war.

A WOMAN LIVING IN THE SHADOW OF THE SECOND WORLD WAR

*Helena Hall's Journal
from the Home Front*

Edited with an Introduction by
Linda Grace and Margaret Nicolle

Foreword by Peter Liddle

Pen & Sword
MILITARY

First published in Great Britain in 2015 by
PEN AND SWORD MILITARY
an imprint of
Pen and Sword Books Ltd
47 Church Street
Barnsley
South Yorkshire S70 2AS

Diaries of Helena Invicta Hall, 1940-1945
(East Sussex Record Office ACC 863/17/1–34

ISBN 978 1 47382 325 9

Printed and bound in England
by CPI Group (UK) Ltd, Croydon, CR0 4YY

Typeset in Ehrhardt by CHIC GRAPHICS

Pen & Sword Books Ltd incorporates the imprints of Pen & Sword Archaeology,
Atlas, Aviation, Battleground, Discovery, Family History, History, Maritime,
Military, Naval, Politics, Railways, Select, Social History, Transport, True
Crime, Claymore Press, Frontline Books, Leo Cooper, Praetorian Press,
Remember When, Seaforth Publishing and Wharncliffe.

For a complete list of Pen and Sword titles please contact
Pen and Sword Books Limited
47 Church Street, Barnsley, South Yorkshire, S70 2AS, England
E-mail: enquiries@pen-and-sword.co.uk
Website: www.pen-and-sword.co.uk

Contents

—⟋⟍—

Acknowledgements

—ɱ—

We have appreciated the assistance of the staff at East Sussex Record Office.

Dr Peter Liddle's involvement has been invaluable. He recognized the unique potential of the journal and encouraged us to study it in depth.

We would like to acknowledge Richard Bryant's involvement in the initial stages of this project.

With his knowledge of military history, Nicholas Grace has contributed useful comment.

Malcolm Grace and William Nicolle must be thanked for their support and advice.

We are grateful to Peter Leigh and Jim Topping for their technical support with the illustrations.

Hilary Whiteside was helpful in proofreading the initial draft.

Preface

—∽∞∽—

As County Archivist I care about preserving records for future generations so that we can learn, first hand, what it was like to live in previous generations. Without those records we would suffer from collective amnesia, living only in the present and with no understanding of how our society came to be. Official records, such as those of local councils and churches, play an important role in recording the past, and central government records give us a national picture of the time. But personal records, like diaries, can often show how national events did, or did not, have an impact on the lives and attitudes of individuals, which can help the reader to identify with them and to make those events more real in our understanding. This is just what Helena Hall's diaries do, taking the reader back in time to relive those wartime years in rural Sussex through the eyes of a remarkable woman.

I am delighted that Helena Hall's diaries, which were deposited at East Sussex Record Office by her executors, have survived to tell the tale of Lindfield at war and that Linda Grace and Margaret Nicolle have undertaken to make them more widely available in this way. The editors are to be congratulated.

Elizabeth Hughes
Chief Archivist for East Sussex County

Foreword

—⁓—

'July 16 (1940) Spent some time today and yesterday putting some papers and "precious" things into a suitcase to have ready in case of necessity.' With 'necessity' being the imminent likelihood of a German landing on the South coast of England, the immediacy of danger is captured in this diary, but with a practical reaction paralleled again and again as Helena Hall daily documents her Home Defence responsibilities, her observation of what happens in her immediate surroundings and the progress of the war as reported by the *Daily Sketch*, other newspapers, rumours and news bulletins.

When I first saw this diary its significance was clearly apparent, its author revealed as one of that special breed of person in many a rural, but not exclusively rural, community, providing, with others, vertebrae in that locality's backbone – cultural, historical, artistic and social contributions. By natural extension such people would have an awareness of the role which a village, in this case Lindfield, would necessarily play in great events which are determining their destiny along with that of the nation. Not altogether, but by and large, the events are rendering the pursuit of self-interest out of order. A positive response is called for and of course someone like Helena will provide it – and this lady, true to form, will keep a diary! How fortunate we are. The hand-written diary was subsequently well-placed in the East Sussex County Archives, its importance discerned by Linda Grace and Margaret Nicolle, who then worked prodigiously in transcribing, editing, supporting with endnotes and promoting the journal's worthiness in assisting understanding of the manner in which an individual, among those similarly or differently engaged, contributed to the work of the most minuscule cogwheels of the nation at war. They have now brought the journal to publication. A huge task and let no one underestimate it. They well deserve our thanks and congratulations.

If you were to have read so far, believe me you have hold of a Home Front gem. I liked, for example, reading that on January 26th, according to a newspaper, presumably the *Daily Sketch*, the Government was not discouraging holidays to France in the year ahead. I suggest that Helena was frequently matter of fact but this was not invariably the case, even though she attends an ARP lecture on 'Panic and Fear' and makes no further comment. She expands on the newspaper comment on Lindfield resident, Marquis of Tavistock, as an ardent pacifist. 'He's much worse than that. During the last 8 years he has been active in Communism, Pacifism, Social Credit, Fascism and National Socialism. He is pro-Nazi and accuses the British Government of responsibility for the war.'

Emotion of a different nature is displayed at news of the French surrender. She expresses 'sorrow for them, dismay for us'. On June 16th (1940), in a packed church, the *National Anthem* was sung and the *Marseillaise* was played on the organ. 'The prayers today were specially for France and her people and heartfelt prayers they were.'

There should be little need to offer further encouragement to delve into this book for illuminating insight into the microcosm of the war revealed by Helena's journalistic microscope, but I cannot resist this for both topicality and the fact that war may change many things but not everything: 'November 23rd. Most of the ARP wardens at Brighton were "on strike" last night, as a protest against the recent decision to dismiss 98 full-time paid wardens. They made it clear that they will come out in an emergency, but refuse to carry out "post" duties except on Sundays, until the men are reinstated.' Over Lindfield, Helena records four air raids during that night.

Well done Miss Helena Hall and well done Linda and Margaret who have served you so well.

Peter Liddle,
Mickley, North Yorkshire

Lindfield

—ᴍ—

Lindfield is a village situated in Mid Sussex, in the southeast of England. In the period covered by this journal the village was in East Sussex. In April 1974 Lindfield was transferred to West Sussex as part of local government reorganization.

At the beginning of the Second World War, Lindfield was a small village with a population of around 3,000 people, with local farms, horticulture, service in private houses, village shops and local businesses providing a range of employment opportunities and services.

During the war, troops were stationed at camps around the village. There was a lot of aerial activity over Lindfield and it was almost a daily occurrence for the sirens to sound, very often several times during the day or night when German bombers were trying to get through to London. A key local target was the Balcombe Viaduct, because it was part of the railway link from Brighton to London. As a consequence many bombs fell in this area.

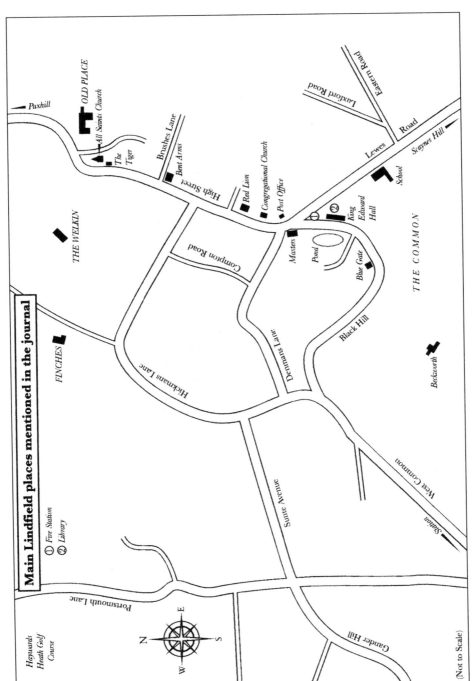

Main Lindfield places mentioned in the journal

Paxhill

OLD PLACE

All Saints Church

The Tyger

Brushes Lane

Bent Arms

High Street

Red Lion

Congregational Church

Post Office

THE WELKIN

Compton Road

King Edward Hall

Masters

Pond

Blue Gate

FINCHES

Hickmans Lane

Black Hill

Denmans Lane

Beckworth

THE COMMON

Lewes Road

Luxford Road

Eastern Road

Scaynes Hill

School

West Common

Station

Sunte Avenue

Gander Hill

Portsmouth Lane

Haywards Heath Golf Course

① Fire Station
② Library

(Not to Scale)

© Margaret Nicolle

Roll of Honour

—ɷ—

Lindfield Urban Parish
Patrick Ahern*
Patrick Bannatyne
Frank Beales
Frank Bedford
John Bigland
Cyril Boston
Wilfred Boyes
Frederick Bray
Herbert Brooks
Frederick Burlong
Ernest Clarke
William Comber
Thomas Dawes
Kenneth Dorrell
David Farncombe
John Gadd
Leslie Harper
Reginald Heasman
John Huddart
Edward Jourdain
Ronald King

Ronald Manklow
Dennis Massey-Dawson†
Ernest Mills
Harold Newnham
Fredrick Pearce
Peter Penny
Kenneth Porter
Albert Prodger
John Rowley
Michael Sturdy
Harold Tanner
Skipwith Tayler
Gordon Winn
Lindfield Rural Parish
Anchitel Ashburnham
George Buxton
Harry Jay
A.J. Pearce††
Charles Scott
Leonard Washer
Ronald Willett

Information provided by Chris Comber

* Spelt Aherne on the War Memorial
† Spelt Massy-Dawson on the War Memorial
†† First name not known

Introduction

—∕∕∕∕—

Helena Hall: writer of the journal

Helena Invicta Hall was a remarkable woman who had many talents and interests. She was a writer, historian, artist and expert needlewoman.

Born in Shoreham, Sussex, in 1873, Miss Hall was the youngest but one of a large family. Her father was an architect and engineer. She was only eleven years old when her mother died in 1884. After attending boarding school in Tunbridge Wells, Miss Hall went to live in Brighton with the family of the Reverend Arthur Gill. One of the children in her charge was Eric Gill, the famous but controversial sculptor, typeface designer, stonecutter and printmaker who was associated with the Arts and Crafts movement. Miss Hall then moved to London and became a student at the Royal College of Heraldry. Following this she developed her skills in flag-making and embroidery. One of her most significant works was a cross-stitch curtain measuring about 10 feet by 5 feet and containing over one million stitches. The curtain depicts the heraldic arms of the noble families of England set against a background of oak leaves and acorns. First hung at the Royal Academy, it is now displayed at Michelham Priory, Sussex.

She moved to Lindfield in 1920 and became actively involved in village life. She was a member of the Lindfield Women's Institute, the Bonfire Society, the Horticultural Society and the Lindfield Players. Miss Hall was the Lindfield Librarian for many years. She was responsible for the periodic issues of the *Lindfield All Saints Church Guide*, which she illustrated with her own sketches.

Miss Hall was a prolific artist. The work of the blacksmith as an artist interested her, and in her younger days she cycled to every parish church in Sussex, often camping out in a field overnight, to sketch all the old church ironwork she could find. A collection of over 350 of these drawings was left to the Brighton Museum, but unfortunately most were subsequently lost in a fire. She designed the wrought-iron altar rail in All Saints Church in Lindfield, having it made by local craftsmen.

Miss Hall was sixty-six years old when the war started. In addition to running the village Library, she volunteered as an Air Raid Warden. She was also involved with fundraising, sending parcels to Lindfield men serving in the forces, as well as helping out in the WRVS canteen. She applied her artistic talents to designing her own Christmas cards, and making flags and posters. Somehow, she managed to find time to continue to pursue her historical and cultural interests, including trips to London to see, among other things, exhibitions at the Royal Academy. Spending time with family and friends was important to her, and she made frequent visits to Brighton to see her elder brother Jock, who lived there.

After the war Miss Hall continued to pursue her interest in local history. Her first book *William Allen 1770–1843*, was published in 1953. Her next venture was to work with the Reverend W.D. Parish on a new edition of *A Dictionary of The Sussex Dialect*, published in 1957. This was followed two years later by her much-respected *Lindfield Past and Present*.

Miss Hall died at Blue Gate, her home opposite Lindfield Common, on June 11th 1967, just two weeks short of her 94th birthday.

The journal

'I expect your war diary is becoming very interesting and should make some very good reading after the war.'[1]

Miss Hall's cousin, Valentine Bassano, described the journal as '7 parcels of exercise books beautifully written and full of paper cuttings of illustrations'. It is fortunate that she had the foresight to recognize the potential importance of this journal and deposited it in the East Sussex Record Office.

Miss Hall started writing a journal at the outbreak of war on September 3rd 1939. As an amateur historian she must have realized the events of the war would be worth recording. We are unable to establish whether she ever intended to publish her journal. Our only clue is in her closing remarks.

The journal covers approximately 4,700 handwritten pages on paper the size of a small school exercise book. It has been bound into thirty-four volumes. Unfortunately, volumes one and two, which covered from the outbreak of war until the end of 1939, have been lost and it is a shame that it is not possible to see how she introduced the journal and how the early stages of the war were recorded. The available text starts with volume three on January 1st 1940.

The journal consists of a mixture of personal experiences, accounts from family, friends and acquaintances, as well as written reports from local and national newspapers, and radio news broadcasts. In addition, a key feature of the journal is the inclusion of material that illustrates and complements the written entries. This includes newspaper cuttings, letters, stamps, greetings cards, leaflets and other items of interest such as a ration book.

Miss Hall wrote in the manner of a reporter. She took a considerable amount of material from newspapers, but also expressed her own views. She liked to include little stories and snippets of information which amused her. The inclusion of cuttings of cartoons indicates a sense of humour not always evident in the written entries. We know she took *The Sunday Chronicle* chiefly for the Raemaeker's cartoons.

One of the ways in which Miss Hall experienced the war outside her immediate locality was through the radio. She liked to listen to the radio, particularly key speeches and important news, in the company of others, even though she had her own radio. This may have been something which people did for mutual support during difficult times, feeling a collective need to share and discuss important events.

An entry is recorded on virtually every day throughout the war until VE Day on May 8th 1945. Entries for each day were written continuously, without paragraph breaks, perhaps to save paper. At times the ink is hard to read. Occasional pieces of blotting paper left between the pages give the thrill of connection with the writer of the journal.

To have written the journal in such detail throughout the war could not have been easy, with so many other demands on Miss Hall's time, and it demonstrates commitment to her chosen task. It is as if the journal became a part of her daily life.

Miss Hall's writing style is engaging, moving between the personal, social, political and military in a seamless and random way. It is this eclectic style, together with her attention to detail, which gives a unique diversity and breadth of coverage, thus making this such an exceptional piece of work. In writing her journal, she defines herself and her position within the local community.

This was Miss Hall's war and was written from her perspective, reflecting how she experienced and understood it through her selection of material. Her skill was in the way she brought events together to tell her story.

When writing about village life, Miss Hall rarely commented unless it was something which either involved her directly, or which interested her. This placed her at the centre of village life as she saw it. Thus she wrote about her work at the Library, her war work and duties as an Air Raid Warden, and how the wider war intruded on her daily experiences. It should not, therefore, be regarded as a complete history of the war as experienced in Lindfield. One example is that there is only a limited mention of the evacuees who arrived and went to school in the village. However, the journal does produce knowledge of the village which may not be recorded elsewhere.

At the beginning of the journal there are accounts of how she enjoyed having tea with friends and playing card games with them. She also wrote about her passion for local history, spending time sorting through local papers. However, as the war intruded on her life, it also seems to have given her a new purpose, excitement and sense of importance and she gradually wrote less about tea parties and historical research and increasingly about her new activities.

Being an Air Raid Warden in the village provided Miss Hall with an opportunity for particular insights, especially on local events. She meticulously documented her ARP training and service experience. As might be expected from her ARP interests, air raids were noted in specific detail, showing their relentless frequency and how disruptive they were, for example to meal times and library sessions. There must also have been an underlying fear and uncertainty, even though she did not directly express it, although as time went on people may have become a little blasé about air raids, continuing to play cricket on the Common during a raid, for example.

Miss Hall wrote frequently about the weather. A subject that on the surface appears to be mundane, was for her of keen interest. Many days concluded with a reference to the weather, almost as a way of signing off for the day. There could be many reasons for this. During the war, there were no current weather reports in the press or on the radio so as not to help enemy invasion plans. Her references could be linked to air raids, as these may have been less likely during bad weather. Additionally, her Air Raid Precaution work meant being outside for long periods of time and bad weather would have made this a far from pleasant experience. However, it could also be simply due to the fact that in the UK our weather is changeable and often commented on, so it is therefore not unusual to find it recorded.

Miss Hall was fascinated by what was happening overseas. As well as using newspaper reports to record events in her journal, she was interested in carrying out further research to fill any gaps in her knowledge, such as spending time on June 29th 1944 trying to identify the boundaries of White Russia.

Miss Hall focused mainly on the war in Europe. She referred to the war in the Far East, but in less detail. There could have been several reasons for this, about which we can only conjecture. It is possible that less news was available from further afield. In addition she may have been less interested in this sphere of the war, which would have appeared more remote because of the limitations of travel at that time. Alternatively, she may have concentrated on the greater impact on *her* life of events closer to home. Whatever the reason, she did not continue the journal beyond VE Day.

The importance of the journal

Miss Hall's journal is unusual and distinctive and has much to offer the reader today. It combines first-hand accounts and personal experiences with reports of issues and events from outside her locality to provide a unique, fresh and fascinating account of the war.

Textbooks of the period have been written after the event, constructed with the benefit of hindsight, and subject to prevailing opinion at the time of publication. Likewise, personal memories of the period can become overlaid with subsequent experiences and changing interpretations of the period. This journal, however, is unchanged and in consequence fixed in time. It therefore offers a window through which it is possible to connect with the past, providing an insight into one person's life as it was being lived. Regular entries provide a sense of immediacy, of breaking news, with events being described as they unfolded and were understood. They show history in the making.

The journal shows us that people did not know how the war would progress and how they would be affected. It gives an impression of how the war intruded, not only into the life of its author, but also into the lives of local people. Air raids, troops billeted in the area, food shortages and other disruptions made it difficult to carry out the usual routines of work, shopping and leisure pursuits.

The breadth of content makes it possible to appreciate the scale of events and their impact throughout the world during the war years, with people being affected in different ways. This is particularly evident towards the end of the journal, where it is possible to gain an insight into the enormity of the upheaval wrought by the war, particularly in Europe, where it is recorded how millions of people had been displaced, and the reader can gain a sense of a sea of humanity on the move, advancing, retreating, surrendering, trying to return home. From the extracts one can imagine the scale of shattered communities and lives, a desperate need for housing, food and employment and the amount of planning needed to ensure the manufacture and distribution of items essential for the war effort and to support and feed the civilian populations.

Living as we do now in a culture where information is readily and immediately available, it is intriguing to note how information was used at that time. There are many interesting examples of lack of information, and indeed misinformation.

Manipulation of information in the newspaper sources Miss Hall used can be detected. It appears that she liked to read the popular press of the day such as *The Daily Sketch*, *Daily Graphic* and the *Sunday Chronicle*. Their journalists' selection and interpretation of material would have been governed by the political stance of the individual paper. Therefore the newspaper reports she was reading may have understated, exaggerated or distorted events. This is likely to have influenced her choice of material.

Lack of information can also be detected: for example, she often noted that a bomb had dropped, but she did not know where it had fallen.

Sometimes the information was incomplete 'In today's *Mid Sussex Times* a map is given showing where fly-bombs came down in East Sussex. But it does not give nearly all of them as one can check in this district'. (October 11th 1944)

It should be borne in mind that news took time to filter through to the public. One of the reasons for this was wartime censorship. The journal provides interesting examples of how it could take some days before an event was reported or confirmed by the government. It is noticeable that Miss Hall was aware of government censorship. When recording the German losses on the Eastern Front she comments on August 22nd 1943 'one is left to wonder what Russian losses have been'. Russian advances, and General Patton's campaign into Germany are other examples of information being withheld. On May 25th 1944 she acknowledges that 'Not much news has come through today – no doubt it is wiser to say little'.

It is significant that propaganda was widely in use at the time. It is fascinating to observe how, when listening to the radio or reading newspapers, she seemed to be unaware of the existence of home propaganda. She was patriotic, and generally did not question or criticize the British government's actions. However, she liked to identify the use of foreign propaganda, for example commenting on August 11th 1940 'German reports always exaggerate our losses and their claims are fantastic'. She showed increasing scepticism, writing on July 5th 1941 about the German/Russian conflict 'Reports are contradictory and one cannot believe either side'. On January 1st 1943 she wrote 'A propaganda film of *Germany's Fourth Christmas at War* shows festive seasons in Berlin, with plenty of food and drink and happy faces. The film was composed of extracts from 1938 newsreels'.

With the benefit of hindsight, her record of some events may appear to be misleading. For example some campaigns were reported as successes, which we now know was not the case. However, it should be remembered that this is how such events were recorded and understood at the time. The Dieppe Raid was 'said to have been successful despite losses.' On reflection we see the raid as a failure, although within this there were successful elements.

The victor in any conflict attempts to replace the cultural values and beliefs of the defeated with their own. The reader can identify this being implemented by the Allies when plans were made for the re-education of Germany after the war. Miss Hall wrote on September 5th 1944 about plans 'for reorganisation of the newspaper press of Germany to give German people the truth'.

Editorial method

This book is our edited version of Helena Hall's war journal. The detailed way in which Miss Hall recorded and copied out information has made editing the journal a challenge.

Miss Hall wrote 'Correspondents send long accounts of what is going on – interesting enough but too long to quote' (June 7th 1944). So she had already engaged in the process of editing when she wrote the journal. Even if at some stage in the future she had wanted to publish her journal, she would have had to edit her material further. In our view the inclusion of the whole or most of the text would have made an end product too lengthy to engage readers as fully as our edited version.

We did not want to produce a military history of the period as this has been recorded elsewhere. It was not possible to include references to every theatre of war, nor was it necessarily desirable, as to attempt to do so would have resulted in a superficial account. A local focus, which we initially considered, would have altered the essence of the journal because it would have belittled her extraordinary achievement.

As editors we acknowledge our personal bias. We have selected extracts which interested and fascinated us. At the same time, by careful editing, we have tried to include a cross-section of the entries to demonstrate the range of material. In order to achieve our aim, some years have been given more coverage than others.

We decided to include entries which refer to Miss Hall's personal experiences and interests as these will not have been recorded elsewhere. We were also anxious to retain as much of the journal's variety, character and immediacy as possible, aiming to keep the compelling sense of involvement which the diary evokes. To do justice to her work it became obvious that we would need to focus on certain aspects of her account. We chose to provide more detailed references to the Battle of Britain, the war between Russia and Germany on the Eastern Front and from D-Day onwards to achieve our aim.

The written entries are remarkable for their neatness, with few crossings out and corrections. However, Miss Hall's writing was not always easy to read, making it hard for us to identify some names and places. She herself may have found it difficult to spell some words which she had heard on the radio. We have made every effort to establish correct spelling.

Her word order and structure at times appear unusual and she often used long sentences with minimal punctuation. If left this could have caused confusion to the reader. We have tried to aid understanding with judicial use of punctuation.

The sentence structure reflects her style and the fact that this is a journal. Some of the material is obviously copied from her sources and is therefore fairly standard in presentation. Other passages are clearly written by Miss Hall and reflect her thought processes rather than being pre-planned. We did not wish to reword these passages as this would have lost their authenticity. We have therefore not altered or adapted the entries.

Every effort, including careful proofreading, has been made to ensure that the material used has remained as close to the content of the journal as possible. Brief endnotes have been included to provide further information where we feel this may be helpful.

However, there has been some inevitable standardization in the interests of clarity. The original text contained some inconsistencies, for example in the use of abbreviations and capital letters, which were personal and added character, but this became lost when transferred to print. Minor changes have therefore been made in the interests of standardization, but without altering the content in any way. We have not altered the way Miss Hall refers to money, therefore retaining the variety of contemporary usage. However, in the interests of the modern reader, minor changes have been made to references to time. The use of ellipses indicates where text has been omitted within an entry.

We loved the cuttings incorporated in the journal. It was incredible for us to see images which may not have been viewed since the day they were published in their respective newspapers. We wanted if possible to allow our readers to share this sentiment.

We found it extremely difficult to select images as there were so many of interest. We wished to present a mixture which would complement the written material and replicate something of the scrapbook nature of the journal. We are aware that the quality of some of the images included is variable. This is because some of them are photographs of newspaper cuttings, which have deteriorated over time. However, we felt they were still worthy of inclusion.

The many sessions spent in the East Sussex Records Office made us feel that we had come to appreciate Miss Hall's style and personality. We grew to admire her drive, enthusiasm, determination and commitment. We observed her at times domineering nature, while at the same time warming to her sense of humour, and sharing her sense of drama.

We feel privileged to have had a window into Miss Hall's wartime life, and to have this opportunity to communicate the magnitude of her achievement to others. Our aim has been to share Miss Hall's war through her own words. We hope that in so doing our readers will experience the events described in the same way as we have, as both a historical record and a shared and participatory experience with an impressive personality.

There is little doubt that Miss Hall would have been pleased that her war journal is now receiving recognition. We feel that we have done justice to both Miss Hall and her journal.

Abbreviations

—∞—

AA	Anti-aircraft
AF	Air Force
AFC	Air Force Cross
AFS	Auxiliary Fire Service
ARP	Air Raid Precaution
ATS	Auxiliary Territorial Service
BEF	British Expeditionary Force
CD	Civil Defence
CO	Commanding Officer
DFM	Distinguished Flying Medal
DFC	Distinguished Flying Cross
ENSA	Entertainments National Service Association
FAA	Fleet Air Arm
FFI	Forces Françaises de L'Intérieur (French Resistance Army)
GPO	General Post Office
HG	Home Guard
HQ	Headquarters
IRA	Irish Republican Army
LDVF	Local Defence Volunteer Force
LI	Light Infantry
LCC	London County Council
MC	Master of Ceremonies
MOI	Ministry of Information
NAAFI	Navy, Army and Air Force Institutes
PoW	Prisoner of War
RA	Royal Artillery
RAF	Royal Air Force
RAMC	Royal Army Medical Corps
RFA	Royal Fleet Auxiliary Service
RSF	Royal Scottish Fusiliers
VE Day	Victory in Europe Day
WAAF	Women's Auxiliary Air Force
WI	Women's Institute
WLA	Women's Land Army
WRNS	Women's Royal Naval Service
WVS	Women's Voluntary Services
YMCA	Young Men's Christian Association
YWCA	Young Women's Christian Association

Glossary of Key Places

—◆◆◆—

It has not been possible to include all local references.

Bent Arms	Public house and hotel
Chafford House	School for six children with learning disabilities at Fordcombe near Tunbridge Wells. One of Miss Hall's brothers lived there until 1936
Hostel of God	A hospice that occupied Beckworth House
Masters	Large shop with a store and yard on the Lewes Road
Oaklands	Local council offices in Haywards Heath
Paxhill	Large country house to the north of Lindfield used as an army camp
Scaynes Hill	A village about two miles southeast of Lindfield, once part of Lindfield parish
The Hall	
Village Hall	Refer to King Edward Hall
The Heath	Local name for Haywards Heath
The Parvise	A room in All Saints' Church which housed many items including parish records, pictures and early photographs
The Tiger	One of the oldest houses in the village, formerly an inn, purchased by the Church in 1916
The Welkin	Large Victorian villa used by the Army

1940

—∿—

January 1st Monday

Everyone is wishing everyone a Happy New Year.... After the Library Peter came and we sorted more of the Tiger papers and even finished the largest lot of those about Cuckfield Union, Removal of Paupers from or to the Village, Overseers etc.[2] This morning I had another letter from Captain Fawssett...

British Consulate General
Salonika

December 23, 1939

My dear Miss Hall

Really you are a wonder with your Christmas cards, year by year you produce a fresh one each one better than the last! This year's I think you have gone over the top for you could not do another to approach it. The one you sent me, for which many thanks, was taken off by the wife of the Consul General within a short time of my getting it, for she liked it so much and wanted to show it to many of her Greek friends as an example of how they do special cards in England.

Yes, do send me a signed copy of the Church Guide when it appears, I would like to have it out here to read and I know that I shall be interested. Fancy all those old papers and records turning up in the Tiger! You can imagine the workman of the day when it was sealed up smiling and wondering who would discover what was to him a pile of utter rubbish. You never gave me the dates of the stuff you recorded but I am guessing it to be about 100 years or thereabouts. Sorry to hear about Jock, remember me to him and pass on some cheery remark for I rather feel that we are all rather down by this terrible war now in progress. However do *not* pass this to Sybil who is doing her share of keeping an end up.... We shall all look forward to the New Year, remember 1940 is the centenary of the postage stamp. Great Britain was to have had a special issue to commemorate but doubt if it turns up now... Fruit of a seasonable and local nature is cheap otherwise things are expensive here especially all imported goods. The shops have stuff of German manufacture... but the German goods as a whole are poor quality rather Woolworth in looks. I am glad I am well stocked in clothes for to renew here would cost a fortune. Good luck best wishes and again many thanks for your card. Yours affectionately

Arthur Fawssett

...The 2nd contingent of Canadians arrived crossing in normal time with no interference thanks to British and French naval escorts. Their song seems to be *Roll out the Barrel.*

January 2nd Tuesday
At 10 o'clock this morning Peter came to help me carry 200 Church Guides to the Tiger. I parcelled them in packets of 50. We each took two but by the time we arrived at Bentleigh I was glad to leave one packet there for they were heavy. We came back for the rest and delivered them all at the Tiger. Just outside my gate we met Captain Cooke, home on short leave, looking very smart in his RFA uniform and taller than ever. As he had many friends to see I thought it kind of him to call on me. I gave him a copy of the Guide and one of my Christmas cards. He is in Scotland attending to some of those raids that so often occur off the Orkneys.... Two Nazi bombers were shot down by RAF machines on coastal patrol yesterday, one after a raid on the Shetlands, and another over the North Sea. The only casualties on the islands were – three sheep. By Royal Proclamation last night men of 19 to 27 inclusive become liable for military service this year. An Englishwoman Miss Clare Hollingsworth, known as the modern 'Scarlet Pimpernel' has rescued hundreds of Poles and Czechs from the Gestapo who were due for firing squads or concentration camps. Today she goes to Hungary saying there are 50,000 refugees there who need help.... Russia has decided to carry on the war against Finland, instead of waiting for the spring. Britain has informed the world through the League of Nations that she is to give Finland substantial assistance. Russia can hardly protest because she says she is not at war with Finland, but is helping freedom-loving Finns engaged in a 'civil war'.

January 4th Thursday
In today's papers we are told that a new *Catechism of Modern History* has been published by the Education Department in Germany, and is being circulated to all German headmasters. It is a great pity for it is one long 'lesson in hate', Chamberlain being the most wicked man in Europe. Two German planes were brought down yesterday by French fighters. It was first publicly admitted that Germany may be involved over Finland. At the Royal Academy this winter there is an exhibition of pictures by the United Artists Club or Society. Every artist exhibiting has agreed to give half the price of his picture to the Red Cross and St John's Fund. People in Berlin are short of coal and in many blocks of flats central heating cannot be used. The shortage is due to lack of transport rather than to

scarcity of coal. Railways are so busy catering for the war, that they have not enough trucks for general use. Some of the people are banding themselves together in small 'home clubs' whose members each heat a room in turn for the benefit of all the rest.... The first five reproductions of army badges are shown in the *Daily Sketch* today.... Mrs Fawssett, John and Bobbie came in to tea. We played the Belisha card game. I showed them some needlework Bobbie being specially interested in cross-stitch.

January 5th Friday
In addition to his main titles Goering is now Germany's Minister of Economic Warfare. A severe form of taxation is to be introduced prescribing the mode of living of every person in the country, fixing a maximum amount of income to be used for personal needs the balance to be subscribed monthly to a compulsory loan. This law will limit all private spending. It means though that the Nazis are taking off their coats to the fight. So of course are we. Some think the war will end soon, but it hardly seems like it. Perhaps the endurance will be the hardest battle of all.

January 6th Saturday
The government have just issued a new gas mask for children aged from 2 to 5, so that makes five different gas protectors or respirators as they are officially called; large, medium, small, this new one, and the baby one a kind of protective helmet. I think this new mask will be nick-named 'Mickey-mouse', for it is made very attractive to a child, a frontal of red rubber, two round 'eyes' close together and a tab piece of the same red rubber like a long nose. The harness is a bright blue elastic. They are expensive to make and are government property. Parents have to sign for them and give notice if they leave the district, and when no longer needed to be returned to us. There are only two children in my sector that will need this size, so Mr Parsons gave me two to take home.

January 8th Monday
Rationing begins today: 4oz bacon, mutton or ham (3½oz if cooked) and 12oz of sugar per week. Coupons will not need to be given up at restaurants.

January 9th Tuesday
Strong measures are to be taken against profiteering. Yesterday a wholesale butcher of Smithfield, Douglas Cooper, was fined £60 with £20 costs for charging prices in excess of the maximum allowed by the recent Meat Order. It was the first profiteering case heard in The City, at Guildhall Police Court.... At 7.15 Mrs Hill, Peter and John came to supper to partake of the chicken that Mabel sent me via Esther Dunlop for a Christmas present. We played Belisha rummy until 12pm, a happy evening, very cold night.

January 10th Wednesday
The Prime Minister spoke at the Mansion House yesterday. He warned the nation that the risk of air raids had not diminished and added 'Every restriction which the country is asked to accept is just one part of the general plan for securing victory in the shortest possible time. We have got to do without a lot of things we shall miss very much.' We have yet a hard and painful road to tread. There is talk of standardising suits and other clothing – it may not 'materialize'.... After the Library this afternoon I looked in at the Hall to see the children's fancy dress for the Infant Welfare Christmas treat: with their mothers they walked round the tree set near the middle of the room. The children looked delightful in their fancy dresses and it was difficult to decide which was the best of them. One little girl was an ATS, another a workbox and needlewoman with everything complete on her even a sewing machine in her hand, an 18th century grandmother by a 3 year old. And the small boys, John Bull, a pie-man, Father Christmas and many more. For a war-time effort and some things not easy to get I thought the result very good and the mothers must have worked very hard.

January 11th Thursday
I walked to Scaynes Hill or rather Bedales Corner and met in the bus Mrs Cooke and Donald for we were all bound for Lewes to choose the next collection of books for our libraries. Mr Ridgeway yesterday afternoon said he would take my ARP place. The bus was 10 minutes late at Bedales, not leaving until about 9.20. We all enjoyed the bus journey and it was pleasant to see the Lewes main street fairly free from motors and other traffic. We left there by the 1.23 bus and chose seats near the front to enjoy the warmth of the radiator. I walked from Bedales arriving home at 2.30 and after a quick lunch prepared the tea table for a small party: Ann Parsons, John and Bobbie Fawssett and Betty Mather. Richard could not come. We played card games and with the exception of Betty I saw them home, stars and searchlights brilliant.... Meat prices are now fixed, also prices of torches. It is still difficult, almost impossible to buy a new small refill, 3d for a small torch.

January 12th Friday
Farmers are having a better time owing to the war. By the spring, about 1,000,000 acres of derelict grassland will be added to the total area ploughed for food production. Since the Ministry of Agriculture granted its £2 an acre subsidy to farmers who plough up their derelict land. One Farmer West in Kent has turned 40 acres of 'bad lands' into a site for grain seeding. Berlin is having 37 degrees of frost. There were 20 here last night.... I went by the 1.23 train to Brighton to spend the rest of the day with Jock who was much better.... Many of the evening trains have been taken off and I had to wait 40 minutes at the station until the 10.28 went out. While waiting, many soldiers arrived on leave all looking well and

happy. At the Heath station the last bus had gone, but it was a fine, still, starlight night and I enjoyed the walk home.

January 13th Saturday
It seemed colder than ever this morning when I went to the Post.... At 3 o'clock this afternoon a demonstration was held of *real* Thermite incendiary bombs in the meadow at Oaklands. Mr Huddart called for me in his car at 10 minutes to 3. Peter Hill came to do the stamping of books at the Library to help Donald who took my place for the final 15 minutes. Misses Staynes, Merry and Bramwell were the operators with a goodly gathering from Lindfield, Cuckfield and Haywards Heath ARPs etc. looking on, screened off by a rope round part of the meadow. The actual bombs are only about 10 inches long. One was set on a piece of ordinary flooring, made for the occasion, then fired burning for 10 minutes or so much like a firework with sudden fierce splutterings one of its contents being manganese. Then the board was shown round by Mr Staynes so that we might see the damage done. Another bomb was placed and fired on a piece of ceiling.... Another was then fired and put out, each time after burning for 90 seconds but using the jet (which is wrong) on the flames instead of the spray (which is right). The demonstration lasted for 1 hour 20 minutes and everyone was very cold. We all stamped our feet, but nothing made us warm. It was pleasant to get into Captain Huddart's warm car and pleasanter still to be home in a warm room drinking hot tea.

January 14th Sunday 20th week
Lord Haw-Haw continues his radio talks which amuse those who listen to him.[3] All leave in the Belgian Army has been cancelled and all soldiers on leave are to return to their units. When I came back from Matins about 12.30 there were numbers of skaters and sliders on the Pond, some playing football, some hockey and all enjoying themselves in the sunshine with no cold wind blowing. I took a few snapshots to remember the Pond in war-time. It is not often the ice remains bearable for so long. It has been continuous now since December 29th. Janet Robertson came in the afternoon and we drank hot tea by the fire. She showed me her badge of the Land Army; a golden wheatsheaf within a circle and a small coloured imperial crown on the top: a colourful badge. No other visitor came. I wrote letters in the evening.

January 15th Monday
Jock's 79th birthday. I met Val in the Post Office and she sent Jock a greeting telegram. I thought I might as well withdraw my small balance at the PO savings bank and buy Savings Certificates with the money.... A letter from Jack Hall bore interesting stamps coming by air mail. He wrote a long letter from Bombay but of course must not hint about his job. All leave from the BEF has been stopped for a

time. Belgium has called up a further 40,000 men. Holland has cancelled military leave. Families living near the border in both countries are moving to safer areas. Holland is testing her frozen area defences; her infantry on skates are practising firing, lying flat on the ice.

January 16th Tuesday
The coldest weather of the winter. Road deaths from the black-out are high. In December 1,155 people were killed on the roads compared with 683 in December 1938. Accident cases are less numerous on moonlit nights. The new street lighting is not installed yet, things may be better when it is.

January 17th Wednesday
Dennis Massey-Dawson was Commander of the *Seahorse* and although we still hope there does not seem much to cling to... it is hard not to grieve although it was the death Dennis would have chosen.... A number of new 'evacuees' arrived at Cuckfield a short time ago. One little boy being taken to school said 'Lummy ain't they got a lot of sky down here'. Another boy was taken to Brighton and naturally his first desire was to see the sea. He stood gazing at it and when his guardian asked what he thought of it he said 'Well, it's the first time I've seen enough of anything'.

January 18th Thursday
No weather reports are issued in the British Isles at all, nor have there been any since war was declared. The knowledge might help the enemy.... I went to Brighton by train this morning... and was met at the station by Connie Hutton, driven to Telscombe in her car specially to see baby Patricia Mary, born December 8th, and say goodbye to them and nurse Betty before sailing to India in the *Britannic*. Connie drove me back to the station in the afternoon and the walk home at 6 o'clock by moonlight was pleasant.

January 19th Friday
This morning from 10 till 1 o'clock Donald and I unpacked and put on the shelves 240 fresh books for the Library, repacking a return lot. Today begins the 4th week in succession of skating on the Pond, quite a long spell for this part of the country. It was a moonlit night and at 7 I went to the Viking had supper with Val Bassano and Miss Papworth and played Rummy afterwards being joined by Miss Daniel who made up the party to four.

January 21st Sunday 21st week
From tomorrow headlamps of motors must be fitted with the official type mask, either to the offside or the nearside headlamp. Whilst 'blacking-out' the other

evening (a thing we all have to do), a little girl who was watching said the curtains must be pulled close together at the top, if not the gap would 'let the black-out in'. I went to Matins this morning. The Vicar, in the notices, said that as the RAMC had commandeered the Tiger the usual mission service would be held at the Vicarage this evening at 6.30.

January 22nd Monday
A year today since I fell and broke my thigh. I went for a walk in the snow to pay rates and leave a small present (a new half-crown) for Elizabeth M. who is 16 today. It was slippery in places, so I walked carefully. At the Library Mrs Allen told me the RAMC had commandeered St John's Hall and she was obliged to move her canteen to the Village Hall where room is cramped in the corridor. She wanted chairs stacked in the Library. I suggested the only place was under the table. The school children, or some of them, are also going to have their dinner at the Hall so difficulties arise all round. Peter helped this afternoon by stamping the books and came home afterwards for an evening's work at the Tiger papers. In today's paper a neutral observer, nationality not given, writes the first of a series of articles on *Inside the German Reich*.

January 23rd Tuesday
This morning Val Bassano brought me in some Savings Certificates for I had taken all I had in the Post Office to exchange into the certificates. She receives small amounts from various people and when they have completed the 15/- she buys the certificates. Rather a lot of trouble, but her War Work. They are stuck into a small book only 5x4 inches, twelve certificates in each book. Sixpenny National Savings Stamps are on sale at any Post Office. They may be stuck in a Stamp Savings Book which is given on application. 30 stamps may be exchanged for a certificate so every inducement is given for people to save. Each holder of a certificate has a registered number, mine is C.I.97.149.... Many MPs are pleading for less severe black-out which is responsible for so many deaths on the road. But fliers who go up at night over Britain to report say that any relaxation is out of the question and many houses, chiefly those out of sight of ARP wardens, are too light. The final decision must be left with the RAF.... This has been a particularly beautiful day, very sunny, quite still and not so cold. Cycling, football, hockey and other games were enjoyed on the Pond, the last snowfall on Sunday not being heavy enough to spoil the ice although it is rather rough. The air is clear. Venus and Jupiter very bright.

January 24th Wednesday
Many soldiers of the RAMC have arrived in the Village and a new arm to the signpost outside Masters' has been added. Black letters on deep yellow read Camp Reception Hospital which is Walstead Place along the Lewes Road.

January 26th Friday

The 26-year-old trade treaty between the United States and Japan comes to an end today.... The BBC is successfully fighting a strong Nazi attack on British news broadcasts now being waged all over the world. Hitler sent protests to all neutral governments against the use by their newspapers of news picked up from British broadcasts. Its accuracy is becoming appreciated in comparison with lying Nazi 'propaganda'. Spain and Bulgaria accordingly banned all news from foreign radios, but within a fortnight public opinion forced them to raise the ban.... Holidays in France this year will not be discouraged by the Government despite the war. This is good news for soldiers in France for those on short leave may find relatives in some French town.

January 27th Saturday

When I went to Warden's Post this morning there were four army lorries outside the garage, getting petrol no doubt. They were all painted a muddy green colour with broad diagonal uneven black stripes by way of camouflage.... At the Library this afternoon Peter did the stamping and helped in other ways because Donald had the afternoon off to go to a Brighton concert. I went back with Peter to have tea with him and afterwards Mrs Hill and I went back by bus to the station and walked up to the Broadway cinema to see *Wuthering Heights*, a good film with excellent scenery. It rained slightly, but so heavily when we came out about 9 that Mrs Hill telephoned for a taxi which stopped at my gate on the way to Bentleigh. In the *Mid Sussex Times* for this week there is a short account of Dennis which I cut out as he is such an old friend. The paper also notes the first summons for using an unshielded hand-torch in the black-out and shining it on a building. Even after being warned 'she' pointed it up at two clocks in South Road. 5/- fine, but more in future.

January 28th Sunday 22nd week

I never remember a day like this. After the heavy rain last evening there was a frost which came before the water had time to sink into the hard ground. The garden paths and the road was like a sheet of ice, icicles were hanging from the slates and reaching to the gutter pipes, 'dewdrops' of ice were all along the telegraph wires, bushes and leaves glistened like glass. I thought it foolish to go out for there was no foothold and for the first time I did not go to Warden's Post, feeling sure Mr Parsons would know the reason. At 9.15 he sent Ann round to tell me not to come. I hope she arrived home safely. I did not go out all day and every time I looked across the Common there was no one to be seen and traffic was at a standstill. There could not have been many people at Church for the simple reason that they could not get there. The paper today says Hitler has chosen the man who will be Nazi dictator of Britain when Germany wins the war: E. Wilhelm Bohle born 36 years ago in Bradford of German parents.

January 29th Monday
Now that it is a fortnight old the weather news, a State secret, may be told. It is the coldest winter Britain has had for over a century. For several days in succession 28 degrees of frost have been recorded here and in many other parts of the country. Rivers have been frozen. There was ice over the Thames. Early in January the sea froze as it lapped the shore at Felpham and the ice stretched along the shore for 300 yards. At Scotswood-on-Tyne the river was frozen so hard that shipping was unable to move for the first time since 1745. The record low temperature was at Buxton, 11 below zero. It is said that every 40 years or so a severe, cold spell recurs, the last was 1895. Yesterday evening a faint breeze sprang up and I heard what sounded like tinkling rustling on a bell-like pitch. It was the frozen small branches and leaves all iced jingling together. I have never heard it before nor seen rain come down and freeze immediately it reached the ground as it did yesterday afternoon. Today the country is white again and more snow fell in the afternoon. Walking therefore is safer and I went to Warden's Post as usual, and later to do some shopping in the Village. I noticed Humphrey's shop had the shutters up and wondered if all was well until I saw a written notice on a small square of white paper 'OPEN. Shutters frozen'. British authorities are complaining to the Low Countries about detailed weather reports showing winds and temperatures in England and Scotland that are appearing regularly in certain newspapers, some of which are subsidised by the Nazis.

January 30th Tuesday
The snow is deep today and the sky still looks greyly full of it. The milk-boy brought the milk on a wooden box sleigh for it was impossible for him to use the ordinary wheeled carrier. Last night the government urged people to economise in coal, coke, gas and electricity: also in beef and pork. Temporary shortages have been caused by the weather and saving helps transport.... In the early afternoon I ploughed my way up the village street to Mrs Hill who still attends to my troublesome toes and about 5 Peter came down for the evening. We went through all the Cuckfield Union papers, dating from 1835 to 1882. We enjoyed scrambled eggs on toast and crumpets for tea at 7. Humphrey's shutters are still frozen so that they cannot be moved.

February 1st Thursday
Slush slush again today and half the road of Pondcroft was ice. By treading in the deep snow and holding on to the low iron railing I reached Warden's Post in safety.... About 9 in the evening Sybil Barrow came in to ask if I could put up her friend Michael B. for the few nights of his leave. I remember meeting him here on Coronation Day when we got very wet watching the fireworks and then dried ourselves at the bonfire. He arrived about 12. He is going through the usual series

of inoculation against typhoid and expects soon to go abroad. He is a gunner in anti–aircraft artillery.

February 2nd Friday
In the afternoon Peter came and we went through the specially interesting *Removals of Paupers* in the collection of Tiger papers. At 10.15 we heard for the first time the bugle call of *Lights Out* wondering at first what it was, for it was not quite close.

February 3rd Saturday
At 6.30 this morning I was awakened by Reveille. I looked out of my bedroom window and saw the bugler just opposite on the Common path. It is the first time since the RAMC came to the Village that it has been sounded. The soldiers at Hillside on Black Hill would hear it. At 7 o'clock I hear them tramp, tramp, I suppose on their way to their canteen at St John's. At 10 o'clock there was a test siren from Oaklands. I pinned a notice of it to a board which I hung on my railing, and warned a few people about it yesterday. As the siren is not taken up by our warnings here, it does not sound at all loud, so folks are not scared…. Sir William and Lady Campion had a meeting at Danny on January 26th when a gathering of local people decided to form two flights of the Mid Sussex squadron of the Air Defence Cadet Corps, one to serve Burgess Hill and one to serve Hurstpierpoint, Hassocks and Ditchling. The kids from the villages joined those of Haywards Heath, Cuckfield and Lindfield and made them over strength. It is good to enable boys between 15 and 19 to do something for their country. At present there are about 230 squadrons in the country, all with an average strength of 80. The Mid Sussex squadron was formed last October and within two weeks there were two flights at Haywards Heath, one at Cuckfield and one at Lindfield.

February 7th Wednesday
Meat rationing is to begin on Monday, March 11th. It will be on a value basis 1/10d worth a week per person with half that amount for children under six. Poultry, liver, kidneys, tongue, oxtail, sausages and meat pies will not be rationed. Neither will coupons be necessary for meat meals in restaurants or canteens, although their supplies must be normal.

February 9th Friday
With Peter's help in the afternoon and evening I finished the Tiger paper of *Removals to and from Lindfield*. There has been a cutting NE wind all day and a cheerless time for the funeral of Ronald Manklow who was buried at Walstead, a military funeral. He had been in training only a few weeks at Hastings where he died of pneumonia, only 22 years old. That is the third 'war' death from this

village: Dark of the *Courageous*, Dennis M–D of the *Seahorse* and now Ronald, training with the Queen's Royal Regiment (West Surrey).

February 11th Sunday 24th week
The *Sunday Chronicle* today contributes a little 'history' in the newspaper world. For the first time a Sunday newspaper is printed simultaneously in London, Manchester and Glasgow. I take the paper chiefly for Raemaeker's cartoon which appears every week. They are always good, very telling. Dr Goebbels, Nazi Propaganda Minister among other titles, told foreign journalists yesterday in Berlin that Hitler had formed a 'complete idea for the future of Europe' and that he would either fulfil that idea or fall together with his regime. Relatives, mostly mothers, of BEF men who are in hospital in France are allowed to visit them under a Red Cross scheme. The first seven left last night. A special 'parents' hotel' has been reserved at the base for the visitors by the British Red Cross. The scheme is for those gravely wounded and in danger.... A number of RAMC men came to Matins and just before service began Dr O'Feely practised some of the hymns with the men. One of them read the 2nd lesson.

February 12th Monday
I walked to Haywards Heath and bought 18 oranges for those ordered from Masters' do not come. If I go to the Council and ask at the Food Control Department there I am allowed 3lbs extra of sugar if the receipt for the fruit is shown. No more is allowed than 3lbs per head, no matter how many oranges you buy. I had a letter from Hugh Hutton this morning. He posted it from Peshawar on January 7. I thought I had posted my Christmas letter and card in good time, but he did not receive them until January 5th. The envelope is stamped 'Passed Census' but does not look as if it had been opened. All good news in a cheery letter, but of course no war news.

February 13th Tuesday
This morning I went to Oaklands and met Mr Wilson, Donald and Mr Evans. Mr Wilson offered me the post of Librarian to the Haywards Heath Library in place of Mrs Cooke who is resigning. With Donald's help I am going to try it for a year. Mr Wilson came back and had lunch with me, returning to Lewes by the 2.16 bus.... Peter came to tea and afterwards we worked a short time only finishing the Poor Law papers. In the evening I cut up the oranges for marmalade.

February 14th Wednesday
Skating and sliding are in full swing again on the Pond. In spite of the thaw the ice did not wholly disappear before this next frost began. About 4.30 I walked to the Heath to see the Library there and Mrs Cooke. We had a talk over a cup of tea

at the Perrymount café and I saw some of the working of the Library which is larger but not so conveniently arranged as ours here at Lindfield. I walked home and in the evening boiled the cut up oranges for marmalade.

February 15th Thursday
I cycled to the Heath to do some shopping, buying an English hare at Sainsbury's for 3/6.... The Government has decided to spend an additional £400,000 on the Secret Service.... It was stated at a meeting of the Cuckfield Urban District Council last week that there were no paid ARP workers in the whole of the district which covers an area of about 120 square miles. The only additional expenditure is on the Fire Brigade Scheme.

February 16th Friday
In a letter today Jock tells me that H. Gill was lost in the *Fort Royal* last week. He was a Sub-Lieutenant, Gordon's third son, 27 years old.

February 17th Saturday
It is stated today, or 'revealed' as the paper would say, for with the writers today everything is 'revealed': its use is getting as bad as 'following'.

February 19th Monday
Slipperty, slopperty, slush and slime! The roads were bad, and the pavements were worse.... Peter helped me in the afternoon and came back with me afterwards. We went through the Lindfield Burial Board's papers, but did not finish all of them.... Sixty thousand ARP workers and volunteers took part yesterday in the largest air raid rehearsal yet held. More than 100 houses were actually destroyed by fire or explosives to give realism, 400 'dead' and 5,000 'casualties' were tended. London was 'raided' by waves of bombers. It must have been an exciting practice.

February 20th Tuesday
Every morning when I go to Warden's Post, and again later, companies of RAMC men are being drilled on the Common, a good place for the purpose and the curious bark of the sergeant major is heard all along the lane.

February 22nd Thursday
I went to London today with Wilma and we separated at Victoria. I went to the Science Museum at South Kensington to see models of a sloop, but the first floor where the models are housed was closed, all the models being packed away for safety. The custodian helpfully told me to write to Greenwich for the information I wanted. I went downstairs to the Children's Gallery, also an air raid shelter, and saw some delightful scenes in colour and models of ancient and other ways of

doing things through the centuries. On pressing a button the scene was lighted. A delightful place for grown-ups as well as children. From the Museum I walked to Central Hall, Westminster and at Hyde Park Corner and Victoria saw balloon barrages, those queer fish-like things poised in the air. Wilma and I met at Central Hall to hear a British Israelite lecture on *Christ or Chaos* by David Davidson. But he was ill, and the Editor of their paper *The National Message*, A.R. Hever, read the paper written by Davidson. It was disappointing and when finished difficult to say what it was all about. The room was very close, crowded with people, there seemed no oxygen at all. It was a relief to get out and walk to the Army and Navy Stores where we had tea. Then we again separated, Wilma to take a train home, and I to see the film *The Stars Look Down* at a cinema near Victoria Station. It was quite good, but gave only a part of Cronin's book, the whole would have been too long. The train I came home by was rather slow, but I was home by 10 o'clock. A mild and fairly sunny day.

February 24th Saturday
The US Secret Service is co-operating with British authorities in routing out a colossal Nazi spy organisation covering every port in the States. Already about 100 secret radio transmitters have been discovered. They were used to convey to an unknown headquarters news of arrivals and departures of British ships.

February 29th Wednesday
There has been a cold NE wind today. I did some first gardening after the snow and dug the ground for over an hour. Nearly all the vegetables are dead: spring cabbages, onions, the autumn-sown broad beans have not appeared and only a few spinach plants look as if they may survive. It is too cold to sow seeds yet. Soon after midday a sleety rain fell and kept on all the afternoon. Peggy Allen came to supper and we talked about the Haywards Heath Library post, which I have now refused partly because the work there would take too much time and partly because of the low salary they offered me. The Committee however must have reconsidered it for they advertised the vacancy in this week's *Mid Sussex Times* and stated the salary was £60 a year. They offered me £40 out of which I should have had to pay at least £6-10-0 a year to a helper on Mondays when our session times are the same. I think false economy was tried. It has failed.

March 2nd Saturday
There has been a good deal in the papers the last two days about the Marquis of Tavistock who lives in Lindfield at Barrington House and known to be an ardent pacifist. But he's much worse than that. During the past 8 years he has been active in Communism, Pacifism, Social Credit, Facism and National Socialism. He is pro-Nazi and accuses the British Government of responsibility for the war.

Another Fascist, William Joyce, working with Tavistock, is thought to be Lord Haw-Haw who one so often hears on the wireless. A leaflet headed *Germany's Peace Terms* was said to be secured by Lord Tavistock but in today's paper Germany repudiates the papers and says it is an invention from Dublin.... In the *Mid Sussex Times* there is a notice of Lady Bagot who died on February 21st. She did so much in former wars and had she been able would probably have done much in this war.[4]

March 7th Thursday
A fresh series of ARP lectures are to be held during this month and part of April. Instructions have been received from the Government that wardens' training is to be speeded up and we are to become fully qualified in the shortest time possible. A timetable has been set and for us here consists of a training course in how to deal with damage by incendiary and high explosive bombs and training in first aid work. The first lecture is tomorrow at 7.30 in the Village Hall. Mr Staynes is giving it.... Another sharp frost last night and cold all day. I made new curtains for the little bedroom which looks better now with a new bed and chest of drawers that I bought at Masters'.

March 8th Friday
Two old inhabitants of the village have just died. Mr George Blunt the tailor aged 74 died on February 29th and Mr Humphrey the baker on March 5th. He had lately passed his 85th birthday and was buried today.... At 8 o'clock I went to the lecture in the Library given by Mr Staines on incendiary bombs. It lasted till 9.45 and a great deal of information was crowded in, far too much to remember. Nearly all the wardens were there and our sector, no. 25, is to go to Oaklands on Sunday morning at 9am, not 10 as first arranged, full ARP kit.

March 10th Sunday 29th week
This morning I walked to Oaklands, meeting Mrs Robertson up Boltro Road. Mr Staines was in command and we numbered 13 altogether with two extra helpers to build up the fires in the large corrugated roofed building in the grounds. We had to put out fires occasioned by incendiary bombs in this building. First we went in companies of 4 one after the other crawling all round inside the building which was full of smoke. This exercise was to prove the truth of the statement that about a foot from the floor the air is clear of smoke, so it is of the utmost importance to keep the head *down* so as to avoid being hurt by smoke from a fire. We formed groups of 3: no.1 who took the nozzle of the stirrup pump, no.2 who worked the pump and no.3 who placed the two buckets of water and kept the one in use well supplied with water. Each one of us had to do all these parts in turn, the most exciting being no.1 who puts out the fires, using the jet for the fires and the spray for the bomb after it has been alight for at least 30 seconds. Also he has a small axe used for getting

furniture or other small obstacles out of the way, just hitting it aside with the axe. The pump has 30ft of hose and will deliver 1¼ gallons of water per minute. The jet carries 30ft and the spray 15ft. In the 'room' were two old arm chairs, some large containers of rubbish and paper and a holder made of wire netting attached to a piece of wood about 5ft tall. After each fire we filled these various containers for the next fire and Mr Staines put in and lighted a bomb. I got on very well in extinguishing my fire which was a large one. I put on another and larger trouser overall over my own, for the floor was very wet and messy and I am glad I did for the wet seeped through both. The practice took until 12.30. Jack Ward took me home in his car with Shepherd and Knight, which saved time for it had been tiring work, but the best practical practice we have had. We know something now.

March 12th Tuesday
At 8 o'clock Mrs Doyle, who is an ARP ambulance driver, went with me to the first of five lectures on first aid given by Mr Eastland in the Library on Tuesday evenings. On the 16th there is to be an exam which ARPs must take if they did not take the previous course at the Tiger last autumn. It was a clearly expressed lecture, followed by practical bandaging. I paired with Nesta Pennethorpe, Mrs Doyle with Mrs Robertson, and we were home by 9.30.

March 13th Wednesday
With Miss Taylor's help, I spring-cleaned my bedroom, and hope to do the guest chamber tomorrow. Among the airmen lately awarded medals was Frank Carey, a Lindfield boy. He has the DFM and was the hero of two encounters with Nazi aircraft both over the North Sea, one in January, the other in February. Frank Carey, called Fuzzy when he was a little boy in the choir because he had such curly hair, is 27 and qualified as a Sergeant Pilot in 1936. When in the choir the organist was Dr Pringuer Mus.Doc. and when I noticed Fuzzy was not in the choir for two Sundays running I asked him if he had left. 'Yes', he said 'I had a little difference of opinion with Dr Pringuer'. Fuzzy was ten.

March 17th Sunday 30th week
Early yesterday there were queues outside butchers' shops to buy the weekend joint. Coupons had been saved during the week and they were keen to get the largest joint possible before the general rush started. Most of them wanted beef, so *when* I draw my ration I shall ask for mutton. I have not used any coupons yet, there are many things besides fish that one can buy without them.... In the afternoon I went to the hospital to see Miss Oram who is rather better and Miss Sherwin who fell down on 'slippery Sunday' and fractured her hip. She has a pin in it. In the bed next to her was a woman from Ardingly who also fell down that treacherous day, broke her thigh and her left wrist. I am glad I did not venture out.

March 19th Tuesday
At 8 o'clock there was a meeting, in the Public Hall, Haywards Heath, of ARP wardens and officials to hear a lecture on Panic and Fear in a National Emergency given by Dr Margaret Grant of London. She spoke for an hour – very well. She gave advice as to the best way of controlling and assisting unstable people who show excessive fear during an air raid. Six of these talks have been arranged for March in different places in East Sussex, but not all by the same speaker. It was a fine evening so I walked to the Hall and Jack Ward brought me home in his car, very kind of him, where I arrived at 9.30.

March 23rd Saturday
Yesterday being Good Friday no newspapers were published.

March 26th Tuesday
Nazi agents have entered Britain with Czech and Polish passports issued by the Gestapo in Berlin. To sift the genuine refugees from the Nazi agents special Scotland Yard inquiries are now in progress…. I went to the lecture at 8. It was on Dislocations and on Haemorrhage.

March 27th Wednesday
The railway line from London to Baghdad is almost completed. From April 1st it will be possible to travel from London to Baghdad (Iraq) in 5 days, 1,500 miles. After getting into a coach in France there will be no change travelling through Switzerland, Italy, Yugoslavia, Romania, Bulgaria to Turkey. At the edge of Europe is Istanbul; the Bosphorus is crossed by steamer and the journey continued by rail.

March 28th Thursday
Captain Anderson, Director of Naval Intelligence is worried about the number of enemy aliens allowed to wander about the country. He says 'They make a marvellous smoke screen for the activities of spies'…. At 8pm all the wardens in our sector no.25, met at Eldon Lodge where Mr Fraser told us our duties on Monday next when we practise co-operation with the Fire Service. There will be one Major Fire, one Minor Fire and two 'No Action' reports to be sent in. We work in threes, Mr Ridgeway, Mr Ward and myself in one set, Mrs Robertson and Misses Shepherd and Knight in the other set. We report to Mr Huddart's Wardens' Post at Froyles, and they to Mr Horton's Post in Lewes Road. We then agreed our parts. Ward looked after the last 'No Action' timed for 9-12: Ridgeway gave in the first 'No Action' at 8pm and will be Producer for the minor fire arranged for at Grange Cottages, Townhill. I am Producer for the major fires which will be held at The Bent Arms and at Everyndens. The Producers wear a

white armlet, so that the wardens from other sectors will know from whom they take their instructions. The scheme is to see how long the firemen take to do their jobs. We Producers have to time all arrivals and actions, that is when they begin and are ready to tackle the fire. I made a copy of the 'No Action' incidents that we arranged. Ours have no gas recorded, but the other set put gas in their 'No Actions'. We are to wear full equipment, so I must go to the Library session with some of mine on. The meeting was over at 10. A very dark night.

March 29th Friday
A Supreme War Council of the Allies was held in London yesterday. They pledged their peace aims and also decided on the future line of action in the war. The new Premier M. Reynaud headed the French delegation. The meeting was attended by the heads of the fighting Ministries and Services of both countries. The joint declaration of peace aims looks beyond field victory to the greater victory of peace and is addressed not only to Germany but to Europe and the world.... A Heinkel bomber was shot down off NE Scotland yesterday. One of our planes, a bomber, found itself by accident over Holland and was forced down by Dutch fighters. One of the crew was killed, the others interned. The Dutch acted in a right and neutral manner; so did the Norwegians who interned a U-boat which went aground on their coast through mistakes in navigation. War on spies in our ports has begun vigorously. Armed soldiers were posted as sentries yesterday beside all neutral ships in 6 East Coast ports, severe restrictions being made. Officers from Scotland Yard are tracking down careless gossipers who are letting out secrets. No actual spying, but innocent leakages of information. As a counter stroke to German diplomatic moves in the Balkans, six envoys have been called to confer with the Foreign Secretary. Turkey, Greece, Bulgaria, Romania, Hungary and Yugoslavia are sending their envoys to London.... Since the Brenner meeting Moscow and Rome have definitely expressed their intention of keeping out of the war.

March 30th Saturday
Nazi agents are being increased in all the Balkan capitals in preparation for the return of the British envoys after they have had their conferences next week with Lord Halifax. So soon as the agents have discovered what our moves are to be, the 'whisperers' are to spread stories to counteract the moves. These counter moves will be so speedily organised that the Nazis hope to check plans before they are 'put across'.... Decisions were taken at the War Council on the 28th to close all commercial routes leading to and from Germany: in fact a land blockade as well as a sea blockade.... For the first time since war and black-out began we went back to the old times of evening session at the Library from 6 to 7.

March 31st Sunday 32nd week
To avoid losing the war of words the BBC is to enlarge the scope of propaganda broadcasts.

April 1st Monday
At 8pm I went to Mr Huddart's Chief Warden sector no.26 for our first practice with the AFS (Auxiliary Fire Service). After Mr Ridgeway had read a 'No Action' paper members of the 26 sector made their comments and requisitions on the incident which later will be sent in to Mr Fraser, Head Warden. Then came the Major Fire for which I was Producer and took the various times the fire brigades arrived and began their operations. Then came another No Action incident and finally a Minor Fire (only one engine needed) at Graham Cottages, Spring Lane, looked after by Mr Ridgeway. Here there was delay for something went wrong with the Compton Road sector, who were also working in other parts and the engine was diverted to Finches. All went well so far as our sector was concerned and I was thankful it was a fine and a mild night. I was home soon after 10.

April 2nd Tuesday
In answer to the Allies heightening the blockade Hitler is moving troops to the Hungarian–Yugoslavia frontiers and rushing commissioners to the Balkans for trade purposes. Every Nazi ship in neutral ports is to be loaded to full capacity and ordered to brave the blockade in a dash to Germany. It is estimated that there are at least 500 such ships in foreign ports and that 60 per cent will get through.... It is said that Germany's food worries are increasing.... Today I have been spring-cleaning the parlour and at 8 went to the 4th First Aid lecture given in the corridor this time as the Library was being used for another meeting. As a soldiers' boxing match was going on in the Hall our lecturer's voice at times was all but drowned. We had 'burns and scalds' and afterwards bandage practice for haemorrhage.

April 3rd Wednesday
The Prime Minister's speech last night warned neutral States that they must give Britain guarantees to limit their trade with Germany. Otherwise they will not receive goods of British, Empire or French origin. The Allies, he said, must deprive Germany of getting materials that enable her to continue her aggression.

April 7th Sunday 33rd week
There are no special headlines in today's paper, but leading articles point out that public confidence in victory is everywhere apparent.... Even so, living is expensive. By way of doing something I have given up taking *Punch* and call for my daily paper which saves the delivery charge of 2d. I propose putting aside the 8d a week and buying Savings Certificates when there is enough money.

April 8th Monday
After the Library I helped Miss Huggins and others prepare for their Home Nursing exam and stayed with those who are sitting for it in the corridor, where it was cold, until 10 when they had finished.

April 9th Tuesday
Just before 4 o'clock Dorrie Robertson asked if I would like to go over to hear the news. I went. Germany has invaded Denmark and Norway, and taken Copenhagen and Oslo. The Premier was speaking in the House of Commons and saying that Germany has made a false step. This evening in the Library at 8 o'clock we had the 5th and last First Aid lecture with bandage practice afterwards. The exam is next Tuesday.

April 10th Wednesday
In the early evening I went to see a neighbour about a light that shows too bright from a first floor window.

April 14th Sunday 34th week
It is serious that enemy aliens, free to live among us, are working against us and the safest course is to intern the lot. Before Hitler invades a country he plants his agents there. They were in Czechoslovakia, Poland and Norway. Holland teems with them. Their operations in Denmark made possible the rapid occupation of that country. A story is told of a little girl removed from London to the country. She burst into the room one evening and said 'I've seen a moon outside just like the one we have at home'.

April 15th Monday
In the afternoon Miss Nesta Pennethorne came to tea. Before and after we practised bandaging for our exam tomorrow evening.

April 16th Tuesday
At 8 o'clock wardens gathered together for our First Aid exam after the five lectures we have had from Mr Eastland. Two took the exam orally. We who chose to write it were in the Library and we had 49 questions to answer. I did not find them difficult. Our practical part was held in the corridor. I was given three breakages to mend: arm, head and hand. We all felt relieved when the exam was over and we could go home. We await results. A fine day with cold winds.

April 18th Thursday
I went by the 8.53 to Victoria to go to a war-time Thrift exhibition with a Nursery School section held at 23 Belgrave Square. It was arranged by Women's Voluntary Services and the rooms contained all sorts of salvage and waste material, garments

and toys made from scraps and items usually thrown away. The meeting was from 2-6. On arriving at Victoria I went by tram to the Tate Gallery as it is many years since I have been there. However I had to be content with seeing the outside only of the gallery for it was closed for the 'duration'. I went back and spent a good 2 hours in Westminster Abbey where there is always plenty to see.... It was a cold windy day, raining all the afternoon and I was glad of a taxi to Victoria after I left Belgrave Square at 4 o'clock. In the paper I bought to read on the train, a useful map was given of fighting preparation in the Mediterranean.

April 20th Saturday
This morning Peter helped me take some of the many bundles of Tiger papers up to the Parvise.... Leaving at home only those I want to transcribe and to make extracts from for my future history of Lindfield[5].... Four journalists have been interned by Nazis in Copenhagen one each from the *Daily Telegraph*, *Sketch*, and two of the *Daily Express*.... Today is Hitler's 51st birthday. Many happy returns to his blunders. World opinion is that he has made a great blunder by trying to conquer Scandinavia.

April 23rd Tuesday
St George's Day and I hung my two flags outside.... In the early evening Mr Fraser called to say I had passed the First Aid exam. He did not know the percentage of marks, but said I had passed well.

April 25th Thursday
Photographs appear in the papers today of the landing of our BEF in Norway. Every troopship was crowded and as a precaution all wore life-jackets and not one man was lost.

April 28th Sunday 36th week
There was a large congregation in Church this morning. Members of the Air Defence Cadet Corps sat in Masset's Chancel and the usual number of RAMC in the north transept. One of their officers read the first lesson.

April 30th Tuesday
In the early afternoon I cycled to see Mrs Loman of Cockhaise Farm in the interest of Marianne Ellis who wants to join the Land Army. Mrs Loman is head of the organisation in this part of Sussex and will see Marianne tomorrow afternoon when interviewing applicants at Brighton at Old Steine.

May 1st Wednesday
This afternoon a practice took place on the Common.... It was chiefly to show the

right and the wrong way to conduct such things as sentry work at night, bringing in stores etc. Many people gathered to look on and all learnt something.

May 4th Saturday
Yesterday evening at 8 o'clock we ARP wardens had the first of eight lectures on gas which are to be held every Friday throughout May and June, with an examination at the end of them. Mr Staines is giving them.

May 5th Sunday 37th week
The papers have many articles and 'bits' about the Norway campaign and of course much criticism of the Government in this country of free speech.... This has been a perfect May day, a summer's day. I sat in the garden to write this journal and a letter to Captain Fawssett.

May 6th Monday
In Narvik our soldiers are fighting in snow-storms and bombarding the town trying to dislodge German machine-gunners on the heights above the town.... Ten thousand prospective German tourists have been barred from Yugoslavia by the Government. Obviously the tourists would be mainly Nazi agents. Other countries do not seem worried about our temporary reverse in Norway and the towns we have evacuated. The first fortunes of war often go against the victor. The US says 'This small defeat will not affect the final issue'. At 8 this evening Mr Cox from the Haywards Heath Gas Company gave ARP wardens a talk on supply gas (not poisonous gas) and how they might help the Company by reporting damage to mains or to supply pipes to houses. All very useful and fresh information making one feel that gas is not so very terrible even when escaping. I did more gardening this morning and being 'bean week' planted my row of runner beans.

May 7th Tuesday
Our RAF and RAMC soldiers practised tent fixing on the Common.

May 8th Wednesday
The Prime Minister opened the House of Commons debate on Norway yesterday and naturally plenty of criticism followed his speech. But no division was taken. Churchill is appointed War Chief and in future is to supervise the operations.

May 10th Friday
Sir John Anderson introduced a Bill in the Commons yesterday providing death for sabotage in this country. Even if one conspires to give assistance to naval, military or air operations of the enemy, punishment may be death, 7 years penal servitude or a fine of £500.... A Dutch 'Fifth Column' leader, Anton Flescher,

was arrested by the secret police yesterday. His palatial villa in Haarlem was raided but no details of the discoveries can be given yet. His chauffeur was also arrested. Flescher is believed to be in the employ of the German Intelligence Service, and to be a dangerous spy…. At 8 o'clock we had our second lecture on gas. I sat next to Mr Ridgeway who told me the news that had come through on the wireless. Germany has invaded Holland and Belgium. Both are defending their countries.

May 11th Saturday
Mr Chamberlain has resigned and Mr Winston Churchill is the new Prime Minister. Mr Chamberlain will be a member of the War Cabinet. He spoke in a broadcast to the nation last night in which he declared that words were not enough to describe 'the vileness of those who have now staked everything on the great battle just beginning. The hour had come when we were to be put to the test'. He also said that Hitler had 'chosen a moment when perhaps it seemed to him that this country was entangled in the throes of a political crisis. If he has counted on our internal differences to help him, he has miscalculated the mind of this people'. Chamberlain made a dignified speech saying that now a drastic action must be taken if confidence was to be restored to the House of Commons, and the war carried on with the vigour and energy which are essential to victory. One salutes a great patriot whose efforts for peace enabled him to lead a unified nation in war, and he will be remembered for his integrity of purpose that made this possible. All the nation is behind Churchill who takes over affairs at the most anxious time we have yet had…. All RAF leave is cancelled and the Whitsun holiday is cut out…. The Dutch Army foiled an aerial attempt to kidnap Queen Wilhelmina. A flight of 16 Junkers, perhaps more, landed near the Queen's summer villa at Ruygenhoek each carrying 20 soldiers. But the planes were set on fire by Dutch snipers. She broadcast a proclamation to the Dutch people from Hilversum 'I and my Government will do our duty'…. All day yesterday and today our RAMC troops have been packing up and departing and only a few are left. I missed their tramp, tramp, marching up the street from Black Hill to their canteen at St John's Hall. A fine sunny day with a cold breeze.

May 12th Sunday 38th week
Nearly all the news in the papers is war news and accounts of battles going on…. I had tea with the Breffits and listened to the 6 o'clock news.

May 13th Monday
Since today is not to be observed as a holiday I thought it better to have the library session from 6 to 7 as usual. So in the morning I stuck a notice to this effect on the time and day plate outside the Hall, for I would not like anyone to think I was not 'falling into line', although it is unlikely anyone will come.

May 14th Tuesday

More soldiers have arrived in the Village. About 50 or more marched past the Common this morning at 6.30 but I could not see their badge. Hayden, who is fixing a geyser, told me that about 200 men of the Duke of Cornwall's LI arrived by train at Haywards Heath this morning, journeying from Cornwall last night. The Common is strewn with soldiers lying down enjoying the warmth and sunshine, all seem very tired.... When I walked up the village this evening I saw soldiers taking in their kit to the Hall so evidently it has been commandeered.

May 15th Wednesday

No Institute meeting this afternoon since the Hall is 'fully occupied'. The foremost war news today is that Rotterdam has surrendered.

May 17th Friday

In the afternoon a stoolball match was taking place on the Common; the girls who were batting teaching Tommies the game, very exciting apparently and many spectators.

May 18th Saturday

The Germans launched a new massive attack in what has now become known as the Battle of the Bulge. Fighting in this area... reached a terrific intensity yesterday and was described by the French as a veritable mêlée.... German troops are withdrawing from Narvik after an allied landing on the N shore of Rombaks Fjord.... Broadcasting House is being guarded night and day by troops. Soldiers were on duty there yesterday for the first time. Many other strategic points are also guarded now. Everyone has to carry their identity card and must show it when asked. Official estimates assert that the Fifth Column in Holland numbered 100,000 men and women. No wonder the country fell. Many of the German women servants in Dutch households were Fifth Columnists. Search in the homes of 3,000 Germans and Austrians in the big round-up yesterday produced many important documents which have been handed over to the Home Office. Many spies have thus been caught.

May 19th Sunday 39th week

Early this morning reinforcements from Britain, men and vehicles, were streaming across France to take part in the 'Battle of the Bulge'.... France has recalled to the Government Marshal Pétain, hero of Verdun in 1916. He is 84, flew from Madrid where he was Ambassador, and is now appointed Vice Premier of France.... A million pounds worth of uncut diamonds snatched in Amsterdam were brought ashore at an East Coast port in sacks slung over the shoulders of two Dutch officials. The officer in charge of the British warship that brought Princess

Juliana here helped to save the diamonds from the Nazis.... Soon after 6 a small party gathered for a service on the Common against Pelham House wall opposite my parlour window. A man held forth from a megaphone, but I shut the window as I wanted to write the journal. Many RAMC soldiers left this afternoon.... At 9 o'clock I went in next door to hear the Premier's broadcast on the War. His speech was full of grim cheerfulness and he emphasised the gravity of the hour. He spoke of the probability that after so much had been thrown in battle the full force of the German powers of destruction would be turned towards this island. If it came we must face it, he said, reminding us that every blow aimed at us is a blow diverted from the men at the front. The fact is we can all do our bit.

May 20th Monday
After the library session there was an ARP and police and special police meeting lasting from 8 to 10. The head of the Haywards Heath Constabulary addressed us and many understandings between both parties were settled especially at the time of an actual raid, and with regard to 'black-out' which has been rather slack the last few months. The room was full, all ARPs turned up.

May 21st Tuesday
At 8 we had a second practice with the fire brigade and the fire patrol, our sector 25 with sector 26. All went off well. I was with Warden Ridgeway and we finished at 10.30 when I was glad to go to bed after so much standing and walking.

May 22nd Wednesday
Bad news came through on the wireless last night and today the papers are full of the serious happenings in France.

May 24th Friday
Empire Day and the only flags flying from private houses have been Mr Jenkinson's and mine. A Jack was flown from the Church during the morning, but it was not up at the proper time. I left a visiting card at the school master's house and wrote on it 'Dear Mr Porter. Empire Day and no flag flying. HH'. I was on my way with Helen to Chailey Common where we took our lunch and as Mr Porter would have been teaching in school I should not have seen him. In the afternoon I received the attached letter from him....

Dear Miss Hall. It was most unfortunate that we could not fly our flag today, the rope having snapped. We held our 'celebrations' – the LCE children in the Reading Room and local children in School.[6] The local children brought pennies for the Overseas League – over 30/- in all. I can assure you that there is no other reason for not having flown the flag. Yours sincerely P.G. Porter p.s. Perhaps you have noticed the flag at my window facing the Common – PGP

At 8 o'clock we had another lecture on Gas by Mr Staines. He brought samples of gases in small bottles for us to become familiar with the scents. At 9 o'clock the King spoke to the nations, one of his best speeches. I went in next door to hear him. The distant boom of guns in France has been more noticeable even than yesterday.

May 25th Saturday
Not much news has come through today, no doubt it is wiser to say little.

May 28th Tuesday
The war news becomes graver every day. The situation in Northern France and Flanders is very serious…. I took Helen into Brighton to see her grandparents, Bertha, Cassie and Jock…. I went next door to hear the 9 o'clock news and before it Mr Duff Cooper spoke. He said that in spite of the bad tidings our army is not defeated and one need not despond of our ultimate victory…. There were not so many soldiers at Brighton as I expected to see. Both piers are closed to the public (we went down to the sea) and behind piles of sandbags we saw soldiers with rifles. Palace Pier was more armed than West Pier.

May 29th Wednesday
This morning a company of stretcher-bearers were having an exercise on the Common, much to Helen's interest. We watched them from my bedroom window and I took a far-away snapshot. They carried 'wounded' men back on stretchers and on their backs and while on one journey a sudden order 'Gas' was given and all masks were quickly on.

May 30th Thursday
Dunkirk is still held…. Mr Parsons called in to say that we must carry our ARP identification card and produce it when required to do so. It is a green card dated 8.4.38.

May 31st Friday
Thousands of BEF have been brought home in scores of ships: paddle boats, cargo boats, tramps and barges…. All signposts and directions which would help the enemy in case of invasion are to be removed…. I took Helen to Worthing this morning to see her mother and 4 days old baby sister Mary Elizabeth Swanwick Hall. We took our lunch which we had on the beach. It was low tide. Soldiers were guarding the pier as others were at Brighton and no one was allowed nearer the

pier than 4 groins away from it. At 8 o'clock we had another gas lecture in the Library and gas mask drill.

June 1st Saturday
There are many photographs in today's papers of the return of soldiers from Dunkirk and the marvellous way it was carried out.... Helen and I cycled to Lywood Common, had our lunch there returning by way of Horsted Keynes. Nearly all the signpost arms had been removed, a few on the by roads were still on.

June 3rd Monday
This morning at 5 minutes to 3 I was awakened by the first of two bombs falling. I thought it must be in my front garden, took my torch to see first if Helen awaked but she was sleeping, went downstairs and found everything in order. Mepham told me that the *Middy* writers said 2 bombs had been dropped at Forest Row, Ashdown Forest but no one was hurt, although particulars are not yet forthcoming. Windows were shattered nearby.... The ESCC sent me a large poster asking for books, magazines etc. for men and women of the army. I have put the notice on a board on my fence, because only a few people would see it on the library door.... Anything sent I take to the Post Office.

June 4th Tuesday
Many little ships have been employed bringing troops from Dunkirk.... Photographs of the bombs dropped in Forest Row are given in today's paper.

June 5th Wednesday
Dunkirk is now in German hands.... This evening about 8 o'clock there was a practice in the newly built Sunte Close, not all finished yet between the Fire Service and First Aid Units. It was not a lengthy affair, and I was home by 9.20. A house was 'fired', bombs were in the garden, 'casualties' brought out of the house, attended to by First Aid and were then removed on to stretchers and so into the ambulance.

June 6th Thursday
There will be many stories of heroism to tell of the great evacuation of Dunkirk when all is over, so many marvellous deeds are yet unrecorded. After leaving Warden's Post I cycled back to Fordcombe with Helen leaving here at 9 o'clock. Much to her delight the car with 'Hitler's Secret Weapon' chalked on part of its remains was still by the roadside.

June 7th Friday
I slept out again last night and at 1.35 an air raid siren sounded. I got up, dressed

and waited in case I was wanted for any job. The men in our sector are on duty at night. Soon after the siren there was a good deal of traffic, the mobile ambulance unit was ready manned at the Tiger, motor-cyclists passed at intervals, searchlights crossed the sky as a plane roared by (for it might have been an enemy one) and at a quarter to 3 the 'all-clear' sounded. There have been no particulars of the raid yet, but several counties were involved: Midlands, East Anglia, Essex, Kent, Sussex and Hampshire.... At 8pm Mr Staines gave the last of the series of gas lectures, our exam evening was fixed for the 21st.

June 8th Saturday
Mr Strachan-Davidson told me that a spy had been arrested in the village this morning. He was obviously a foreigner, had been watched as he always carried a bag and wandered up the Lewes Road. What he was after is not known.... The main hall in our Village Hall has been taken by the military for a store room and the officer in charge has locked the room. Unfortunately for me the keys of the library doors are missing so I cannot lock them at closing time, Foster thinks the officer locked them in the main hall by mistake.

June 9th Sunday 42nd week
An even more terrific battle is being fought in France.... Distant guns rumbled from about 3 o'clock to 20 to 4 in the afternoon. I supposed there was aircraft off the south coast. Mrs Scott-Symonds came to tea in the garden, and to talk over notices for her sale. She has arranged to have a one week's sale of antiques and bric-a-brac at her shop in the High Street, from June 17th to 22nd, all the takings to be for the British Red Cross. I said I would do her 4 posters and in the evening I designed it on paper 19x12 inches.

June 10th Monday
The Battle of Paris continues in all its fury.... A special National Savings week begins today. Val Bassano who collects here brought me down a board and poster, I made the board longer with a piece of stout cardboard and hung it on my railing.... I have spent all day doing the posters for Mrs Scott-Symonds for her Red Cross sale.... They take a long time to do.

June 11th Tuesday
Several friends here are reported missing and some killed during the Dunkirk episode. Colonel Willett's son and Albert Woodcock (RAF) are killed, and 'missing' ones include Kenneth Seth-Smith and Mrs Jourdain's son.... I finished all the 4 posters for Mrs Scott-Symonds and took them to her this afternoon, fixing up one on cardboard for Canon and Mrs Lea to display on the Manor House gate. I took one to the Post Office, and put one on my fence which is fast

becoming a hoarding. Books, papers and magazines are left with me every day for the forces abroad. The response has been very good. I take them over to the Post Office where they are collected every day.... At twenty to eight in the evening I cycled to Muzzell's Yard, Gower Road, Haywards Heath for another 'incident' staged by the Heath ARP. I thought it a poor affair, very slow and lifeless: no information was given about anything we were specially to notice and it was imagination to say we had learnt anything. It was a fine evening. I cycled home calling in at 9 to hear the news with Sybil Fawssett. Some people on Black Hill, newcomers, showed too much light last night, so I called to see them.

June 13th Thursday
I again slept out last night and heard many lorries passing along towards the Heath. I suppose some more of the soldiers here are being sent out.... Several dug-outs are being made here by soldiers. I have seen two thus far, one on the west part of the Common and another in Denman's Lane in the shape of a rough isosceles triangle. These are cover for soldiers to shoot from. At 10pm I made two calls on people who had forgotten to hide their lights.

June 14th Friday
If Britain is invaded we are advised to stay where we are. Certainly I should not leave home. Crowds of refugees on the roads have handicapped the soldiers of France.

June 15th Saturday
The delightful hot weather continues. I got up at 5 this morning to do some watering for I was too tired last night besides it is never a clean job and easier only half dressed in the early morning. News came through on the radio yesterday that the Germans have entered Paris, and today's papers report that they have advanced 20 miles south on both sides of the capital. And so after 70 years Paris is again under the German invader.

June 16th Sunday 43rd week
I went to Matins after going to early service and the Church was packed. For the first Sunday no bells are rung. Before singing the *National Anthem* (which we have done at the close of the service ever since war began) the *Marseillaise* was played on the organ. The prayers today were specially for France and her people and heartfelt prayers they were.... The war news is not good this morning.... Cellars in shopping places are now available as shelters for people caught in the streets during a raid. There are two here, one under Masters' shop (50) and another under Edmond's shop (60). They are intended only for those caught away from home.

June 17th Monday
At one o'clock today the news came through on the radio that France has given up the fight. It has filled us all with sorrow for her and with dismay for ourselves. At 3 o'clock I went to help Mrs Scott-Symonds at her shop for the Red Cross sale week. She had done well in the morning and taken £8, but only a few came this afternoon, no doubt the news accounted for that. I left soon after 5 for the Library where the usual number for a Monday came in. Now that raids are more likely to descend on us I have decided to pack away my favourite china ornaments and put them in a box under the stair cupboard where they will be better protected. They would soon be bumped off a shelf or mantelpiece with a near bomb. This morning's paper told us that Pétain is the new French Premier.... This morning at 6 o'clock a big company, I should guess about 3 to 400, of soldiers were drilled on the Common just opposite my house. I watched them from the window. The sergeant was severe 'Well if *you* call that a straight line I *don't*' and so forth. They dispersed at 7.40. After the Library I went to see the Robertsons and had a 'scratch' supper with them and heard the 9 o'clock news which was opened by a short speech from the Premier. He said that what had happened in France makes no difference to British faith and purpose and that we should fight on unconquerable until the curse of Hitler is lifted from the brows of men. 'We are sure that in the end we will be well'.

June 18th Tuesday
Although on one page of the paper it is said 'France gave up the fight yesterday', on another page we are assured that 'the battle continues along the whole front'.... We are told that the British Government on Sunday proposed to the French Government a solemn act of union, that France and Great Britain should no longer be two, but one Franco–British Union, the subjects of each country becoming citizens of the other.... This evening I criss-crossed 12 panes of glass with strips of linen pasted on to the glass: the hall door, work room windows and those in the little room. All the other window panes are small and protected by the wooden divisions.

June 19th Wednesday
Last night at 9 the Premier broadcast a speech lasting half an hour. He warned us that the 'Battle of Britain' was near and on it depended the existence of Christian civilisation.... I have fixed up my old garden hose length on to the tap over the sink which will be useful if there is a fire nearby. Keable has put a chain to secure the brass end to the tap so that when adjusted it will stand a pull. I shall leave it ready fixed every night and have decided not to sleep out any more in case I need the spray. It will be safer to sleep indoors with my equipment close at hand to get into quickly. At 8.30 there was another 'incident' staged by Lindfield ARP in

Masters' yard opposite the Fire Station. Mr Burn of Portsmouth Lane was the organiser, the lot drawn having fallen on him. Kent Street is very narrow and I thought it quite wrong to allow so many people, especially children to gather there and stand against the wall, baby in a pram, Dan in his invalid chair, children in arms, all were there. I did what I could to keep the line back, for it was more than the three police on duty could manage. Mr Merry, head organiser, was to blame for he said he wanted as many as possible to see it.... When I was at the Library this afternoon, and just before 2 o'clock, 8 or 10 military police came tearing noisily past on their motor-cycles. One thought they must have received orders for some important duty. Not at all, they turned off at the Common and had lunch under the trees. Swank. One came to grief by the Church. He crashed into a car, had his hand damaged and was taken to hospital in the ambulance. The WI members' meeting was held in the corridor, but I did not have time to go into it as Donald, his mother, who saw the accident to the soldier, and Miss Brazier came to tea in the garden. The WI notice board on the poplar tree outside Box was headed 'Lindfield' and as all names of places are forbidden to be shown I told Mrs Allen it must be taken away. The name of the Post Office is already away. It has been a fine day, rather windy.

June 20th Thursday
A lady lost her way in Sussex a few days ago and asked an 80 year old rustic to direct her. He said 'I bain't givin' no information'. He had a basket of chickens and was evidently going in the same direction, waiting for the bus. He was being cautious. The lady said 'Perhaps you'd like a lift?' He readily assented and they went together without any more ado. This morning I gave more notices to people with the name of Lindfield on their vans etc. One of the most difficult jobs is for Masters' to obliterate the name on their sun-blind.

June 21st Friday
At 6.30 Mary came and after tea in the garden I went for our ARP gas exam at 8 in the Library. Out of 8 questions on the paper, 6 had to be answered, 3 being compulsory. I answered 7. The papers took 1½ hours to write.

June 24th Monday
I went to the School where Mr Staines and Mr Merry spoke to the public about what to do in an air raid. Stress was given to defending one's house and to the choice of the safest place in it.

June 25th Tuesday
This evening I pasted linen strips on all the windows I had not already done.

June 26th Wednesday
At 10.45, just after I had gone to bed the siren sounded. I dressed quickly and went to the Post where we were all soon assembled. Mr Ridgeway and I patrolled our part of the sector, found a few people on their doorsteps whom we advised to take cover. One window showed too much light although it was not brilliant. About 1.30 a heavy sounding German plane was overhead and from its noise we thought it must be flying low, but it was high in the clouds and invisible. It dropped nothing here. At 3.30 the 'all-clear' sounded and we all went home, cold and rather hungry. I made myself a cup of hot Bovril and had some biscuits, and soon after I was asleep. I did not get up until 6.45, and none the worse for the 'outing'.... A travelling cinema has been lately touring Mid Sussex in the interest of the War Savings Campaign. It visited Lindfield Common last Wednesday evening and our WI President Mrs Allen spoke about National Savings, mainly to the women of the village.

June 27th Thursday
Today I made 2 boards to fit into the framework of the glass in my front door. I had to join two pieces of 3-ply for each glass and took them round to Wickham to saw. I covered the edges with velveteen to make a better fit and nailed on two tabs of the material to pull them out with. If the glass were broken the 'shutters' will be some protection against the weather. I shall put them up every night.

June 28th Friday
This afternoon I collected 10 gas masks from Beckworth, which have been given out to patients there, but had never been used by them. I took them on my cycle to Mr Fraser. The Mother Superior envied me riding a bicycle saying they were not allowed to, but they were allowed to ride a horse (if they had one!). Ellmer's, the fish shop in the High Street, was closed on Tuesday. The fat man who presided there has German tendencies. He has not been interned *yet*, but is being watched.

June 29th Saturday
The village seems quiet with nearly all the soldiers gone, doubtless more will soon be here. Mr Parsons came round about 8.30 to say that if I saw unusual yellow lights in the sky tonight I should know they were some new signals being tried for the first time.

June 30th Sunday 45th week
Mrs Pellet told me that at Paxhill last night a sentry shot his own officer. Apparently no reply was given to the sentry's challenge and the sentry thought it was someone raiding their camp.

July 1st Monday
I then went to see the Vicar about removing notices with 'Lindfield' on for there are many in the Church and in the south porch.

July 3rd Wednesday
The Premier has been inspecting coast defences and visited Brighton where many thousands cheered him. Large bodies of local men will be mobilised to help in the great drive to strengthen coastal defences. A new order bans civilians from beaches on all the West Sussex coast. This is because soldiers who are preparing the defences came from Dunkirk and know only too well how civilians can hamper military operations. For two days a curfew has been sounded from 5pm to 5am on Brighton beach and southern promenades. Whole areas of the countryside and beaches have been changed to a war zone. Camouflage guns command them and the sea. Some of the troops are armed with tommy guns from America, just arrived.... All this week newspapers have been one sheet less. They may get less still.

July 4th Thursday
I have never yet been asked to show my identity card, but many have. Only police in uniform or military officials have the right to demand it. Fifth Columnists, under various pretexts, try to steal the card.... Miss Carter who came to tea in the garden told me that bombs had been dropped at Brighton. One bomb fell in the garden of a Mr and Mrs Jennings. Mrs had a narrow escape. Mr Jennings' comment was 'The blighters have blown up my crop of potatoes'.... About 11 o'clock last night I heard either guns firing or bombs dropping and at least 3 thuds. On Tuesday night I heard one thud. On Monday at 1am there was a peculiar noise like a siren and I partly dressed and then decided it was not a siren, but what else I do not know. Then a very heavy lorry went by making much noise. It carried a huge gun. Yesterday I received a certificate that I had passed the Gas Exam about which I have been doubtful. However Mr Fraser wrote me a note very kindly a few days ago in which he told me I had passed and that I had written a good paper.... An accompanying note said I had received 47 marks out of a possible 50. I should like to know the points I dropped but papers are not returned. I think they should be, with comments.

July 6th Saturday
On the road just outside my gate, and at intervals on the Haywards Heath roads, there was painted today a circle in white with 20 enclosed in it. I suppose these marks are to show we are within the 20 mile limit of the coast.

July 8th Monday
Holiday visits to Eastbourne, Seaford, Newhaven, Hailsham, Peacehaven and

South Hampshire are forbidden under the new control of movement directions.... When I went to the Library after a tea party in the garden this afternoon, I found the door locked. The 'Army' had been in the Hall that afternoon and not content with locking up the main room which contains army stores, they locked all the doors. So I could not get into my Library, nor the men into their club. The caretaker was out, so we could not get his key and Mary Gibbs who had kindly cycled there then went for Mr Robertson who had not got a key and said he did not know what could be done. Finally the boss of the club was found at home and his key was fetched but it was not until 6.20 that I could get in. The gathering of readers who all wanted to 'help' take down the grills were sadly in the way but we got going at last. Later I saw Foster who will get Wickham to make me a duplicate key for which I have repeatedly asked. This is the third time the door has been locked 'by mistake'.

July 9th Tuesday
At 8 o'clock this evening the ARPs in our sector 25 gave a demonstration of how to use a stirrup pump. There was a goodly number of people. We got water from the tap in Captain Fawssett's garage and performed on the Common just outside his home. It lasted an hour and then Mr Ridgeway and I went to Beckworth and made an appointment to give the people there a demonstration. As I had been gardening all the morning, and out in the afternoon, I was particularly thankful that we had a quiet night with no sirens.

July 10th Wednesday
At library time this afternoon some soldiers were at their stores in the Hall, among them the man who locked the main door. He was very sorry about it, he did it without thinking.

July 11th Thursday
Canadian soldiers arrived in the village today. It now seems normal to have them again. We had another stirrup pump demonstration, in Pondcroft Lane this time, and after that I went with Mr Ridgeway to a fire practice chiefly staged for the men to know the alternative way to Backwoods Lane, which is through Beckworth gate and two fields.

July 12th Friday
Mr Duff Cooper broadcasted an appeal last night for recruits for 'an imaginary regiment, the Silent Column' composed of men and women resolved to say nothing that can help the enemy. He emphasised the danger of dropping scraps of information, sometimes vital parts of a vast jigsaw puzzle being pieced together by the enemy. As part of an 'anti-rumour' campaign a new poster is published.... I

have often wondered how the term Fifth Column came into being and what Fifth Columnists meant originally.... A Fifth Columnist, properly so called, is a man or woman who works against his or her country for the aid and comfort of the enemy, in fact a Fifth Columnist is a traitor.... Many of the most precious art treasures of Paris are to go to Berlin for 'exhibition'. Herr Otto Greif has arrived in Paris to make the selection. He went on similar missions to Vienna, Warsaw and Amsterdam, and treasures from there are all 'on exhibition' in Germany. Three girls came to the door yesterday saying 'ARP for animals, have you a dog?' 'No' I said, 'but there's a cat next door I'm always shooing off my garden'. They were taking account of all animals. More details of the central jam making are given in this week's '*Mid*'. It was begun in the Village Hall here last Wednesday, the 10th. The jam is made on Tuesdays and Thursdays in each week. Fruit must be brought on those mornings when it will be weighed and paid for at wholesale prices. The jam will be sold at retail prices. Mid Sussex dairymen have formed a Mutual Aid Assistance Pact. If an air raid causes damage to a dairyman's business premises, arrangements will be made for his customers to be supplied. On the Emergency Committee formed, Barnett represents Lindfield, and the district comprises of this village, Cuckfield, Haywards Heath, Burgess Hill, Danehill, Hurstpierpoint and Ditchling. Nearly all the dairymen are joining the Pact. Recruits for the LDVF no.5 Lindfield Platoon are needed. All between 17 and 65 not already serving in Defence may enrol at the Headquarters, Red Lion Yard, any evening between 7.30 and 9.30. I went to Brighton today and was told that in all the streets near the sea, curfew is enforced at 9.30, the time altering with sunset time. Sentries go along the streets to see that they are clear. No one is allowed on the beach, guns and forts abound. The London children who were evacuated to seaside places last autumn are to be removed further inland, North Sussex or South Surrey.... Boy Ellis has been called up. He gave me his printed letter of welcome from the War Office signed by the Foreign Secretary Anthony Eden. I think it an inspiring as well as useful letter. It was the first time I had been to Brighton since the names of the stations had been removed, no station names are now to be seen.

July 13th Saturday
Yesterday was Marshal Pétain's first day as Fuehrer of France, subject of course to the ruling of Berlin. Tomorrow the 14th is the anniversary of the fall of the Bastille, a day of rejoicing, but it will be observed as a day of mourning to celebrate the appointment of the new Fuehrer. His henchmen are: Laval, Vice-Premier; Baudouin, Foreign Affairs; Weygand, Defence; and Darlan, Navy.

July 14th Sunday 46th week
The Vicar is having another exit made from the Church in case of an air raid. It is through the most easterly south window in Massett's Chancel. I think it

unnecessary, our people in Church would not panic and many would remain put.... French fighting men are celebrating the 14th today by marching through the streets, laying a wreath on the Cenotaph at noon. They will march down Whitehall and along Victoria Street to put a wreath on Marshal Foch's statue in Grosvenor Gardens. They are General de Gaulle's French Volunteer Legion.... At 9 I went to Pelham House to hear the news.... The BBC commentator was Mr Charles Gardiner and the recording unit was on the cliffs, when the Germans, diving almost vertically, loosed their bombs on shipping in the Channel in the afternoon.[7] The RAF and anti-aircraft batteries combined shot down 5 Junkers 87 dive-bombers, and 2 Messerschmitt 109's. About 40 Junkers 87 dive-bombers used in Poland and in France were in action here for the first time. The action lasted an hour, our Spitfires and Hurricanes swinging about like trapeze artists. Millions throughout the world heard this wonderful battle, bombing and firing clearly heard and then the commentator 'Bang! Wallop! That was a bomb. There's another bad miss. That Hun is dropping wide – Hear that one? Good! We've got him! Down he goes' and in less time than it takes to run the Derby, Mr Gardiner was saying: 'Well it's all over. That's six of them down!' It was the first air battle I have heard on the radio, and thrilling it was.

July 15th Monday
Nine thousand children have now left the Sussex coast for the Home Counties. Many were sent to Brighton, but all have left now.... At 8.15 I went to our post for a meeting of all our sector to arrange about the distribution to the people of notices on the new Contex filters which are attached to gas masks.[8] We begin at the Tiger on Thursday the 18th, the days for those in our sector (no.25) being Saturday 20th and Monday 22nd. I promised to be there every morning from 10 to 12, the other times fixed for the work being 2 to 4 and 6 to 8pm. A deep trench is being dug at Scrase Bridge, for soldiers I think.

July 16th Tuesday
I spent some time today and yesterday putting some papers and precious things into a suitcase to have ready in case of necessity. Widespread havoc by the RAF is reported in today's paper.... I have spent most of today going to every house in my sector to give them the leaflet with instructions about the new Contex filter.

July 17th Wednesday
A former influential English businessman of Paris is acting 'Scarlet Pimpernel' to British people stranded in German occupied France. He has formed an Underground Organisation and emissaries escort them out of the German zone, provide them with papers and take them to and over frontiers.... No traffic passes along the road outside my house from Black Hill to Lindfield. Extra special police

are diverting it along other roads. It is a military practice, or as they call it 'manoeuvres'. So it seems extra peaceful.... In the evening Mr Parsons, Mr Ridgeway and I went to Beckworth and gave the nurses and staff there the stirrup pump demonstration which had been postponed on three occasions owing to wet evenings. The Hostel has its own pump and plenty of water buckets, the roof attics have been cleared and sanded, in fact everything possible has been done from headquarters for the safety of the patients. When I came home I wrote out a list of the houses and names of those who have gas masks needing the new Contex filter, 179 in my patrol portion, Pondcroft Road to Black Hill.

July 18th Thursday
I went up to the Tiger this morning and from 10 to 12 helped to fix the Contex filters to gas masks, a simple procedure only needing slight practice. Two feet of sticky (very sticky) black paper is cut off a large roll and bound round the two pieces, the new piece being a transparent bright green, then smoothed down with a toothbrush handle or like object. Mr Fraser has made us two little gadgets of wood for the purpose which are very easy to use. Today's paper gives an account of the wreckage of one of Germany's main canal systems by our RAF bombers.... French people are not allowed to read the truth in their own newspapers. But they are getting it from papers delivered to them from Britain by air. These newspapers, prepared by General de Gaulle in London, have been dropped over France by plane.... The other day in the street a little girl saw a one-armed soldier and asked her mother if his arm would ever grow again. On being told 'No' she said 'Well if the Lord made us I think he ought to keep us in repair don't you?'

July 19th Friday
Goebbels' latest piece of humour for Germans is 'Britain is so terrified of invasion that she is burying all tombstones for fear they will give information to our parachutists'.... Today and onwards our Chief Wardens have their helmets white and the W black, just the reverse of ours. The reason for the alteration is to make the Chief Wardens easily distinguished.

July 20th Saturday
In a letter to the paper it is suggested that the public should be taught German for 'Hands up. You are my prisoner' (in case of parachutists).... I went up to the Tiger from 2 to 4 for gas filter fitting, the first day of our sector. We were fairly busy. Mr Parsons in the chair, that is he checked the names and addresses of the people for there are many alterations since our list was made nearly 2 years ago. Mr Ridgeway, Knight and I fitted. When library time was over, John Ash came in looking very well in his seaman-rating uniform. He is training at Skegness and doing well and enjoying the 2 day leave.

July 21st Sunday 47th week

There is a great deal in the paper about Hitler's speech and peace terms, but Britain's official reply will not be heard until tomorrow. No German peace will be made anyhow, so details are unimportant.... In Northern France churches are compelled to distribute a leaflet as worshippers leave headed *The New State Order and Religion*. It declares 'In future the symbol of your faith is the hooked cross' (swastika). Under it, the State of Adolph calls to the Church and the Church must listen to its call.

July 23rd Tuesday

Lord Halifax spoke last night giving Hitler the official answer he was waiting for before deciding on his next move against Britain. Lord Halifax said 'Britain will not stop fighting till freedom for ourselves, and others, is secure'. Almost before he had finished speaking the Nazi radio offensive began urging us to accept Hitler's so-called appeal to reason, emphasising that this was Britain's last chance to save herself.

July 24th Wednesday

Pétain's Cabinet last night deprived all Frenchmen who left France between May 10th and June 20th, without authority, of their citizenship, property and fortunes.... Beginning today, Brighton beach between the 2 piers, will be open for bathing from 9.30 to 6.30 every day. During that time all the promenade to Black Rock and the promenade at Hove will be open.... About 9.30 just after lighting up time, I went to Mrs Whitley's to find out about a Luxford Road light and stayed till 10.40, but no light showed this night.

July 25th Thursday

I went to Brighton to see Jock before he goes to the Eye Hospital for his cataract operation. On account of constant raids many people are leaving Brighton and Hove. The two largest hotels, the Metropole and the Grand, have been forced to close.... We had some tea that was new to me called Maté, drunk without milk, something like other herb teas, quite pleasant but not tea. Probably one would get to like it better in time. At 10.15 I went along Luxford Road with Mr Parsons to see about the window light there.

July 27th Saturday

I cycled to Mr Fraser's this morning with another unused gas mask from Beckworth. On the way I passed a car with the latest slogan on it in red letters across the windscreen, the first I have seen, 'Stay Put'. People are far too inclined to move about thinking one place is safer than another. Often they come back to where they lived before.

July 30th Tuesday

I receive a number of letters now with a 'saving of paper' on the envelope flap, an economy that will disappear with the war. The slip makes the envelope easy to use again for it is not stuck down.... Pétain and his Government have passed death sentences on all Frenchmen serving with de Gaulle. But it has not made much impression on the loyal troops.

July 31st Wednesday

For three hours this morning soldiers, chiefly New Zealanders, their equipment, armoured cars and Bren guns made their way through the village from along the Lewes Road towards Ardingly. The Women's Institute had a good Produce Show at Mrs Hobbs, Tall Oaks, very well staged in her garden. I showed my American yellow stringless beans grown from seeds Phyl gave me. I am trying to find out their proper name and where to buy the seed so that others may grow them too. Seeds are not to be had here, nor anywhere.... This was the last afternoon at the Library before closing for August, until August 31st when we open again.

August 2nd Friday

This morning three mounted Bren guns rode down the street towards the Heath. The carriages, men and guns all were the same inconspicuous khaki, difficult to spot I should think. About 11 when I was gardening yesterday I heard the noise like an electric Hoover that announces a fire practice over the Pond. I ran upstairs for my camera and went out to take a few snapshots although the weather was dull for good photographic results. Eight army lorries were drawn up by the side of the hedge on the Common at Black Hill. A number of soldiers of a Scotch regiment arrive in the village tomorrow and on my way to the station to go to Brighton Eye Hospital to see Jock after his operation, I saw several lorry loads of soldiers going this way. A good number are billeted at The Welkin, the Jourdains having left their house, so it is said but the Welkin seems too good a house for ordinary billeting.

August 3rd Saturday

A vast Japanese espionage network operating against the British Empire has been discovered and accordingly arrests are being made.... General de Gaulle has been sentenced to death by a military court in France, the charges being treason, desertion and an attempt against the outside safety of the State. He says he will settle with them after the victory. German leaflets dropped in Southern England and Wales yesterday were looked upon as a joke and found a quick sale as souvenirs to aid the Red Cross. I should like to pick up one of them for this journal. I hope he will drop some more.... More air raid shelters are to be made in the village, one for the schoolchildren on the Common adjoining the school, and another at the Tiger which would hold 32 people, the estimated cost £25. It would be made in the Tiger cellar. I saw two men from the Council descend there one morning when we were fixing the mask filters. It is the cellar where the drink used to be stored when the Tiger was an inn. The hook for the chain for lowering purposes is still to be seen.... Our identity cards are to be more often asked for, but I have never been asked to show mine. A cautious Sussex villager, of whom a motorist inquired the way, replied he had better see the driver's identity card. The motorist complied. 'And now hadn't I better see yours?' he said. 'Oh no' replied the villager 'Oi knows who oi be'.

August 4th Sunday 49th week
Queen Elizabeth is 40 today, but because of the war the bells of St George's Windsor will not ring and there will not be the usual ceremonies. She has already given away most of her birthday presents.

August 5th Monday
The leaflet *Stay where you are* was in the letter box this morning. Copies are being delivered by the postmen to every house in the country. At 7.30 a company of Scots were being drilled on the Common opposite my house. I took a snapshot from the front door and did not care to go closer for I think it is not allowable to take snapshots of the military, harmless though the scene is.... Concrete emplacements are being built in many places now, chiefly at crossroads to make motor or other traffic difficult. There is quite a collection of them at Sussex Square where the road crosses the Scaynes Hill, Ditchling, Lindfield and Haywards Heath roads. I should think the barriers would also impede our own motor units, like many ideas it will hit both ways.

August 6th Tuesday
The US have declined to send food to the hungry peoples of Europe which would only undo our blockade, much as we dislike helping to starve those we regard as friends and hope still to benefit. No doubt Americans will find it just as hard as we do.... The red Cross of Lorraine, the emblem carried by Joan of Arc, has been adopted by General de Gaulle for his forces in addition to the national flag. Warships will fly the Tricolour at the stern and the Cross of Lorraine at the bows.... Before going to see Jock in the Eye Hospital this afternoon I went down to Brighton sea front to see if the rumour current here that the piers or one of them had been blown up for our own defence was true or not. Both the piers are standing but in the middle of each a space has been made by blowing up. Palace Pier was blown last night, West Pier early this morning. It is a clever piece of work, for any one going on to the pier, or landing at the sea end, could not possibly see the vacant place. If therefore the Germans did try the landing stages they would not get far without disaster. One can hardly recognize Brighton beach, at this time

of year usually crowded with holiday folk all gay and happy. And now there is first, nearest the sea a line of barbed wire festooned entanglements supported at intervals on posts. Next on the flat beach there are mines, all fairly close to one another, circular with white tops, then another line of barbed wire similar to the other. The place was alive with soldiers, some laying the mines. In one place were a number of blocks, wood I should think, painted white and in red letters 'danger, laid mines'. Along the sea front in several places are erections with holes on all sides, obviously for men to shoot from. Shops are holding their sales just the same, but one misses the usual crowds.

August 8th Thursday
Lindfield Fair Day, but there is no fair this year.... Worthing Council has now banned bathing along the whole of its sea front thus following Brighton's example.

August 9th Friday
A new British radio station from which multi-lingual broadcasts will be made is to be erected in Singapore. It will be an important link in the British world radio chain.

August 11th Sunday 50th week
When I came down from Church this morning I saw a motor army lorry treated in a new way. Over the jazz pattern was a net to which was attached fluttering pieces of green material. When stationary no doubt it would look just like a bush. The Nazis are accusing us of two crimes, of prolonging the war (because we refuse their peace terms) and of starving Europe. But if Hitler cleared out of his conquered territories and gave them back their freedom all would be well and no starvation. This evening after the 9 o'clock news J.B. Priestley gave one of his interesting talks. His subject was the introduction by the Minister of Munitions of entertainments during the off-time of workers in the factories where both men and women work. The innovation is a complete success, or as Priestley said 'sound as a rock'. German reports always exaggerate our losses and their own claims are fantastic.

August 13th Thursday
We are soon to have a French newspaper, prepared by de Gaulle's experts, supervised by the Ministry of Information, Treasury financed.... Bradley and Vaughan suggest that people should have an inventory of their goods and chattels for if one's house was bombed it would be difficult to assess values.[9] They have brought out a pamphlet *War Damage to Property – Government Compensation Scheme*. It is a practical suggestion and this afternoon their Mr Egerton came to make an inventory of my property.

August 14th Wednesday
I went to Brighton by the 12.22 train and first called in at 1 Montpelier Crescent to collect a copy of the *Sussex County Magazine* that I lent to Miss Haddan. Just before one, as I was leaving, the siren went so I stayed there in the first floor flat until the 'all-clear' sounded at 1.20, so it was a short raid. On the roof of a house opposite, soldiers were posted with two guns mounted on the roof. The whole, being on high ground was a good vantage post. Other people in the flats above came down and said they did not go down below until the guns began firing or bombs were dropped. I was late arriving for lunch at Cassie's. She told me the bomb dropped yesterday was in a cornfield at Lancing so it must have been a little away from the sea[10].... At 3 o'clock I was at the Eye Hospital and just as I had returned from buying Jock an eye shade, the siren sounded again. We, like other patients, trooped down two short flights of stairs to the large underground room which is well lighted and furnished with plenty of chairs and forms. Some of the patients were moved in their beds and everyone nursed their gas masks. The raid lasted from just before 6 until 7.15.

August 15th Thursday
The notion of a French newspaper prepared by de Gaulle's experts seems to have fallen through.... There have been two air raid warnings here today, one at 3 o'clock lasting about an hour and another at 6.45 until 8. I patrolled with Mr Ridgeway most of the time. Many children playing on the Common but living at the Heath or Bentswood we told to shelter in Masters' cellar so all were well. Two women with babies in prams were walking along West Common when the siren went and were uneasy about their children playing on the Common. I told them they were safe enough and knocking on Heasman's door the women and babies sheltered in his house. We always ask the nearest people to give shelter when it is necessary. We heard a battle overhead, very high up, and guns firing and at least one machine came down. I do not know where. A lady was cycling back to Franklands village but I told her to shelter in my house and go when the all-clear sounded. She brought some books for my collection for the forces. In this week's *Mid* there is a short account of Frank Carey, Pilot Officer in the RAF who last March was awarded the DFM after fighting over the North Sea, and later DFC and Bar. When in France in one week he shot down 9 enemy aircraft, four in one day. He himself was shot down, but although wounded he landed safely by parachute. His hospital ship was bombed at Dunkirk.[11]

August 16th Friday
At 11.30 last night, just after I had got into bed, guns and bombs were heard, the nearest we have yet had. No siren sounded. I dressed and was ready in case there were fires, my stirrup pump and two pails of water in their places ready in the hall.

The searchlights were numerous and brilliant. As there were no fires I did not think it necessary to go out, but stayed up until the guns stopped. Mr Parsons told me this morning that bombs had been dropped just this side of the bridge at Black Brook (Backwoods Lane) and about 11, I cycled to see the hole. A bomb could scarcely have fallen in a safer place, the field was soggy so the hole is full of water. The trees near are marked in many places with splinter bits and pieces picked up by souvenir hunters are heavy and sharp, no wonder they damage people. In America Lane another bomb fell but made a smaller hole damaging tree trunks.... Nazi agents in the US have begun to offer secretly to Americans some of the most precious of the Louvre's art treasures. Secretly, because the US would be likely to bar the sale of stolen pictures.... The siren sounded here at 12.30 this morning and the all-clear at 1.50. It was a quiet raid here for we heard only a few planes high up. But at 5 o'clock the sirens were out again. I was collecting a library book at Sunte Avenue and the siren was clear enough there.... I went on patrol with a messenger, Stafford and we heard guns and bombs and the rat-tat-tat of machine guns. The planes were too high up to see but they seemed to be all around us.

August 17th Saturday
A quiet night for which we were all thankful.

August 18th Sunday 51st week
A new half-crown War Savings stamp has been introduced. It will not be on sale to the general public at Post Offices but will be sold only by National Savings groups to their members. I shall buy one from Val Bassano. Four Southdown motor buses have been commandeered by the Government for transport for the Scotch soldiers here, and perhaps others, who are not yet fully equipped. These buses are camouflaged with nets like the lorries, tied with strings of buff and green canvas material, and marked private in the front. Yesterday was a flag day for 'Comforts for the Forces'. Members of the WI are doing different things to collect money for it: whist drives, parties, tennis tournaments and so forth. There was a 2½ hours' raid today from 1 o'clock just as people were going to have lunch, until 2.30.... I patrolled with Mr Ridgeway and we heard guns and bombs, but nothing was dropped here. There was a long pause after the all-clear siren, 'sireen', as the villagers say, before we were allowed to return and I did not get back till 3 o'clock.... Jock and I went to see Mrs Hill and Peter in time to listen to the 6 o'clock news which was chiefly of successful raids in Libya.

August 19th Monday
No wonder we had a 2½ to 3 hours' raid warning yesterday, for there was a big raid in the Channel at the time, one of those mass raids on the country. The morning paper says that out of 600 Nazi bombers and fighters 'more than 100 were

destroyed.' At Warden's Post this morning Mr Parsons said the 7 o'clock news reported the number 140. Sixteen of our fighters were lost, 8 pilots of which are safe. For the first time Londoners, who had two raid warnings, heard their AA guns open fire. Batteries were in action along the coast from Essex to Hampshire. Several of our airfields in the SE were bombed, some service personnel killed and others injured. Many bombs were dropped in open country.... The Germans in Paris have stripped the Place de la Concorde of all its bronze statues, lamp-posts and ornamental balustrades and have removed all metal valuables from private houses. All art shops are being denuded of treasures, which are being sent to Berlin.... A story by the Air Ministry has excited a good deal of controversy. Briefly, the pilot of a British airplane on patrol at night, near Borkum, spotted something on the surface of the sea beneath him and discovered it was a Heinkel at anchor. The machine could have been easily polished off, but the British crew thought it unsporting to attack a 'sitting bird'. So it flashed its headlights in invitation to the Nazi to come up and fight. The invitation was accepted and the Heinkel was destroyed. It is said we cannot fight this war with the ethics of the old school tie, and when one thinks of the way Nazis bombed and machine gunned helpless refugees, sunk lightships and shot our sailors while struggling in the sea the attitude of 'an eye for an eye' is understandable. For my part I think it better to keep free from the German taint and retain our national characteristics. After all Nazi philosophy is the lowest ever known, our own is the highest. But people will differ.

August 20th Tuesday
When I was cycling in the Heath this morning I noticed on several gate posts the notice *Stirrup Pump*.... It is a good notion to know which houses have stirrup pumps. I had to go to Oaklands to get Jock's ration card, or book, so that I could use it here since he is registered at Brighton.[12] They gave me three emergency cards each available for a week, three being the most supplied for the purpose. They have the advantage of being honoured in any shop so it is not necessary to register at any particular one. The girl in charge at Oaklands cut 3 week's coupons from Jock's book so there could be no cheating by using two for one rationed article!

August 21st Wednesday
More than 50 of the old guns which have stood on Tower Hill by the Tower of London for more than 100 years are being removed to be broken up and made into modern war weapons. It seems a pity to remove historical things like guns when there are so many useless iron railings about. There are tons of railings in Brighton doing nothing useful at all, lines of them down steps dividing houses as well as rails on the other side of steps.

August 22nd Thursday
I finished designing a poster for Val Bassano which is to be put up in the Post Office for helping in the War Savings Certificate effort. The aim is £5,000 for a Spitfire *How soon can we get there*, the sums to be recorded beginning from August 1st. A Sussex regional gift store has been started by the Red Cross Society. It is at Little Farlington, Oathall Road, where depots and working parties throughout the county send their gifts which are distributed to hospitals in Sussex. Mrs George Clarke of Welcombe, Lewes Road, is the head of the scheme and all the work is voluntary. Everything needed in a hospital is received, not only garments and first aid appliances.

August 23rd Friday
By Hitler's order the *Marseillaise* is to die. Pétain's government will shortly produce a new and tamer anthem. The *Marseillaise* is to be kept alive by General de Gaulle, who will use it on all necessary occasions and will ignore the new one....
At lunch time this morning a loud speaker paraded the High Street announcing that from 9 to 12 midnight there was to be a curfew for all traffic. The reason was for certain army manoeuvres taking place at that time. People could walk about on the pavements but I did not go out, it was a pitch dark night and inclined to rain.

August 24th Saturday
I bought one of the new 2/6 Savings Certificate stamps from Val and also one of the ordinary blue 6d stamps stuck on cards until the investor reaches 15/- when the card is exchanged at the Post Office for a Savings Certificate.... A p.s. by Leipzig radio says 'Goering's planes are producing such panic in Britain that the mental hospitals are full of new patients'. I wonder what the Nazis will next think of to say! They also said yesterday that bombs had been dropped on 'the important railway junction of Southwold'. But Southwold never had a railway junction, the nearest station is Halesworth 11 miles away. Sorry Dr Goebbels.... Potato flour is being tried in Germany as a substitute for paper. One newspaper is now being printed on potato paper. (When done perhaps the newspaper can be put back into a potato.) The names of all Germans and Italians have been removed from the lists of British honours. Therefore King Victor of Italy is no longer a member of the Order of the Garter. The ceremony of degradation takes place at night. The banner and shield are taken down, the banner is trampled on by officials of the Chancellery of the Order and then removed to the vaults beneath, the shield to rust, the banner to decay.... This morning Mrs Wadham gave me some leaflets which I said I would distribute for her to homes in my ARP sector.[13] Like many other places we are beginning to collect for a Spitfire to present to the Government. It is apart from the war savings that Val is interested in. At 4 o'clock just after I had made tea which I was taking into the garden the siren sounded. I

patrolled with the messenger boy Stafford and with Jack Ward. Stafford and I saw 7 spitfires evidently chasing the German machine which had gone over south before the sirens went. The all-clear was at 5.20, when I came back to tea.

August 25th Sunday 52nd week
Planes flew to and forth at intervals all last night, few could have had much sleep. I often expected to hear the siren but it did not sound. The paper tells us that London suffered most. There were 3 warnings in 24 hours. Forty-seven German planes were brought down yesterday although battles were still going on when going to press. The battle raged all over SE England. Dover, Ramsgate and Portsmouth all suffering.... A long stretch of Hove sea front has been declared a forbidden area and was closed to the public yesterday.

August 26th Monday
In yesterday's air battles over this country, the paper says 39 were brought down but Mr Barrow told me this morning the correct number was 55.... *France*, the first daily newspaper for Free Frenchmen to be published since France capitulated, appears today. It is produced by a group of independent French journalists in London and aims to provide news for the thousands of French people, soldiers or not, in England.... There was a warning at 12 this morning, but it was a short one. I patrolled with Messenger Charlie Ellis and the Common cleared of people in about two minutes. Last night 3 bombs were dropped in Paxhill grounds fairly near the house and fairly near together. One is sentry-guarded because it is a time bomb and deep down. At 9.15 this evening, when I was reading to Jock Sir Neville Henderson's book *Failure of a Mission*, the siren again went but neither of us heard it. The sirens are not nearly loud enough, many complaints are justifiably made about them. I dressed and went out and thoroughly enjoyed the sights I saw during this long raid which was not over until 4am. The searchlights were a marvel in themselves. I counted 19 congregated and they kept politely bowing to one another and they followed the enemy planes far above them. It must have been disconcerting to have lights dazzling your way like that. Then fire flares were dropped in the NW and lasted in the sky, lighting up everything like day for over 5 minutes. They are dropped, of course, in order that the enemy can see where he is and also if any damage has been done. The light over the Pond was truly beautiful, reflections clear, the lights themselves looking like glorified fireworks only keeping quite still and sending down little bright sparks. Later on, about 2.30, when patrolling with Mr Ridgeway, we saw quick flashes of gun-fire in the SE. All the enemy planes were from the SE and all went northwards. We think two of their objectives are the railway and Balcombe Viaduct, with possibly Gatwick airdrome thrown in. One brightest light in the western sky suggested an incendiary bomb, and we heard the Haywards Heath fire

brigade 'somewhere'. We all took turns to sit down at Warden's Post and about 1.30 Mrs Parsons kindly made a pot of tea which we much enjoyed. It was a perfect night, still, mild and clear although there were clouds in the sky. We watched the moon rise in its last quarter and very beautiful it looked. All the bombs we heard drop were some distance away, there were no near ones, nor even near concussions. None of us were sorry when the all–clear sounded but we had all enjoyed the eventful evening. When I came home I made a cup of hot Oxo which I drank in bed and slept well until 6.45 when I got up not having noticed the curtailed bed hours.

August 28th Wednesday
A new splinter-proof bowler hat has been made both for women and for men. This is light compared with our helmet. I handled one at Beckworth when I was patrolling last Monday. It belonged to Burgess their gardener. It is a good design and needs no chin strap.

August 29th Thursday
This morning I took to Warden's Post a list I made yesterday of those houses that have stirrup pumps. The printed notices on cardboard, such as I saw in the Heath, are to be given to us for fixing on to the gates of these houses. Already there are 5 in my bit of the sector, Four Acres, Little Pelham, White Gates, Chievely, Beckworth, as well as my own.... Our Spitfire Fund is getting on, Masters had a large table outside his shop yesterday with many useful things, chiefly of glass and china, for sale and all takings were to go to our Spitfire Village Fund. I bought a blue and white ½ pint milk jug and new well shaped drinking glasses.... There was a short air raid warning this afternoon from 3.30 to 4.45. I was in the Library, beginning the annual cleaning of the book shelves before Saturday's reopening. There was a short dog fight over the Common although it was too high up to see clearly. At 8 o'clock there was a meeting of wardens in our sector with Mr Fraser presiding to talk about raising money for the presentation of a Spitfire to the Government. It is agreed that we join forces with Cuckfield and Haywards Heath, the object being to raise £5,000. Since the whole district is divided out into sectors the easiest way is for each warden to undertake a collection in part of his sector. We have each been provided with a receipt book and I hope to begin next Monday.

August 30th Friday
We had a raid warning at 11.30, again as I was busy with my library shelves, and it lasted until 12.45. We heard the enemy aircraft overhead before the siren sounded. The noise sounded like many machines. All the gun-fire, or perhaps bombs, we heard were in the northeast, but before 10 in the evening much heavy firing was heard, and although there was no warning here I dressed and went to

the Post. So did many of the wardens, but not all of them. I stayed an hour, firing in the N and NE continuing all the time, searchlights busy and one plane picked out, which one does not often see, and red and green signal lights falling at intervals. I went down into Mr Parson's 'dugout', their cellar, where Ann was in bed. She has adorned the walls with notices and pictures and the whole place, with 4 candles alight on the table, looked quite inviting.

August 31st Saturday
Polish civilians are in future to pay double the fares paid by German civilians on trams and buses. The double fare is for German soldiers to ride free.... The Library reopened this evening and five minutes after I got there a raid warning sounded at 5.45. I hailed Anscombe who was passing by and sent by him a message to the Post that I was at the Library and would stay there. Several came in to shelter and as all–clear did not sound until 7 there was then a long queue of people and I did not get back until 8.50.... Readers were glad they could change their books after having had none for a month.

September 3rd Tuesday
Today is the anniversary of the war, also a flag day for soldiers, sailors, airmen and their dependents. Collections are made from door to door and Union Jack buttonholes given in return.... There were so many planes about last night between 10 and 11, I thought we should be called up, but we were not. However night raids were over London.... Thousands watched what was described as the 'sight of the century', German raiders fleeing pell–mell before the defences of London. Over 200 planes were in battle over the Kent coast. Barrages were continuous and formations approached at different routes, one being in the form of a swastika. By tea time 300 had tried to cross and there were dog-fights in a dozen places at once.... I began Spitfire Fund collecting.

September 4th Wednesday
More attacks were made on London yesterday and more by our RAF in Germany and France. While at tea in the garden this very day we heard a loud report at 4.30 and thought the time bomb dropped in Paxhill Park on Sunday night August 25th had gone off. People on the Common and elsewhere saw a column of black smoke. Sergeant Avis told us in the evening that we had destroyed it. So now we shall not know whether it was a time bomb or a dud. It had been guarded all the time so it was well to be done with it. I collected more for the Spitfire Fund, all the cottages in Pelham Place gave me something. Thus far I have had only one refusal, Mr Bannantyne of White Gates. He does not approve of the thank-offering effort at all and says we pay taxes for Spitfires which is true enough, but I just think he is mean about parting with half a crown.

September 6th Friday
A Guernsey father and son came over to a SW port in a 20ft auxiliary engine cutter, which they bagged, swimming out to it. There was only enough petrol to start the engine, but they found some paraffin and when that gave out they used a sail. Life is terrible now in the Channel Isles.

September 7th Saturday
While Jock and I were having tea in the Samuels' garden at Little Pelham the siren sounded so I left hurriedly. The raid which was a bad one over London lasted until 6.45 which was very inconvenient for the Library. I kept it open until 8 then came home and had just made Jock's porridge for his supper when the siren again went at 8.20. I dressed in ARP full outfit then and put on my winter coat not knowing how long the raid might last. It was well I had for the all-clear did not sound until 5am. It was the longest raid we have yet had and this time far more planes were overhead and seemed all round us, not only on the E or the S side as formerly. We saw two lots of coloured lights but no flares. We ran to earth lights from a house in Black Hill that had puzzled us before and the owner promised to attend to them. We saw many gun flashes in the NE and a glow from a fire in the north. Mrs Parsons made us a pot of tea about 1 o'clock which we much appreciated.... Mr Fraser got some extra tea for the Wardens' Post from the Food Control Office saying we ought to have it. Mr Fraser does get us things.... Yesterday there was put up by the Post Office a large wooden frame to mark the progress of our Spitfire Fund, a blue plane marking the amount raised which has now reached £1,000.

September 8th Sunday 54th week
As I was not in bed until ¼ to 6 I did not get up till 8.30 this morning. I made up my Spitfire Collection, £6.7.0 and took it to Mr Parsons who is taking all the collecting books to Mr Fraser. The names of those who have contributed are to be published in the *Mid Sussex Times*.... After a quiet Sunday with a slight shower of welcome rain in the afternoon, the siren sounded at 8 o'clock.... As half our number was on duty on Saturday night, the other half remained on duty tonight, so at 10 o'clock Mr Ridgeway, Manton and myself and one of the messenger boys returned home, but ready to come out again if summoned.

September 9th Monday
The siren all-clear sounded at 5.30 this morning so the raid was the longest we have had yet.... No papers came through this morning until nearly midday and Sunday's papers were also delayed. More intense raids against us are threatened for this week.... Again this afternoon the siren sounded about 5 just as we had finished tea with Elizabeth Parsons and Mrs Lister. The all-clear at 6.25 made me

late for the Library but in the morning I stuck a notice on the door that the Library would not be open during a raid for on Saturday some people were foolish enough to go there then. At 8.20 there was another call and as it was my night on duty the others left about 9.30 excepting Mrs Robertson, who having rested during the day, took the place of Mr Ridgeway who has a bad toe and had been to see the Doctor. There was more gun-firing and bomb dropping than ever before. Several times we saw planes picked out by searchlights. The nearest bomb that fell was about 3 o'clock. Just after 4, I was on the Common with Mr Parsons and Dorrie Robertson when we saw in the north the glow of a fire which gradually heightened and brightened. Sparks from shell fire darted about in and around the glow. We had never seen a distant fire so distinctly. I hope we hear where it was. I am sure a lot of damage has been done tonight. At 5 minutes to 5 came the all-clear and as it was then rather cold I made a cup of Oxo and enjoyed it in bed.

September 10th Tuesday
Both Victoria and London Bridge stations were put out of action on Sunday evening and yesterday Mr Parsons was 4 hours getting up to town and 4 hours returning. Later in the evening Victoria was 'mended'.... This photograph of the glare of the fire in Thames Dockland 30 miles from the Capital is similar to the glow we watched from the Common in the early hours of this Tuesday morning. The 3 streaks are parachute flares dropped by raiding planes[14].... There was the now usual tea time raid this afternoon, from 5 o'clock until 6.25. During this time Mr Parsons, Charlie Ellis and I watched a Spitfire and Hurricane attack and bring down a Dornier. The fight was near Brook House and the machine fell in a field at Sheriff Farm. We saw it just over the Village Hall. Knight, on leaving his work at the mill, went to see the wreckage. The plane seemed to be in three parts and 3 of the airmen were killed.

September 11th Wednesday
This morning various bits of metal from the Sheriff Farm plane are being sold for the Spitfire Fund. The papers were not in until noon.... Ryecroft, in the village, is now used as a soldiers' canteen and recreation house. All the stores have been removed from the Village Hall which is now used by the soldiers for amusement. And a good thing too, or they would be bored stiff through the winter. White Cottage, I am told, is taken for Officers' quarters. This afternoon we had two short raid warnings, each only an hour. At 8.30 the now usual warning for the night sounded and as it was my turn on duty, I was out patrolling either with Mr Parsons, Charlie Ellis or Mrs Robertson.... Planes droned all the time and I watched a battle in London that must have been terrific for us to have heard and seen so much, 40 miles away. What must it have been like there? Barrage fire and bursting shells were kept on from 2.35 until 5 o'clock. We heard two bombs at least

fall, one sounded as if it fell at Burgess Hill and the other at Balcombe, both probably trying for the railway line. The all-clear was at 5.25.

September 12th Thursday
The papers say this morning that last night's 9 hour raid on London was 'less effective than any of those since Saturday'. Mr Parsons, who went to town today, said London was jubilant because in that battle we watched last night, our barrage was so incessant they could not hear any bombs falling and a new anti-aircraft weapon was in action.... In Wednesday night's speech the Premier said that Germany's effort to secure daylight mastery of the air over England was the crux of the War. So far it had failed. He warned us that the threat of invasion remained and that shipping concentrations were being gathered in harbours from Brest to Hamburg and in Norwegian harbours. Behind the ships stood large numbers of troops ready to set out for their uncertain voyage across the sea.

September 13th Friday
There was no tea time raid this afternoon, but the evening 'sireen' sounded at 9 o'clock.... The incessant barrage continued and we watched it from high up Beckworth Lane. The shell fire sparks were brilliant and all that part of the northern sky illuminated.... All-clear sounded at 5.40, so it was a good long night but I enjoyed it as I do all the night raids. The day raids are very inconvenient, coming at meal or Library times.

September 14th Saturday
Dumps of sand have been put in convenient places in our sector for people's use. Each household may take one bucketful of the sand, its use being to put on bombs to smother them out. The dump for this house was at the grass patch outside Pelham House and this afternoon I went with Jock to fill my bucket. I was supposed to tell the people in my part of the sector, but Mr Parsons did this job for me yesterday and called at every house.... We enjoyed the first peaceful night since Friday the 30th of August, which made seven successive nights of raids, and all but one (the 12th) continued the whole night until dawn. I have been too busy to do any Spitfire collecting this week.

September 15th Sunday 55th week
The terrific RAF bombing of invasion bases is believed to have caused Hitler to pause in his plan.... From just after sunset on Friday until dawn yesterday morning, our bombers gave Germany's jumping-off grounds for our invasion the most terrific 'pasting' of bombs ever yet hurled in a comparable period. Londoners may take consolation in knowing that what they suffered was as nothing compared to what our men showered in a continual inferno on the ports

where troops and material have been massed. The full story of this 'Olympian raid' is not yet published, but it is known to be the most devastating ever carried out.... The first warning we had this Sunday was a short one, from 12.20 to 1 o'clock. The second was in the afternoon from 3 to 4 when the Scots Band was playing on the Common so it was useless to get people to take cover. The third warning was at 8.30 and lasted until 3.30am. I patrolled with Mr Ridgeway and at 2 minutes to 9 we saw, due east, a red light and a green light both dropped from above. I went back to the Post to report them and stayed to listen to the 9 o'clock news which told that 165 German planes had been brought down today, that we have lost 30, ten pilots being saved. I left at 10 o'clock as it was my off night, but it was a noisy night, I did not sleep till long after the 3.30 all-clear sounded and then for only a short time. I sleep better when I am out all night and come in tired, and when all is quiet. A bomb which seemed fairly near dropped just before 12.

September 16th Monday
While I was writing to Captain Fawssett this morning, Mrs Cresswell came in to see me. She told me Terence Phillip had been to Tangmere to see Frank Carey and with his police credentials had no trouble in being allowed to the aerodrome. Frank was having a bath. The signal came there was an enemy plane over. Frank jumped out of the bath, flung on his clothes, hurried into his machine, and brought down the German plane. I don't know how many that made to his credit. We have had no day warning here today and I got through the library work in peace and was also able to make Jock's porridge before the wail began at 8.15. It was a cloudy night with a driving mist at times, but no rain.... There were no searchlights at all. Probably by this time they give too much indication of land and may help the enemy. Mr Ridgeway and I patrolled the second time for 2 hours. Some new people from Cooden Beach named Mason had arrived at St Lawrence in the afternoon, and were having difficulty in obscuring lights. We went a different way this evening along the grounds of Beckworth. We climbed over iron fences, negotiated barbed wire and came out in Beckworth garden, all our sector the whole time. We watched one of our planes on patrol with a bright light flying rather low. At 1.10 we returned to the Post and had some tea and biscuits and a rest while Mrs Robertson and Charlie Ellis went out. All-clear sounded at 2.15, the shortest raid night we have had. Conditions could not have been good for the flight over. The nine o'clock news said that 185 planes were brought down on Sunday (the morning papers gave 175) we lost 30, but 10 pilots are safe. It was the most costly day for Germany.... This day Monday the 16th is the 'Invasion Day' but it has not arrived.

September 17th Tuesday
When Bobbie Fawssett was going to bed the other night he said to his mother 'I hope I shall go to sleep, because if not I shall be thinking'. His mother thought the

bomb had got on his nerves and he would listen for the planes. 'Why what would you be thinking about?' she asked. 'I should be thinking about those jellies Ada's made, and she won't tell me what they are'. On Saturday afternoon there was a children's matinée at the Odeon in Brighton. The cinema was bombed, 6 children were killed and others, I do not know how many, were injured. The mother of two children who did not return was naturally very anxious. In the early evening they walked in and in answer to her questions said 'Oh the Odeon was bombed, so we went to the Prince's'.... The siren sounded soon after 8 and I patrolled with Mr Ridgeway until 10. A typed sheet at the Post gave us an explanation of the coloured lights: red emitting red means engaging the enemy on land: green emitting green means engaging at sea.... All-clear sounded 3.35.

September 18th Wednesday
Invasion preparations go forward, although the late SW gale makes it unlikely that Hitler will use his flat-bottomed boats during the next few days. Ships are being massed on the Continental coasts, only awaiting a favourable opportunity. In his speech last night Mr Churchill said that although much damage has been done in London and elsewhere, injury to our war-making capacity has been surprisingly small.... There was a short time raid today lasting only from 1.45 to 2 so the library session was only slightly delayed. The usual evening one began at 8.15 for which I was all ready and waiting. It was a fine night at times perfectly still with no sound and not a leaf moving. But most of the time we heard the droning of planes and saw not only the barrage fire in the north, but a fire in the SE which may have been off Seaford, although we could not tell that. Mr Parsons went to London, but had difficulty getting there partly by train and partly by bus. All the London terminus stations are closed and undergoing repair and are reached only by bus from outside places.... A corrugated iron shed was erected yesterday on the Common alongside the path close to the dairy. It is for ARP fire stirrup pump demonstration, the day for which is not yet fixed. Mr Fraser joined Mr Parsons and me as we were patrolling on Black Hill and together we inspected the shed. Mr Fraser says he has lots of old furniture to burn. All-clear sounded at 3 o'clock.

September 19th Thursday
This is how the Barrage looks nearer. From here we do not see the separate fires. It is one long glow in the sky, with the hearing of gun-firing and sparks flying incessantly[15].... When I went to the Food Control Office at Oaklands to renew Jock's food emergency cards I saw a number of posters of slogans giving advice on all sorts of things especially on economy.... This evening's news tells us that 48 planes were brought down yesterday to our 9 with 5 pilots saved. The usual 8 o'clock siren arrived at 8.15, but Mr Ridgeway and I left early for it was our off night. Cloudy at five, rain at times. At 9.20 there was a loud report. It was a heavy

bomb dropped between the golf links and High Beech, no doubt another attempt on the Viaduct. All-clear sounded at 5am. There was a deluge of rain between 12.30 and 3 o'clock. Mr Parsons said the cricket pavilion made good shelter and one could see a good part of the sector from under its cover.

September 20th Friday

One constantly hears that the opinion of experts is that if Hitler does not invade us now he has lost the war. It is suggested that if put off an attempt might be made next spring. There is no question of our men falling back. If enemy forces did gain a foothold on our beaches our men would fight to a finish. We are now, since Dunkirk, fully prepared for invasion and meanwhile our own offensive somewhere in Europe is being prepared behind the scenes.... One is amazed at the rapidity with which air raid damage is repaired. Mr Parsons told me today that both Victoria and London Bridge stations are open again. Within a few hours people in the badly hit West End were, in some parts, shopping normally again.... The usual evening siren (the first today) sounded at 7.50 and much to our surprise all-clear was at 10 o'clock. Very strange. We expected a call later, but none came and we had a quiet night. We have to speak to several on Black Hill about lights showing through curtains, the worst and most persistent offenders being the military, especially those at Hillside.

September 21st Saturday

As usual there was a raid warning at library time this evening, but on and after next Saturday the 28th we begin the time adopted last winter 2 till 3 for all the three sessions. The night warning sounded at 8.20, the all-clear at a ¼ to 5.... At 11pm, when I was patrolling on the Common with Mr Ridgeway, a bomb fell with a loud report, followed by another. We did not know how near it was, it sounded close, so we both laid flat and afterwards walked to the end of our sector northwards to make sure we could see no fire. Later on Mr Parsons was told that the bomb fell at Saucelands Farm near Ardingly College. On the large-scale map I see there are 2 farms near together, Great Saucelands and Little Saucelands Farm. After 1 o'clock we heard no more planes nor yet any barrage fighting, everything seemed quiet. Miss Abby from Meadow Lane is now a warden and has taken the place of Mr Manton who had to leave. She will be in Dorrie Robinson's division and Mr Knight will come into ours. So we shall now be 3 on each side with one messenger boy for alternate night duty. Raids and patrolling up to 10pm do not count as night work.

September 23rd Monday

A letter from Mr Broadbridge came this morning. He says Oxford Street and other streets of London look like the devastation of an earthquake.... This morning we have the terrible news that a liner carrying children to Canada was torpedoed 700 miles off the Irish Coast. 83 evacuees lost their lives among the 294 missing[16].... There was a hailstorm at the time and the sea was very rough, the conditions... were so bad that there was little chance of survival.... This evening the siren did not sound until 9.15, but made up for it by all-clear at 5.40am. However, it was a glorious night. I enjoyed being out, the moon just at half, stars bright, all very still with no wind the air cool. Jupiter seemed extra bright and when Mars rose he seemed to take possession of all the part of the sky he was in. Planes zoomed all the night, many just overhead, but no bombs were dropped near here. We heard only two some distance away. There was continuous barrage and gun-firing in the north. Poor London again.

September 24th Tuesday

It is said that a candle placed alight in an ordinary pot and covered with a smaller pot upside down makes a useful heating apparatus for an Anderson shelter. I shall try it with two flower pots.... Crowds of people in the early morning gather before the premises of London astrologers to gain information on England's fate. Fortune-tellers are charging as much as £10 for a consultation.

September 25th Wednesday

We have been warned at our Post the last few days about a new weapon now being used and today it is announced in the papers. It is a web-like substance which burns and blisters when touched. It is so quickly dispersed in certain weather conditions that it has been difficult to get good samples from which British experts could decide its composition and action. Mr Knight saw one of the 'cobwebs' on Monday night hanging and blowing about from the lamp post near Beckworth. It spreads over several square feet, but if the ground be wet it quickly disappears.... It has been another fine sunny day. It was so clear that yesterday morning I took snapshots of reflections in the Pond and this morning of the ARP temporary shed for stirrup pump demonstrations and of the Spitfire poster on my fence.... The evening warning sounded at 8.30, but none in our sector heard it for the Heath siren did not function. Those higher up the village heard Mr Fraser's and blew their whistles. It was a specially active night and the raids lasted until 5.40am. There was a fire NW Horsham way or Dorking. It seemed as if a number of incendiary bombs had been let loose all at once. Another fire we saw a little further NW. The barrage continued all the time. There is one German plane we call DI meaning District Inspector. It comes regularly every night, drops its eggs, usually 2, about midnight and then departs.

September 27th Friday

The first raid warning here this morning was at 9.15 until 10.10. With Mr

Ridgeway I watched on Black Hill the most exciting fight I have yet seen. There were about 10 machines that we could see and one was brought down. They looked like silver birds darting about in the sky. The fight was over Cuckfield and we heard later that 2 were brought down there. Also 3 at Danehill, one just escaping the Church and another down on Ditchling Common. The next raid was from 12.10 to 1.10. We heard gun-firing and a bevy of planes that came over, but did not see any fight. The third raid was about 3.50 until 4.30 when many were gathered on the Common watching soldiers playing football. But they stopped the game and dispersed on hearing the warning. At 6.30 I went to Beckworth Hostel of God to fit a gas mask to one of the patients, Miss Hoy. Planes zoomed all around all the evening. The nurses, staff and patients have all contributed to the Spitfire Fund generously. I still have some houses to call at, but there is much to do. The 4th warning was at 8 o'clock and all-clear not until 6am, the longest night raid we have yet had. It was a noisy night with planes and bombs, some very loud ones dropping at 10.15, 12 and 4am.

September 28th Saturday

At 8 o'clock the usual evening siren sounded. We heard the whistles, but few heard the siren. It is a pity it is so faint for I am always on the listen for it especially in the evening, and then I seldom hear it. Mr Porter told me they never hear it at the schools. There was more bombing and firing in this night raid than we have ever had before. Heavy bombs were dropped at Horsted Keynes, where the waterworks are the attraction and others, with far more of a crash sound at the Heath about Ashenground Road. Possibly glass and tiles falling accounted for that crash. We saw it from Black Hill. Mr Fraser rang up to say that another loud explosion came from Stone Cross, another later from the Mental Hospital. Quite close there is the hospital for those soldiers who were shell-shocked or otherwise injured at Dunkirk. It was a beautiful night, light only from the stars shining everywhere with no cloud, no mists, not even on the lower part of the Common. When the all-clear sounded at 6.10 it was dawn, with the last of the harvest moon very bright and the complete circle clearly seen, Mars brilliant above and all in a yellow golden sky. Somehow it seems a pity to turn in! At the Library Donald told me he had been to see the crater in Hales' Farm, Wivelsfield. The bomb fell in the middle of a field from which the crop had been gathered in so it did no harm. It measured 42 feet across and was from 10 to 20ft deep. Souvenir hunters had been lucky. One boy said 'I've found 15 bits'.

September 29th Sunday 57th week

The first raid warning today was at 4 o'clock this afternoon. A noisy battle soon began and we saw many planes and were told that one was brought down at Ardingly. People were stranded on the Common and seeing 9 coming up Pondcroft Road when I was standing just outside the Post, I brought them in there to shelter. Four were staying in Compton Road, one was over from Brighton and the others from London 'for a little peace and quiet'.... All-clear was at 5.15. Stafford, one of our messenger boys, told me he cycled to the Heath this morning to see the damage done by the bomb last night. It fell in Haywards Road scattering glass there, in Ashenground Road and South Road. Among the shops damaged was the 50/- tailor's and a tea shop. An ARP's house in Haywards Road was hit, the windows smashed and the beds where his wife and children were asleep were covered with glass. But no one was hurt in any of the area hit. The night warning sounded at 8.20 and at 9.30 we heard 8 bombs dropped one after another quickly in a northerly direction, perhaps Balcombe way. I went to bed at 10.30. There were no more bombs dropped within hearing. Mr Parsons said the barrage firing London way was incessant. One saw the reflection in the Pond of the firing sparks. All-clear was at 6.22.

September 30th Monday
We have had 5 raid warnings today. They began early for the first was at 9.30 until 10.25. Immediately after the all-clear had sounded there was another warning at 10.28 until 11.15. The next was from 1.30 until 2.25 when I patrolled with Mr Parsons and saw many planes overhead travelling north. There was a collection of lights like silver Roman candles, eleven of them trailing horizontally, probably engine exhaust and fairly near there were 9 planes possibly Spitfires travelling north. Another warning was from 4.40 to 6.08. I stayed to hear the 6 o'clock news with Mr and Mrs Parsons. The evening warning was at 8.14 and the final all-clear at 6.05. It was my night out and I patrolled with Mr Ridgeway most of the time. It was a darkish cloudy evening, not cold, with incessant barrage over London.... As usual the dawn was beautiful.

October 1st Tuesday
The big report we heard on last Saturday's noisy night was a bomb dropped just behind the cottage opposite Lywood Common. The crater it made was 48 feet across and about 20 deep. A plane fell in the hammer pond by Cinder Hill and the airmen were drowned. Many parts of their bodies have been picked up today, for there was an explosion after their plane had dived.

October 2nd Wednesday
There have been raids on and off all day today beginning at 9.08 this morning. We heard little activity in the sky the reason being that the Nazis were kept from coming further than the coast by our RAF. Here is my record of the warnings, 8 in all: 9.08 to 9.50; 10.05 to 10.52; 12.10 to 12.38; 2.10 to 2.27; 3.05 to 3.30; 4.35 to 5.10; 7.45 to 9.25; 10.40 to 12.20. During the 3 o'clock one I was in the Library dressed ready for a raid that I thought would probably take place as soon as the

session was over. We had just finished tea when the 4.35 warning sounded. I was on Black Hill with Mr Ridgeway who had not had tea. Mr Samuel of Little Pelham kindly gave him one on their verandah. All the people who live here are kindly to us wardens and grateful for what we do although we do so little. In the pause in the night raid from 9.25 to 10.40, we did not go home feeling sure there would soon be another. Nor did we retire at 12.20, but had a sweepstake guessing when the next warning would come. There were the five of us, Messrs Parsons, Ridgeway, Knight and the messenger boy Stafford and myself. We all staked a penny, but no one won the 4d because no other warning sounded. We none of us understood the reason, for the barrage was on, planes were zooming on all sides, there was gun-fire and a bang in the NE about twelve-fifty. We had some tea, Mr Parsons went to bed as it was his night off and we four stayed at the Post. At 3.30 two bombs were dropped not so very far away in the NW. Ridgeway and Knight went out in case of accidents, and at 5 o'clock as there was still no warning we decided to leave and go home.

October 3rd Thursday
I was told this morning that the 3.15 bomb we heard at the Post in the early morning fell on the cottages near the Church at Ardingly. All 5 occupants were killed. No more children are to be sent overseas until further notice. The weather conditions are not good. 2,650 have gone thus far.... In the *Mid Sussex Times* there is a story that when an exciting air battle was raging in a Mid-Sussex town recently a resident aged 70 opened his door and hailed an ARP warden, a gardening expert, with 'Just a minute. I want you to tell me the name of this apple.' The warden's comment was, 'That's the spirit that's going to beat Hitler'. A Brighton restaurant keeper experienced a bomb dropping near his place of business. He said 'It saved me half a crown for the chimney sweep. The concussion brought down every bit of soot in the chimney'.

October 4th Friday
Brighton was badly hit on Tuesday afternoon September 24th. No siren had been sounded, but when the scream of falling bombs was heard many people fell flat and two heavy explosions shook the town. A lone Nazi raider had flown in from the sea and dropped its bombs. About 30 houses were demolished or badly damaged and many windows smashed. Buildings wrecked included two public houses. Casualties would have been heavier but for the fact that many houses were empty, the women being out shopping and children playing in the streets. But many of these children were injured.

October 6th Sunday 58th week
The Spitfire Fund now points to £2,100. This has been a day of rain and squalls

for our Harvest Festival at the Church. As Jock is in bed with a bad throat I could not go out yesterday until after Dr Dodd had been. I then cycled up with 6 of my biggest Charles Ross apples. It was 10 to 1 and the decorators had left excepting Miss Abby. I put the apples on the top ledge of the pulpit, just to make Mr Buckingham's mouth water. They had not been moved this morning. The Church looked very cheerful with so many apples and flowers and 4 big loaves of bread on the screen. Wonderful to say there was no evening warning. I laid down with my clothes on all ready thinking one would come later. But at 3am I undressed and had a good night.

October 7th Monday
Much attention is given in today's papers of the havoc wrought in Germany by our RAF…. We have had 4 raid warnings here today. The first was 10.30 to 11.25, the next at 1.30 until 2.35 which delayed the library session. The next came before I had finished the library work at 3.50 until 5.05. The evening raid was earlier, 7.35 and the all-clear at five minutes to 3. I came home then but did not go to bed until ¼ to 5 because I had not written this journal. With Jock in bed with a sore throat there is no time for writing, as I read to him in any spare time.

October 8th Tuesday
After a day of non-stop air battles, during which Hurricanes, Spitfires and Messerschmitts fought six miles above London, Goering's raiders resumed their attacks on London shortly after dusk last night at the same time that we had our warning…. There were 5 companies of soldiers being drilled on the Common, RAMC, who I think were just in, and the RSF under their very enthusiastic sergeant-major, the man who swears so readily and naturally. Another sergeant told me they were expecting the Brigadier.

October 10th Thursday
The Home Guard is on every night in two shifts, 9 to 1 and 1 to 5. We often see them cycling, usually on their way home.

October 13th Sunday 59th week
The first warning this Sunday was at 1.30 just as I was finishing cooking the lunch. It lasted just an hour and in the sky just over the Common we saw signs of a battle with many trails of white circles, I have not seen so many so widespread before. They travelled from N to S. We saw nine planes, apparently ours travelling north and soon after they had passed the all-clear sounded…. There was the usual night warning 7.05 and about 8 o'clock three bombs were dropped in Burgess Hill district. Ten minutes later four more were dropped but further away. After that we heard no more bombs, only planes to and fro. It was a beautiful evening, moonlight

and clear until about 3.30 when everything clouded over. There were spells of complete silence but the all-clear did not come until 6.05am. At 5.15 this afternoon Princess Elizabeth made her first broadcast, speaking especially to children who had been forced to leave their homes. Her voice is like her mother's. She spoke naturally, not at all as if she were reading her set speech. As she finished she called 'Come on Margaret', and Princess Margaret in a small high-pitched voice, said 'Goodnight children'.

October 14th Monday
The bombs we heard yesterday evening fell at Hurstpierpoint and the later more distant ones fell at Moulsecoomb. We have not yet heard what damage they did.... Mr Parsons could not get to town by train today and Peter Hill returned from the station and went by bus from East Grinstead or rather by bus there and then on by train. A luggage train was derailed and its engine was flung across the line somewhere this side of Three Bridges.

October 15th Tuesday
Raids began early today. The siren sounded first at 8.10 and all-clear at 9.25. We heard a gun firing in the north but not in our sector. The second siren was at 10.10 but only until 10.30. These day raids are annoying, no doubt partly designed for that purpose. I prefer the night raids when I am not hindered in the ordinary day's work of shopping, cooking, fireplaces, Jock's eye and his meals etc.... The evening raid warning here was at 7.30 and the all-clear at 5.15am.... Bombs were dropped in the SSE and on three occasions in the north, but none near us. We saw a new light in the northern sky, vivid like a sudden golden fiery sunset, flashed on and once, about 4.30, a red circular light in the middle of the 'sunset'. We did not know what they were, perhaps fire bombs. The barrage was a wider range than usual from NW to NE and planes flying to and fro without the customary quiet pauses. No pause was longer than five minutes. It was a beautiful night, no wind at all and mild.

October 16th Wednesday
The famous ornamental garden at Blenheim Palace, seat of the Duke of Marlborough, is now without its flower beds. Beets, cabbages, carrots and lettuces are planted round its privet hedges. I am working similarly on a smaller scale. My lavender hedge was partly killed by last winter's frost. Yesterday evening Taylor and I dug it all up and I am going to sow a line of turnip tops in its place. I have taken many lavender cuttings and hope to plant them there next autumn. Onions lately have been very scarce and priced at 1/- per pound. The Ministry of Food will impose a maximum price shortly and the price will be less by increasing imports and improving distribution.

October 17th Thursday
Eastbourne is going to make a formal complaint about lack of air raid warnings. They often have none, or one is sounded after the raid has begun. That happens here too.... The following gems are from Goebbels' 'Propaganda Factory' about their raids. October 10th 'Londoners are queuing up in front of lawyer's offices to make wills'. October 7th 'Churchill is enjoying the sight of burning London from the heights of Primrose Hill'. October 6th 'The Underground is exploiting the disastrous shortage of shelters by issuing monthly season tickets entitling the holder to use the station as a shelter. Needless to say, such tickets are quite beyond the means of London's poor'.... For the third time we heard a rifle shot ring out at Scrase Bridge. The Home Guard are there and perhaps their challenge was not answered. Of the plane brought down at Cuckfield on Tuesday night only the engine was found. One assumes that the bomb exploded and blew all else to bits.

October 19th Saturday
The War Office is considering pros and cons of letting troops quartered in London take over some of the work now done by over-worked air raid wardens. The scheme would give the wardens short periods of rest. There was a raid this afternoon during the library session thereby keeping up its record. It lasted from 2.30 until 3. A number of planes went across to the north just before the siren sounded. The evening raid began at 7.05 and lasted all night until 6.10am. Sunday morning, I was glad it was my night on patrol for it was one of the most beautiful nights I have ever experienced, a nearly full clear moon, Jupiter very bright and Mars rising brilliantly. About 3.30 everything very still, only the planes zooming overhead. About 7.45 bombs were dropped Burgess Hill or Ditchling way and about 9.30 we heard 4 much nearer and louder ones. We thought them at Freshfield or Chailey. The bright moon shining on a window often looked like a light from within, several times we have been deceived in that way.

October 22nd Tuesday
This morning there was a warning at 10.30, the short raid here ending at 10.45. Another followed at 2.45 until 3.30. Mr Ridgeway and I watched the smoke-trails of 8 machines travelling high up and flying fast. It looked rather like one machine after six travelling first from the E to W then back again, hiding behind clouds and then appearing again. One zig-zag tail suggested a fight, but it was all too high up to distinguish anything. The evening raid began at 7.20 and a loud bomb fell about an hour later. It was between Chailey and Plumpton. I have not heard the exact spot. The all-clear sounded unusually early, at 11.10. Afterwards no more planes crossed this way. While we were out in the afternoon raid we noticed white gossamer floating about, some of it caught on telephone wires, some in the trees and much on the grass. We were warned about the 'cobwebs' in the paper some

weeks ago, but here they have not been in evidence until this afternoon. We know nothing about them or what they are supposed to do. Presumably they are dropped from planes. We asked a soldier on the Common if he had received any warning such as we wardens had. He said 'No' he had heard nothing of them at all.

October 23rd Wednesday
Dorrie Robertson came in this morning to say that as their night was so short and we had such a long one they had agreed to go on duty tonight, so that we could have the night off. Very kind of them, for we can do with it.... For the last two days the Scots Fusiliers and the RAMC have been leaving the village and artillery arriving in their place. Many heavy lorries, mostly closed, have been through to the Welkin where some of their guns will be stationed.

October 24th Thursday
For the first time the Air Ministry last night told a little of what the RAF learned of Hitler's invasion plans and how they were wrecked. Pilots of the RAF have kept watch on all the German sea bases from Narvik to Bordeaux, 2,000 miles, and havoc done by their raids has done much to undermine the confidence of the enemy. Barges, 150ft long and carrying about two train-loads of men or materials were concentrated in the ports. There were also ocean-going submarines, small warships, tugs and merchant vessels. At one time there were 45 merchant ships at Le Havre. Then began our non-stop day and night offensive, each invasion base in turn came in for bombardment and damage.... The black-out in this country is unlikely to be modified this winter.... All round about here it often happens that the places where bombs fall are where lights are seen. That is the reason we are so severe in our sector with those who show lights. The restrictions therefore will be strictly enforced during this winter, and no needless risks will be taken.

October 25th Friday
There have been warnings and raids nearly all day today. The first was at 9 until 10.45am. We did not see it, but one of our Hurricanes caught fire and fell in flames on the golf course. It was not hit at the time by the enemy. The pilot, a Belgian, was saved. The next raid began at 1.40 and when all-clear went at 4.10, I was glad for the north wind was cold and I looked forward to a cup of tea. But not yet! At 4.25, before I had even left the Post another warning came through and lasted until nearly 5. I happened to be the only warden on duty this afternoon.... It was announced yesterday that Summer Time will be kept through the winter. I am glad, for it will make the most of day light *all* the time.

October 26th Saturday
Ear-plugs have been distributed by the Government and are available at Warden's

Posts. I am told Mr Fraser has them but they have not yet been sent to our Post. They effectively deaden the sound of planes and bombs. One old lady was sent a pair of well-made pale pink plugs. They were marked 'L' and 'R' so that each should be put into the proper ear. She wrote a note of appreciation to the makers, 'My hearing loss has improved beyond belief since wearing your excellent plugs'.

October 27th Sunday 61st week
Marshal Pétain has agreed to collaborate with Hitler. The King sent him a message assuring him of Britain's sympathy for the sufferings of the French people. It was one of encouragement for France and expressed confidence in ultimate victory, the benefits of which would be shared by the French people. A French broadcast announcer said that her position would not be on the basis of a conquered nation, but on the basis of a partner with complete equality. The terms are: 1. Alsace-Lorraine to return to Germany; 2. The Riviera as far as Nice and Corsica to go to Italy; 3. Italy to have joint control with France in Tunisia, and Spain to have joint control with France in French Morocco; 4. France to co-operate with the Axis, politically and diplomatically in the creation of the 'new order' in Europe. The position of the French fleet has been left open. De Gaulle says by his representative in London 'We cannot believe that Hitler will find a single Frenchman who will willingly consent to the mutilation and subjugation of his native country. As for us, the Free French Forces, we declare in the name of France that we hold null and void any carving up of the land which is our national heritage'. He ended by saying that whatever extortionate terms the enemy might impose on France he and his forces would continue to fight on the side of the Allies…. The near bomb on Saturday night was near the railway in Copyhold Lane, but it did not hit the line nor did the others that followed it.

October 28th Monday
There was a warning this afternoon during library time lasting only from 2.40 to 3.20. Another came at 4.30 to 5.27 during which time a parachutist was seen bailing out Chailey Common way. We heard afterwards it was a German machine that had been shot down in a field at Wivelsfield Farm, just bordering on Chailey. The night raid began at 6.45 and I patrolled first with Mr Ridgeway. Bombs fell in the direction of Crowborough and a fire or fires lit the sky for a time. Incendiaries probably. Up Beckworth Lane we saw another fire in the SE and a bright red light rising from near the ground. We walked on along Backwoods Lane and at the end of it a man came through the kissing gate and I stopped on one side and said 'Good evening, what *have* you got there?' He was carrying a heavy, rather long staff in his hand. 'Well,' he said 'I'm not taking any chances, I carry this about with me'. 'You wouldn't attack wardens though would you?' I said. 'No, certainly not. I've captured a German airman this evening,' and he told us of the man who

came down at Wivelsfield Farm. He knew only two words of German, but he indicated the man was to put up his arms which he did, and there was no trouble. I think he was a Home Guard. A policeman came and took the airman to Haywards Heath Police Station. Half an hour later there was a bright light in the NW but no bomb fell, nor did I hear gun-firing there. The light cast a curious lurid glow over all the SE making the Common look unreal. Then we heard more distant bombs, gun-firing and barrage over London. It was a short night though for the all-clear sounded at 2.48.

October 29th Tuesday
I have been at the Infant Welfare Annual Jumble Sale today, held in the Congregational Room. Although there was not nearly so much 'stuff', Mrs Bevan made over £16 and the money this year is to be given to the Soldiers' Comforts Fund. She asked me about a Christmas Greeting Card from Lindfield to put in the many parcels we are sending. Fortunately I had some copies already printed from a block showing the Church and street. I am going to paint in the sky and add Christmas Greeting in red on 120 of the cards. The evening raid began at the usual time, and about 8 a loud report, followed by two more startled everybody. It was not my night on but the house shook so I hurried into my outdoor things, put on my helmet and went to the Post in case there was a fire and extra help was needed. The bombs sounded even nearer than they were. The first fell in Walstead School rugger field and exploded before it reached the ground so that the crater was small. The others fell in the fields between the school and Paxhill and in Court Wood, Paxhill. No one was hurt. Some windows were smashed. I have not yet heard of any other damage. Mr Parsons went up Black Hill while I stayed at the telephone and soon after he returned I went to see Sybil Fawssett to tell her where the bombs fell. At midnight and at 3.15 I heard more bombs but not so near as Walstead. Planes were droning all night.

October 30th Wednesday
Mr Parsons told me there was a blockage on the line. It took over 2 hours to get to Purley and from there he reckoned that by the time he reached London Bridge he would have to leave in order to be home again in reasonable time. So he came back. It turned out to be a wretched wet night, but as the wind went to the SW, I could hear the siren, which I so seldom can here and have to rely on the wardens' whistles like many others. It seems impossible to get this failure remedied although Mr Fraser does his best.... Mr Parsons patrolled with me after supper, and we sheltered from the rain under cover of the cricket pavilion. I suppose the weather was too much for the enemy. We heard no planes for an hour and at 10.20 the all-clear sounded. As the warning was at 7.20 it was about the shortest night raid we have had. I listened with Mrs Parsons to the 9 o'clock news. A warning

was given that small objects about the size of a Mills bomb or a 50 cigarette tin are being dropped by German raiders. They must not be handled for they may be dangerous. This mysterious 'bomb' may have a wire attached. They may explode and kill anyone within 10 yards radius, or they may contain a corrosive substance which would be distributed on the object being moved. The Ministry of Information asks that the public will report to the police or wardens immediately if they find such objects.

November 1st Friday

Owing to the danger of confusion with air raid alerts there will be no two–minute silence on November 11th. There will be no official ceremony at the Cenotaph and the Government feels that all large services should be dropped. Sunday November 10th, will be a Day of Remembrance.

November 3rd Sunday 62nd week

A letter in last week's *Mid Sussex Times* drew attention to our grievance at not hearing the sirens, which has been a worry to us ever since the raids here began. We have been constantly assured that 'the matter is being attended to' but there is no improvement and we always have to be on the listen which adds unnecessarily to our work.

November 4th Monday

There was a short raid this afternoon, fortunately after the library session, lasting only from 3.50 to 4.12. There has been steady rain for 48 hours. This evening at sunset it cleared up and it was fine for our long night raid from 7.05pm to 7.08am. Mist came up about 3am, but it was a beautiful starry night after the moon, nearly at first quarter, went to bed. The barrage continued all night long and planes flew from all quarters. We heard distant gun-firing but no bombs either near or distant. At 5 o'clock, as we were rather cold I made some Oxo using half a square to our tea cup. As biscuits are difficult to buy anywhere we had bread and cheese with our midnight tea and very good it was. There has not been any cheese in the village for over a week. The cheese we had was in the portions done up 6 in a round shallow box. I read in the paper that cheese will not be rationed, but sometimes it will be scarce. There is some breakdown on the line just the other side of Balcombe Tunnel, whether a bomb, or land from an explosion I do not know. Mr Parsons decided not to go to London, passengers travelled by bus after Balcombe station. Mrs Roberts came in to see us after tea and told us the story of a wounded Nazi airman and a doctor. The Nazi, although badly wounded was troublesome, truculent and unkindly in his speech. He was given a blood transfusion and when the operation was finished the Dr said 'Now I hope you will be a better, kinder and nicer man, for we have put into you a pint of Jewish blood'.

November 5th Tuesday
I finished painting the Christmas Greeting cards for Mrs Bevan that are going to be put in each parcel sent to a Lindfieldian serving in the forces.[17]

November 6th Wednesday
It is against the law now for anyone to use a lighted torch during an air raid. Users are inclined to flash them.... The night raid began at the earliest time yet, 6.15, but we had an unusually short night, the all-clear sounding at 2.25. I did not get home till past 3 o'clock because Messrs Ridgeway, Knight and myself had to measure for waterproof coats that the Government is to supply for night work. It took some time to do because the tape measure Mr Parsons lent us was frail and began at 6 inches. There were 5 measurements to take for each of us. The coats are to be shared: Mrs Robertson and myself, Miss Abby and Knight, Ridgeway and Ward.... Of course there were no Guy Fawkes celebrations yesterday.

November 7th Thursday
Lindfield's siren complaint was discussed at the Cuckfield Urban District Council meeting on October 31st. Mr Masters, one of those who represent Lindfield, spoke up well about the complaint and referred to Mr Fraser's Sunte Avenue siren as sounding, 'if one heard it, like a baby squeaking. If it were in Lindfield instead of a mile away it might be of some use.' He proposed to install a lion of one at the Fire Station. People are always asking 'Has the siren gone?' Mr German, a Haywards Heath member, suggested that the matter be referred to the Civil Defence Committee and this amendment was carried. At the same time it means delay and Mr Masters said it was shameful that nothing should be done in the matter until the next Council meeting.

November 8th Friday
Raid warnings today have been 10.15 till 11.10 and 1.40 to 2.37. In the afternoon raid there were many planes in the east leaving smoke trails in wonderful patterns all over that part of the sky. The top arch as it were of a rainbow was noticeable in the NE. There must have been a big battle in the east. I heard the 9 o'clock news when I was at Warden's Post this evening.... The night warning sounded at 6.25 and the all-clear at 2.50. At 7.15 when on patrol with Mr Ridgeway, bright flashes came from due east and eleven bombs were dropped there, the plane travelling north. We were told later they were at Freshfield and Horsted Keynes.

November 11th Monday
Poppy Day. It was Remembrance Day at Westminster Abbey yesterday but with a difference. A small civilian army was being honoured 'To remember those civilians who have died owing to the war'.... A gathering at 11 o'clock was

arranged at the war memorial here, but an air raid was in being at the time, the second one this morning.... Neville Chamberlain died on Saturday night at Highfield House.... He was 71. He dedicated his life to peace, but was not afraid to face war when honour would allow no other discussion. The country is the poorer by the loss of his high gifts of integrity and purpose.... A party of 6 Frenchmen have just arrived in London from Nantes. One of them says a stiff resistance is being put up and a shopkeeper at Nantes whose daughter went to the pictures with a German officer had to close his shop. Not a single French person would pass his threshold. There are more British in France than was at first supposed. The Nazis have gaoled them, putting them on starvation rations. Even men of over 60 have been interned.

November 13th Wednesday
The stormy weather and anti-aircraft guns prevented more than a few Nazi planes from reaching London during yesterday night. There was little damage and few casualties. A bomb that fell yesterday afternoon, making us feel the shock, made a crater, said to be 80ft across, in a field near a hotel at Burgess Hill. In a raid this afternoon Mr Ridgeway and I watched a chase. There were 3 planes, one of ours after a German plane turned quickly and got very close to it. We lost sight of the third plane a little way behind. I think it climbed in order to get above the plane being chased which was not flying high. It took place in the SE.... We have had three raid warnings today: 10.52 till 11.54; 1.10 till 3; 6.25 until 7.25. The second raid made me very late from the Library and I did not get home till nearly 5. The evening was certainly the shortest we have ever had and no wonder! It poured with rain and blew half a gale that continued all night. The recent rain and winds have played havoc with the sandbags round Mr Parson's house. All the Chief Wardens' Posts are sandbagged for telephone protection. Last Saturday some of the bags on the NW side gave way and on Monday morning there was a loud thud outside the front door just as the newspaper boy was leaving the paper. Mr Parsons dug frantically thinking the boy was buried underneath! However he was not. Men from the Urban Council came and on the third day all the sand bags and the loose sand was taken away. I don't know whether it is to be built up again. It is pleasant to look out of their front door and see across the Pond again. It all made a horrid mess for Mrs Parsons.

November 15th Friday
Germany is not making progress in her efforts for French co-operation in the 'new order'. Terms accepted by Laval have been rejected by Pétain.... Mr Neville Chamberlain's ashes were buried in Westminster Abbey yesterday. The broken stained glass windows let in a chilling draught. Just as the coffin was entering the Abbey the sirens began their wail. That was his funeral music.... Many people say

'History will say that he saved this country.' What nobler epitaph could any man have?... I spent from 10 to 1 o'clock today with Donald in the Library putting away the fresh collection of books. Lewes Library, in spite of the war and being short-handed, keeps up well with the new supply every two months.... The night raid beat the record for length, beginning at 6.12 and all-clear at 7.05am, thirteen hours save 7 minutes.... I was out with Charlie Ellis at 3.20 when two land bombs fell in Rocky Lane direction. I made some hot Oxo at 4.30 for Mr Ridgeway and myself, but Charlie was asleep then. I came home at 7.15, had breakfast and then wrote this journal for it was not worthwhile going to bed. Mr Samuel, whose son is now stationed at Winchester, told me that thus far the city has not been bombed. I hope she will be spared.

November 18th Monday
There was only one day raid today beginning at 1 o'clock. As many readers object to the Library being closed during an air raid and do not like the long wait before all-clear sounds, I have decided to carry on in spite of them. It will be more convenient for me anyway and the other wardens will be out while the raid lasts. This raid was over at 1.25. The night raid was again very short. The warning sounded at 8.55 and the all-clear at 9.50. A bomb fell, after a vivid flash, in the district of Rocky Lane. Bombs have fallen there before perhaps aiming for the railway and the bridge nearby. Neither has been hit yet.... I was saddened today to see in the paper the death of my old friend Eric Gill. I did not know he had been ill.

November 21st Thursday
This morning Dorrie Robertson came in to make mutual arrangements about our day time on for raids, which Mr Parsons said we could do as we liked. We have made equal divisions ignoring Sundays when the men are at home. We each have a whole day off, I on Wednesday. I am on all day Tuesday and on Monday morning, Thursday, Friday and Saturday morning. This leaves my library afternoons free, and the arrangement will save us both being out together which is unnecessary.

November 23rd Saturday
Most of the voluntary ARP wardens at Brighton were 'on strike' last night, as a protest against the recent decision to dismiss 98 full-time paid wardens. They made it clear that they will come out in an emergency, but refuse to carry out 'Post' duties except on Sundays, until the men are reinstated.... After our long night... the siren warned again at 9.15. Mr Parsons came out meeting me just outside the Post and said he would go out and I could go home.

November 24th Sunday 65th week
Another Lindfield boy was killed lately, on November 10th, Aircraftman Ronald King of Sunte Avenue. He was 19 and only a fortnight before was posted to a Squadron as a flight-mechanic. That makes the 5th name on our village Roll of Honour.... Parish registers are being filmed in case they are destroyed or damaged by bombs. Each film has a trailer giving the county, parish and then the dates of the entries. The films are being stored in special strong rooms.... The Post has now been sandbagged in a better fashion this time. They are built up to the same height as before, but are protected from the ground by block bricks of concrete, the sacks themselves being treated with a reddish preservative before being filled. The work was done by the Council's men who finished last Friday morning.... Although I heard gun-firing in the north and a few planes over about 7 to 8 o'clock we had no warnings here. At 10.20 we went to bed. I did not take my clothes off in case of having to turn out, but I slept quite well all the same.

November 25th Monday
No siren has sounded today nor was there any night raid. So this time I took off my clothes, knowing Mr Parsons would ring my bell if the warning was not heard.

November 26th Monday
The reason for London and for us having no alert was, it is thought, because in Northern France the ground mists make landing aircraft impossible without crashes. A small formation reached London's outskirts where AA defences and Spitfires turned them back.... There was a very short raid this afternoon... and again no night raid, the 3rd night in succession.

November 27th Wednesday
3,000 building workers are being released from the Army to help repair air raid damage.

November 28th Thursday
The poor women of Poland are having a terrible time. Those living in Warsaw have appealed to the women of the US begging them to help in their struggle to throw off the Nazi yoke. They say they are living through a Calvary for the Germans are trying to exterminate their race, and 3,000,000 Poles have perished already. The number increases as famine grows apace. Their men folk have perished in mass murders, their sons either with them, or else are taken away to labour camps in Germany, whence there is no return and their daughters are apprehended on the streets or abducted from their homes.... To make up for the last few days' freedom from air raids there were two long ones before night, from 10.47 to 12.50. Dorrie was out for that one, then another in the afternoon when I

was out from 2.55 to 4.25. Both times there were many planes overhead and wonderfully interesting sky trails. It is now said that those trails are not made by the exhaust from the engine but from the wings, but the explanation is not clear. About ¼ of an hour after the all-clear sounded in the afternoon I saw a formation of planes, flying from west to north that looked really pretty. They were silvery-grey in colour, with a bright golden light at the end of each one.... I think a battle was being fought Newhaven-Seaford way, I saw planes and heard the gun-firing. The evening raid, the first since last Saturday, was at 6.20. At 7 o'clock we met at the Post to try on new suits, the usual 'battledress' pattern made in the same dark blue drill material as our old suits. These new ones that we are to have are easier to get on and off, have sleeves and buttons down the front, mine is size 5. Mr Fraser has taken a lot of trouble to get them for us. We heard nothing about the waterproof coat we were measured for a short time ago.... The all-clear was at 3.12am, but I stayed to make some hot Oxo and toast for Mr Ridgeway and myself.

November 29th Friday
The new siren for Lindfield was installed.

November 30th Saturday
I heard the first warning from it very clearly, quite a treat after all our worrying for it and complaints of not hearing either the one at Oaklands, Haywards Heath, nor Mr Fraser's baby one. The first raid was at 10.20 to 11.05, and I went to the Post, whistled along Black Hill and then joined Mr Parsons on the Common. He stayed out so that I could get on with the many Saturday morning jobs.... On the Common with Mr Parsons this morning we watched a fight in the SE. We could not see the planes, but only the many streaks from them. One lot, at least 8 we thought, climbed above the others, came down and mingled with them. It was evidently a big battle.... There was no evening warning nor raid, so although ready I did not have to go out this cold frosty night.

December 1st Sunday 66th week
For two nights in succession a mysterious blue beam has been seen piercing the sky over London. It is suspected to be a secret signal to German raiders. We have not seen it here yet and its cause is not yet known. It may be sheet lightning, or the reflected glow of incendiary bomb fires, or a reflection on clouds of our own searchlight beams.... The evening raid was from 7.35 and the all-clear 8.55 and a very foggy time it was, one was scarcely able to see a thing. I piloted a few people home, or on the right way and then was with Mr Ridgeway when he helped guide the traffic. On the way down he had stopped a bus going into the Pond. We guided a car along Black Hill and then took up our post at the crossroads by the pump and prevented a car driving on to the Common. Traffic so often in a fog gets lost just

at that turn at the foot of the hill. As it was so densely foggy and cold we were glad of so short a time out. Mr Parsons gave me my new suit which looks very nice with its convenient shape and pockets. He also gave me a new First Aid Post and Clinic notice to put on my railing.... In today's *Sunday Chronicle*, Beverley Nichols writes about one of our planes that came down a short time ago and was left to burn away on a golf course because the Fire Engine was not sent just because of its being 'urban' or 'rural'. A disgraceful affair altogether and unfortunately it happened at Haywards Heath and the Belgian who was forced down, landed on the golf course at High Beech. The accident happened on October 25th.[18]

December 3rd Tuesday
For the first time since the Soviet Union was formed foreign correspondents are to be invited to take trips with a Soviet battle fleet.... It was a dark evening, inclined to rain, but only raining at intervals. Some gunners got their car stuck at the end of Backwoods Lane for they took the wrong turning at Black Hill, their destination being Bolney. We could do nothing to help them, but went with them to Mrs Poet's tea rooms and told them to come to our Post when they telephoned to Bolney after their tea. There were 3 men. I left them waiting with Mr Parsons... who entertained them until help would arrive from Bolney.

December 5th Thursday
The Great Dictator, Charlie Chaplin's masterpiece film, arrived in London yesterday. A duplicate print, a negative and an ordinary print were sent separately, in case of accidents.... After a day free from air raids we again had only a short night warning, 6.23 until 9.20. It was a horrid wet murky night. About a week ago the shed put up temporarily was taken down. We are sorry for although it was ugly, it gave us protection from rain and wind from the SW. We used to lean against it sometimes. However it has fulfilled its purpose of stirrup pump and fire demonstrations, and that corner of the Common looks nicer without it.

December 6th Friday
British and German long-range guns fought a two-hour artillery duel across the Straits of Dover last night. No casualties or damage occurred.

December 7th Saturday
There have been no raid warnings today, not even a night warning. Hitler must have heard it was Janet Robertson's wedding day. Luckily it has been fine all day, too, and sunny.

December 8th Sunday 67th week
Mr Parsons came round early this morning and told me there was no raid warning

last night throughout the country. London for the first time for months had no day alert either. The RAF returned yesterday morning from the biggest of a series of attacks which are believed to have put a check on night raids across this country. Just after dark on Friday night when Nazi raiders were preparing to take off an avalanche of bombs fell on their aerodromes. It was a blitzkrieg against the blitzkriegers. For 9 hours the RAF attacks continued deep into Nazi occupied France and along the line of German air bases from the Plain of Orleans, through Holland and Belgium. This RAF hammering and the weather conditions are thought responsible for no raiders coming over here.... Two Portsmouth policemen were each sentenced yesterday to 10 years' penal servitude for looting. The Home Guard in a North London district are so indignant at the looting there that they are asking the War Office, through their Commander, for the right to shoot looters on sight. In the *Mid Sussex Times* of last Tuesday, December 3rd an account is given of a meeting of the Urban Council. They say the mackintoshes for us wardens are due in 3 weeks' time. Our new suits are called 'boiler suits' and are far warmer and more comfortable than the old ones now discarded. The siren sounded early this evening, at 5.45 and the all-clear not until 7.18 on Monday morning. It was the longest but one raid and the worst we have had this far with fires constantly recurring in the north and NNW and NNE. One fire caused by incendiary bombs we saw in the Chailey direction. The nearest here dropped at Cuckfield about 2am and another at or near Balcombe so far as we could tell. Many red flares were sent up in the earlier part of the night and the barrage was exceptionally loud and constant.

December 9th Monday
I saw Mr Parsons again this morning about 10.30. He said the line was blocked between Balcombe and Three Bridges. No doubt caused by one of those bombs we heard last night. So he did not attempt the journey to town.

December 11th Wednesday
Hitler made a speech to German workers yesterday, obviously for home propaganda, in a Berlin arms factory. Among other things he said 'If we lose this fight then it is the end of the German people'. But that is nonsense. He means it will be the end of the Nazi system. Germans existed long before Hitler, as a prosperous and happy community and can do so again.

December 12th Thursday
I heard that Brighton was bombed and as the paper mentions 'one slight casualty and damage to property on a SE town' I expect it is Brighton. The puzzling intermittence of night raids in England is thought to be due to Hitler's desire for a mutual discontinuance of night raids. Hitler's raids are said to be retaliatory.

Goebbels threatens greater raids if we continue. A certain lack of confidence has been read by analysts into Hitler's placatory speech to the workers on Tuesday.

December 13th Friday
One bomb in London unearthed two hollowed tree trunks, each 10ft in length and with iron collars at the ends. British Museum experts think they are water pipes laid by Sir Hugh Middleton in 1609. There has been no raid during the day nor yet an evening one. I was dressed ready for the siren but being a cold night was glad enough there was no call.

December 14th Saturday
Today's paper says there were no daylight raids in any part of the country yesterday, and London's first night alert lasted only a short time…. Another day and night without any air raid. The bad weather may account for it.

December 15th Sunday 68th week
This afternoon Christopher Stone invited all soldiers and ARP wardens to an entertainment at the Perrymount Cinema. I was told 2 o'clock, but it did not begin until 2.30 and lasted two hours. I sat between Mr Mossop and Mr Ridgeway. It was a good show, first class artists and no vulgarity. It was a pleasant and mild afternoon and I enjoyed walking both ways.

December 16th Monday
The film most talked about today is *The Great Dictator* by Charlie Chaplin. As part of the King's birthday celebration on Saturday he, the Queen and the two Princesses saw this film. A number of troops were his guests. Again no raid either day or night.

December 17th Tuesday
The Great Dictator spoke to Germany last night. Points in the film now showing in London were broadcast by the BBC to Germany, Belgium and France. 'This will pass away. Dictators will die and the power they took away from the people will return to the people'…. This evening at 7 o'clock there was a cinematograph show at the Public Hall, Haywards Heath, for ARP and 'allies'. Photographs were shown of the use of stirrup pumps putting out fires by incendiary bombs, of first aid help and methods and of the work of rescue squads. All were interesting especially the rescuing parties. One showed rescue work carried out at a bombed house in Trafalgar Square…. I walked both ways coming home with Mr Ridgeway. People are inclined to pull up blinds in the morning, before black-out is over, which now is at 8.34am. When I went to post a letter at 8.15 this morning one window was brilliant. This evening when I got home about 9.15 I called to warn the transgressor.

December 18th Wednesday

The Whirlwind, mentioned in Lord Beaverbrook's broadcast last night, is one of the best-kept secrets of the war, destined soon to become as much a household word as Spitfire or Hurricane. It is one of the fastest planes in the world, the very latest in design with many new features. It is only one of our many new types of fighters and bombers. Lord Beaverbrook said we must recognize the enemy is making preparations for invasion even before spring time comes, by land and sea, but principally by air. He likened the German leader as sitting on a three-legged stool. One leg was superiority in the air; 2nd mechanised forces; 3rd Fifth Column. On our side we have one sure defence, control of the sea. We have knocked off one leg, supremacy in the air. This Whirlwind is among the machines with which Britain has seized control of the air.... Still no raid day or night. One wonders what this peace from raids means. Oil shortage? Getting ready for a grand slam?

December 19th Thursday

German pilots who fly over Britain are now wearing civilian clothes under their flying kit, so that if they bale out they will have a chance of escape. This is believed to explain the reason why the 2 German pilots who landed nearly 3 weeks ago have never been caught.... Compensation for death or disablement by enemy action is extended to every adult civilian in the country under the scheme announced in Parliament yesterday by Sir Kingsley Wood, Chancellor of the Exchequer. It comes into force on Christmas Eve and the entire cost will be borne by the State. Until now Government payments have been made only to those members of the Civil Defence or to people gainfully employed. Up to a late hour last night no sirens had been sounded in London for 48 hours, the longest time since the air war began last September.

December 20th Friday

There was a raid siren this evening at 5.52, but no bombs were dropped in our hearing. I was patrolling with Mr Gilbert in Meadow Lane when the all-clear sounded at 7.10. But the siren sounded again at 9.30 and the all-clear at 2.05am. It was the first time our warden's party had had a second call.... Mr Ridgeway was out when the all-clear went and came in very cold. I made some toast and some hot Oxo which warmed us. When I got home at a ¼ to 3 I did the cooking, or rather prepared it, for the weekend knowing I should not have time for it tomorrow. We heard no bombs and only a few planes all the evening.

December 21st Saturday

At 7.30 I went up to the YMCA canteen.... Mrs Clarkson is in charge on Saturdays and is there from before tea time until closing time at 10pm. We use the kitchen of the flat on the first floor and the large room with the minstrel's gallery for the men. There is a piano, a gramophone, and opposite the counter where tea is made is a shop with useful things for the soldiers to buy: cigarettes, chocolate (there is none in the village shops now), 2½ stamps, razor blades, polishing creams, dusters, handkerchiefs (khaki), aspirin, matches and so forth. They are allowed to have ping pong balls for the game in another room but must leave 3d for each ball borrowed, which sum is returned to them when they bring back the ball. I looked after the shop for some time and found it a cold occupation with a draught that gave me a stiff neck.

December 22nd Sunday 69th week
An early attempt of the invasion of Britain is expected and warnings are repeated over and over again…. People in the Channel Isles are becoming poor because German troops there are buying up all goods and giving in exchange nothing but Nazi credit notes which have no value except for purchase of goods from Germany. But no German goods are being sent to the Islands so the people are landed with so much waste paper and are being denuded of all their property. Guernsey milking cows are killed for meat. The bulk of potatoes and most of the butter and margarine stocks have been sent to Germany. The loud bomb we heard last night was at Cuckfield. It fell just outside the gates of West Hylands destroying a cottage opposite. The three people in it felt the plane uncomfortably near and got out of their cottage just in time and were not hurt. Another bomb fell in the Recreation ground at Haywards Heath and although nearer did not make our windows rattle like the Cuckfield one. I walked to the Hospital to see Miss Beard, it was too cold to cycle. When I got to Sydney Road I opened my eyes. Dr Kilpack's windows were all blown away, the Forest Stores windows a blank with all their stock removed and no glass at all, Dewhurst the butcher lost the glass in his main window and at the corner of Paddockhall Road, Hilton's shop and office windows were gone and much glass swept up in heaps. After I left the hospital I went to see how Louie Stevens had fared for her garden adjoins the recreation ground. She had 43 windows broken as well as her skylight, and the classroom ceiling was down. Then I went into the grounds to see the crater made by the 500lb bomb that had been dropped in the trees close to the cricket pavilion, most of its windows blown away and the cricket ground covered with debris and lumps of earth. The crater looked about 20ft deep, was quite round and about 30ft across…. During the day I collected the last signature for the card I had prepared, with a branch of painted holly at the top, to accompany the rug I bought at Masters' for a Christmas present to Mr and Mrs Parsons from us 7 wardens. It is a pre-war one bought before the new 'purchase tax' was in force about a month ago. I hope they will like it, also the other wardens when they see it. We have all helped to wear out the rug in the 'office' which is our Wardens' Post.

December 25th Wednesday
The 4 'bachelor' members of our Sector, Miss Abby, Mrs Robertson, Mr Ridgeway and myself had decided that the 'family' members, Messrs Parsons, Ward and Gilbert should not be allowed to come out on Christmas night. As it so happened there was no call. Mr Parsons came round in the morning to thank us for the rug, bringing letters of good wishes and thanks to our warden efforts from the Council authorities. They sent to our Post four bottles of beer for a Christmas present. We shall enjoy that one night during our patrols. I went to early service, 8.30 and found the Church prettily decorated although there is not much holly berry this year.... The Church was dark and very full, but at 8.35 the lights were turned on. Most people spent a quieter Christmas than usual. There has been a shortage of a few things, chiefly sweets of any kind and chocolate. One of the reasons of the shortage is the restriction of sugar to the manufacturers, half pre-war requirements. The second reason is the great demand made by the voluntary services and works canteens which get preferential treatment. It is very hard on the retail confectionery trade, there are no sweets at all on the shelves usually laden with large glass bottles full up with different kinds.... I have not received so many cards as last year, 48 against 82 and few are topical.

December 27th Friday
Yesterday, Thursday, which was Boxing Day, was quiet and there were no raids here, nor were newspapers published.... On Christmas afternoon the best present for many parents was hearing the voices of their children in their new Empire homes speaking to them over the radio.... The sirens sounded this evening at 6.37 and I went out with Mr Gilbert and after supper stayed at the Post for a while. We saw lights that we had not seen before, a bright light, then a round red flare then a 'plonk'. We heard no plane above, and whether it was ours or the enemy's we did not know. Mr Parsons telephoned to Mr Fraser, who had not seen them and he came along to the Common from where we saw them in several different places. He tried to get information about them from headquarters, but they had received no message about them. But we hope to hear later on. The all-clear was at 10.45.

December 28th Saturday
The attack on London last night was one of the heaviest for some time. We heard the barrage guns and many planes going over from the S and SE.... In one district 100 bombs were dropped.

December 29th Sunday 70th week
The papers today give photographs of our 'invasion' preparations, showing the various methods of getting troops and vehicles across a river in small collapsible boats.... P.G. Wodehouse was captured by the Germans at his Le Touquet villa last

May. He is now detained in a Silesian lunatic asylum converted into an internment camp. There in his padded cell he is writing another book. At a certain bomber station there were a number of Poles who drew up at the door to bid goodbye before starting on a hazardous mission. Their spokesman had in his hand an English dictionary. He stepped forward saying 'God pickle you, gentlemen' (Note pickle and preserve). On Saturday evening, the 21st, when the bomb was dropped in the Heath recreation ground, 100 incendiary bombs were dropped at Broadhurst Manor. A haystack was partially destroyed but the blaze was got under by the AFS. The electric light cables that fell in Perrymount Road were repaired as soon as daylight dawned on Saturday morning. The siren this evening sounded at 6.07. It was not my evening on but I went to the post and patrolled a while because Dorrie Robertson had been to Crowborough Hospital to see Janet after a motor–cycle smash on Christmas Eve.... There were many planes about and extra bright flashes in the northern sky. We heard distant bombs. Planes were flying low.... A woman living in Vichy writes to her sister in England that although the Nazi overlord is supreme, Germans fear that the French people will aid Britain. She says everything has been taken and all that has been bought paid for with valueless money. Finding food is all the people are trying for, and it will be surprising if there is not a famine this winter.... Northern France is now a forbidden area; it is certainly because they are massing their forces there. How the French hope England will win!

December 30th Monday
We know that when the morning papers are delayed London has been 'getting it' the night before and probably some part of the railway disorganised. There were no papers this morning. Those extra vivid flashes and fires we saw from the Common in the North are, no doubt, responsible. About midday the papers arrived. London had its most severe raid since September, when the City blast began.... The Royal Academy will have no winter show this time.... Rudolf Haybrook, of the AFS, paints London fires and his pictures of them have put him in the forefront. The LCC has just bought 4 of his canvases. Preparations for invasion by glider-borne troops go forward in East Prussia, 1,000 old bombers could each tow 2 gliders with 35 men each. It would be possible to send from Sicily to Benghazi, 450 miles, as many as 35,000 men in a night.... The gliders might be intended for an attack on this country.

December 31st Monday
Yesterday afternoon, while I was in the Library a lorry drove past carrying a German machine that had been brought down. I do not know where. It was not much damaged and its national markings could be clearly seen. Again no raid. The year 1940 finishes on a mild but sunless day. Everyone wonders what 1941 will bring forth. The first thought and wish of everyone is that there will be peace. I wonder.

1941

—✺—

January 13th Monday
The meat ration for this week until further notice will be 1s 2d a person for adults and 7d for children…. The price of rabbits is controlled but one is seldom able to get a rabbit. There are still no sweets of any kind nor yet any chocolate to be bought. The keepers of sweet shops in the village print on their doors in white chalk 'no sweets'. It must save them many journeys to their door.

January 14th Tuesday
Onions are still a rare luxury and there are none for sale in this village. One which weighed no more than 2oz was first prize in a raffle at Uxbridge the other night. Tickets were 2d a time. The result was £2 for a local Comforts Fund. Again no raid either day or night.

January 19th Sunday 73rd week
Fully half an hour before the siren sounded at 8.25, we heard several bombs fall, but I could not find out where they fell. It was a dark night, rather rainy and slippery in shaded places. The all–clear was at 11.50 just as Mr Parsons had made the tea. For the first time we all four had tea and bread and cheese together, Misters Parsons, Ridgeway, Knight and myself. We talked and smoked over it until 1am and then went home to bed.

January 21st Tuesday
There was an air raid warning this afternoon at 3.42, the first day one we have had for about a month. No planes were heard…. The all–clear sounded at 4.20, so I was not out in the wet too long.

January 22nd Wednesday
There was no raid warning last night and for the second night in succession there were no raids in the country.

January 23rd Thursday
It is said that if there had been more spotters and more fire parties ready, the fires in London would not have got such a fierce hold where incendiaries had been

dropped. We are profiting by that experience and fire parties properly organized are being formed throughout the country. There was no raid warning this evening, that is the 4th night in succession without a warning.

February 1st Saturday
For the third time since Christmas, eggs are down by 3d a dozen. It makes no difference in this village for no eggs are to be had.

February 2nd Sunday 75th week
We have had a short warning this morning from 12.17 to 12.37. Two of Louie Stevens' pupils and a teacher came in for shelter on their way back from church. They all carried their gas masks. There was no raid this evening. A clear fortnight now.

February 4th Tuesday
A firm is experimenting making carrot marmalade flavoured with bitter orange oil. It will be several weeks before Seville oranges arrive. I asked Masters if he would be likely to have any. He did not know but thought not. Most will go to manufacturers. This afternoon I helped Mrs Lister at the Heath library and on my return went to some of those in my sector to tell them the 'fire fighter' day chosen.... Our siren at the fire station sounded very loud, for I was out to post a letter when it sounded. The all-clear was at 10.50.

February 5th Wednesday
This morning at 8 o'clock about 200 RA soldiers, equipped with a very small band playing marched towards the Heath. They looked ready for embarkation.... Burgess at Beckworth told me he had seen flares just before the siren sounded and as planes were going over. But when he showed me the direction of them I found it was a light from the greenhouses between Beckworth and Backwoods Lane. Mr Ridgeway whom I met on the Common went to inspect and found the 'flare' is due to the construction of the heating apparatus. It can easily be covered.... Bitter oranges are to cost 6d to 8d. I wonder if any will come this way?

February 9th Sunday 76th week
The Prime Minister spoke on the wireless at 9 o'clock this evening for 45 minutes. I went in next door to hear him and his speech came through clearly. His speech was dramatically moving and encouraging. He ended with his message to Roosevelt 'Give us the tools and we will finish the job'.

February 14th Friday
This week the two bags of sand put at the foot of lamp posts have been hooked on to a cord tied about one third of the height of the post. This position keeps them

drier, but for most people I consider them useless. They are so heavy that only the strongest wristed person could take them down and throw them on an incendiary bomb. I met Mr N. Strachan-Davidson on Monday on Black Hill and I asked him to 'take one of those bags down and throw it on that bomb burning in the road.' He could not lift it off the hook. I have mentioned the matter to Mr Parsons and asked him to speak to Mr Fraser about the too-heavy bags. The sand in each bag would make two bags that everybody would be able to deal with.

February 21st Friday
There was no raid warning here this evening, but as the weather seemed to be in favour of a raid, I did not undress, but as nothing happened I took off my boiler suit at 4.30am.

February 22nd Saturday
News reached London yesterday that 100 Polish Jews were shot because one prisoner, Kott, had escaped and was not found in the 24 hours time limit given. Kott could not have known of what was threatened.

February 23rd Sunday 78th week
Although the evening seemed favourable there was no air raid warning. I again slept in my clothes thinking there might be a call later, but there wasn't.

March 2nd Sunday 79th week
Yesterday afternoon, about 3 o'clock a tank, or a lorry fitted with tank cog-wheels, came round the corner too fast, skidded and knocked out the lime tree that I see from my parlour window just on the other side of the pavement. I shall miss that lime because when docked the boughs and branches made a curious 'animal' like a cat.

March 4th Tuesday
I called to see Mr Masters today about the lime tree and suggested that the Army provided another tree to take the place of the one they knocked down.

March 5th Wednesday
A notice board was put up today on the side of the Common at Black Hill, 'Drive slowly Military Camp'.

March 6th Thursday
This morning, because three helpers were ill, I went to the Hall to help with the children's dinners which they have in the corridor. There were 70 to 80 children, all evacuated and they have a good dinner. Today it was minced meat, pease

pudding, cabbage and mashed potatoes and a milky rice pudding. Serving them and clearing up took just an hour, from 12.15 to 1.15.

March 9th Sunday 80th week
Britain will buy 400,000 crates of oranges from Spain under an agreement between Madrid and London yesterday. I wonder if any bitter oranges are included.... Mr Parsons came in this morning with a foolscap sheet for all of us wardens to sign our names to a letter of thanks for the 'comforts' lately received. I find my gloves very comfortable and warm. From about 11.30 to 1, Beckworth was on fire (in imagination) and the fire brigade from the Heath dealt with it. The practice was chiefly for the nurses at Beckworth.

March 10th Monday
In the afternoon while I was at the Library a military conference was held in the Hall, chiefly officers and several military police on motorcycles. The conference lasted about 2 hours.... Washing tanks and lorries in the Pond has now been stopped although the surface is still oily. The swans hate the oil.

March 13th Thursday
In the morning soldiers had put upon the Black Hill part of the Common a big camouflaged affair for, one supposes, guns and ammunition in practice for invasion. Many tall posts made of steel or iron were fixed in the ground and nets covered with green and grey pieces to resemble leaves were placed in an irregular manner on top. The 'hidden' effect was excellent. In the early evening it was all taken down.

March 15th Saturday
Jam, marmalade, treacle and syrup will be rationed to 8oz per month from next Monday, so perhaps I shall now be able to get some treacle, which can often be used instead of sugar.

March 22nd Saturday
From next Saturday the 29th until the 5th of April is War Weapons Week in Mid Sussex. Mr Ling, who has recently bought Heasman's Estate Agency business in the High Street, is lending his shop for those who are organizing the work and taking the savings. I have been asked to do the decorations and as usual in these cases more work is added. A piece of material 2ft deep is to be slung across the street, 54 foot span and painted in the middle *Our War Weapons Week March 29th to April 5th inclusive*. In addition, Mr Fraser, who is at the head of the scheme, wants also 'Buy your National Savings Certificates and Stamps here' and then an arrow pointing to the shop. Then to make the line attractive some flags. As the flags I have are long I have had to make

most of them... to correspond to the lettered material. On working it all out I find I shall not have time to do the second long line, far too much to read anyway. I have fixed up one of the posters on my fence, but I shall ask for more.

March 26th Wednesday
From today Brighton and the coast area for 20 miles around become a no–man's land for visitors, holidaymakers and trippers. There were two day raid warnings today, both short ones from 10.22 to10.50 and from 3.40 to 4.10. All was quiet here and only a few planes passed over. Riots in Belgrade are even more serious. At Sarajevo more than 1,000 people clashed with the police in a revolt against the signing of the Axis pact by the Government. British newspaper men were told by the Government they would be expelled if they continued to write about the disorders.

March 27th Thursday
The last few days I have been working all day at the street decoration for War Weapons Week which begins on Saturday. The material, unbleached calico, I have made 2ft deep and painted in orange, the colour Mr Fraser gave me, in Roman letters 10½ inches tall *Our War Weapons Week – March 29th – April 5th inclusive*. Then I made 16 flags about 2ft long red, white and blue, St George, Andrew and Patrick and one Union Jack, 8 flags each end of the lettering, to go across the 54ft span of the High Street from Mr Ling's shop to the Red Lion. I don't think much of Mr Fraser's cord. Twisted wire would have been better.

March 28th Friday
This morning and some of the afternoon I spent decorating with flags Ling's shop for War Weapons Week. I took flags that I had and all were useful...the fire brigade slung the line across the street. Some excellent photographs of war subjects were brought from Oaklands by Mr Fraser and these we put in the window and in company with Mr Ling's house advertisements look very good.... The rationing of cheese begins on Monday May 5th and one must register tomorrow. The allowance is one ounce per head per week save for miners and agricultural workers who will get 8oz a week.

March 31st Monday
I cycled with 7 unused masks from Beckworth this morning and left them at Mr Fraser's house. When I was at Muster Green I saw two formations of planes, 12 in each company, travelling east flying high and looking as if they were made of silver. I bought 3lbs of carrots at Waltons. No bags or papers are provided for such things but the girl lent me her brass scales to take them across the road to put them in my bicycle basket. How strange that would have been thought a year ago! Instead of turning out for every raid, our sector has now agreed to every other

night, an alteration I proposed myself as it is often inconvenient not to know that you are certainly free every other evening. Many times I have had to 'dress up' because I was due for the next raid, but now it will only be necessary to don battle dress every other evening raid or no raids. There was no call this evening.... The war savings posters are good. I don't care much for the one entitled *Keep it up* showing a blueish inflated balloon aloft, an ugly thing but all the others are good. I am showing two on my fence during this War Weapons Week.

April 1st Tuesday
I am 'on' all day Tuesday so I went to the Post where I saw Mr Parsons. I hoped Pelham House would give a little shelter from the icy wind but it didn't. I went over to the Pavilion and took the little shelter that gave without destroying the view. But the raid did not last long, only from 9.13 to 9.33.... There were no more calls so got on with spring cleaning the parlour. There was no evening raid.

April 8th Tuesday
I was out with Mr Ridgeway and Mr Olphert, a fire watcher, for some time and we investigated the land adjoining the north side of Beckworth Lane as Mr Olphert had seen a light there. We found no light. It may have been moonshine on a piece of glass left in a broken window of a barn there. I made cups of Oxo for Ridgeway, Knight and myself and got into bed just before 5 o'clock. At 5.50 I was surprised to hear the siren again, so dressed as quickly as possible and reported at the Post where I found Mr Parsons ready and waiting. Mr Ridgeway did not turn up. I expect he did not hear the siren. Mr Parsons went on the Common but the all-clear sounded in half an hour, at 6.20. I went home, got some breakfast and as Wednesday is my busy housework morning did not go to bed again.

April 12th Saturday
In a letter this morning Jock tells me of damage done at Brighton last Tuesday between midnight and 1 o'clock. Norfolk Street and Edward Street suffered the most. The air raid shelter in Norfolk Square got a direct hit and was 'blown to bits'. No one was in it at the time. The heavy bomb shook the floors in his house. This morning I cycled to Ardingly to take Mrs Musgrave my short account with sketches of our holiday in Cornwall in August 1939 just before the war began. I came back along Stonecross Lane and Park Lane, after going down Burstow Hill Lane to see the big crater made by a bomb last autumn. Paxhill Park is being made the site of a large camp and already many tents have been put up, brown camouflaged with black, broad, curly splashes. I saw them well from my bicycle when riding down Park Lane. The military has also taken Finches, very soon after old Mrs Savill's death.

April 13th Sunday 85th week
Four soldiers and four airmen had a surprise yesterday while travelling north by train. A retired London stockbroker handed each a wax-sealed envelope telling them not to open it until he had left the train. They found each contained £50 in notes. The donor said his gift was an Easter offering of thanks for the escape of himself and his family in the last raid on Coventry.... So that more cheese and condensed milk can be made milk supplies are cut to six-sevenths of the sales in the week starting March 2nd. It means that anyone taking one pint daily must now take only half a pint for 2 days of the week. Milk for schools will be the same. In church this Easter morning special prayers were given for Yugoslavia in addition to other 'war' prayers. The Church was delightfully decorated, daffodils being the chief flowers used. There was a full congregation. Mr Buckingham preached a very short sermon. Being Easter Sunday I was surprised there was no raid.

April 14th Monday
Again there was no raid this evening, all the same I did not undress.

April 15th Tuesday
Mr Parsons called to tell me that the fire fighters are to be provided with tin hats. Also that at Oaklands at 3 o'clock next Saturday there is to be a fire practice for firewatchers. Some do not yet know how to use a stirrup pump. I went to meet the firewatchers in my sector to get the size of their hats and to tell them about Saturday and wrote it down on slips for each one so that they can mind the day and the time. There was a late raid, from 10.21 to 4.28.

April 16th Wednesday
I was having tea in the garden, after the Library, with Donald when the siren sounded at 5.11 but it was short for the all-clear was at 5.35. The evening raid was a long one, 9.08pm until 4.55am and one of the worst we have ever had, including one of last autumn's raids. The droning of the planes, gun-fire flares, sparks and flashes were incessant until nearly 11 o'clock and even then the lulls between were short. London was the objective, and no doubt we shall hear of damage done.... Welsh Fusiliers are the new soldiers just arrived in the village. Mr Knight and I had some chocolate when we were patrolling, quite a treat for there is so little to be bought.

April 17th Thursday
The papers did not arrive until the afternoon. I was told that both Victoria and London Bridge Stations were closed so suppose they were 'plastered' last night with other places. When I was walking down the garden on my way home this morning from the night raid at 5.05am, I heard the cuckoo for the first time.

However tired one may get later on of hearing that bird, the first time is always a pleasure.

April 18th Friday
More details are given today of Wednesday's dreadful blitz on London.... Eight hospitals were hit. One of the districts most affected was the West End. Mansions, flats, offices and shops were shattered. Three big stores were damaged and only the walls 'of a famous church remain'. Many rescuers died before dawn. I cycled this afternoon to Oaklands to take part in the fire practice for fire fighters in our sector. Mrs Robertson, Mr Ridgeway and I managed the first fire to demonstrate the method to the uninitiated and then all the others took a part and did very well. I lent John Fawssett my boiler suit while he used the hose. It is always a dirty job on the floor of the shed and I cannot use the suit again until it is washed. But I can use the old suit in the meantime. After the library session I went up to the YMCA canteen to give Mrs Pellett a hand for she was short of helpers and we had a busy evening. There are such numbers of soldiers in the village just now, among those who came in were soldiers of the Royal Welsh Fusiliers lately billeted here. It is a pleasant canteen to work in for we change about and one does not always do the same thing, and the work is divided into attending to men's wants at the tables, serving tea at the counter where the money is taken and doing duty at the 'shop' where many useful things are sold to the soldiers. Mrs Tallis and Mrs Pellett did the cooking. This evening there were fried eggs and chips 9d and sausages and mash 4d, bread and butter 2 slices a penny. All the helpers worked happily together and we divided the washing up between us. The canteen is supposed to close at 10 but it was 10.20 before the last left. Then the clearing up had to be done and the cloths washed before we started the dark walk home each one holding onto a neighbour. A raid was on all the time, it lasted from 9.15 to 4.48. I got home at 11.10 and was glad to go to bed.

April 21st Monday
Tobruk, Verdun of the Western Desert, has smashed a third Italo–German tank attack, putting four completely out of action. Indian troops are among the Imperial forces holding the seaport.

April 23rd Wednesday
Ten tons of bombs were dropped on Tripoli harbour when the RAF carried out a raid in support of the Mediterranean Fleet bombardment of the coast port on Monday.... This afternoon, after the Library, Jean Parsons and I took round 9 of the new tin hats issued to our fire watchers. In colour they are greenish–grey and trimmed with a narrow black braid of bootlace width.

April 25th Friday
Mrs Roosevelt has sent from America a present to all Women's Institutes in this country. I saw ours last Wednesday at the meeting, which was held in the Congregational Church because the military was again using the Village Hall. There are 2,000 soldiers in the village now, more than there have ever been before. Mrs Roosevelt's present to each WI was a packet of seeds, a pint of peas, a pint of dwarf French beans, ½oz carrot and ½oz of onion seed. I suppose they will be sown on the ground the Institute has acquired near the Bent Arms. I have promised to do some hoeing when the time comes, an important item not always valued. Mrs Slack spoke at the meeting on Canada, where she came from, especially in reference to the care of the children there who had been sent from England. There was no raid warning here this evening.

April 28th Monday
Four houses in our sector showed lights. People are still very careless about the black-out. I was at the Post when the all-clear sounded. When Messrs Parsons, Gilbert and Ridgeway came in, Mr Parsons made some tea and we stayed talking till 12 then went home. It was very dark but it had been a quiet raid here I heard only one plane.

April 29th Tuesday
Today soldiers have been practising camouflaging and working their guns. There were numbers of both men and guns on the Common. It was rather far away but I took a snapshot from my bedroom window, for I don't think photographing of troops is allowed.

May 2nd Friday
The siren at the Fire Station in Kent Street has been placed on a high platform so that it may be heard in the north part of the village street. In its first place against the station wall intervening buildings cut off the sound. Many times Mr Ridgeway failed to hear it. There was no raid this evening here, so to bed in my clothes.

May 3rd Saturday
Tonight the two hours Summer Time begins and clocks are to go forward at 2am. Of course some people are against it, but after the first week they will get used to it and probably not mind. After the library session I went to the YMCA canteen at the Tiger where we had a busy evening. Long before closing time at 10 the tea gave out and we used Oxo instead. Then the Oxo gave out so we could do no more drinks. 16 long sandwich trays were cut up for bread and butter, the chief dish being haricot beans on toast. We could have done with more food, sausages and chip potatoes, we had only a little of these. The siren sounded at 10.10

although we do not hear it at the Tiger, far too much noise, the all-clear was at 3.10am.

May 5th Monday
In the afternoon I cycled to Plummerden Lane to pick some wild flowers to make a cross for Mrs Bottrill who died on Sunday. Up Park Lane I saw many more tents up in the Paxhill Camp, a big affair now.

May 7th Wednesday
No cheese will be allowed to public houses or for school dinners and there is no prospect of an increased ration, 2oz a week. Agricultural workers may have ½lb. Our local Spitfire Fund is now closed. The sum collected was £3,500 although our aim was £5,000. No raid warning tonight.

May 10th Saturday
This morning two new notices were put up on boards on the upper part of the Common, in red letters, *Lorries and cycles prohibited*. The Common was getting into a bad state with deep ruts in many places, quite spoiling it for games, so the notices are welcomed…. This morning Mr Parsons gave me 18 forms for the fire-spotters in my special part of the sector to sign, which signature makes them recognized fire-spotters and entitled to receive compensation if hurt while carrying on their duties. There was a fierce raid over London this evening and all night. It began at 10.50 and lasted 7 hours, all-clear at 5.50am. Like the heavy London raid on April 16–17, the planes seemed to be all around. From the Common we saw 2 brought down, so knew that the numbers destroyed would be high. It was a very cold night but still and at dawn the scene from the Common looked like a Christmas card, the white frost was snow-like then, the trees and buildings without detail and the flushed sky mingling into gold behind them. The Pond made another charming picture. I was home soon after 6, too late to go to bed… but I laid down for an hour to get my feet warm.

May 13th Tuesday
There is startling news in the papers this morning. Rudolf Hess, Hitler's deputy and 'dearest friend' has landed in Scotland in a Messerschmitt 110 and given himself up…. On Monday afternoon I worked for 2 hours with Mrs Barrow and Mrs Lazell at the Women's Institute plot of ground behind the garden of the Bent Arms and which is approached down Brushes Lane. The plot is only 4 rows and we are growing chiefly root vegetables, a few rows of peas and have edged the plot with parsley. We sowed peas and carrots and took a layer of weeds off the paths. A large piece of ground there is divided off into plots for other workers besides us.

After the library session I planted my own monte d'or beans down the front garden dividing 'hedge', formerly lavender.

May 22nd Thursday
This afternoon while I was having tea with Marjorie and Edith who had come down for the day the Haywards Heath siren sounded but not ours. One bomb was fairly near, 2 others a little further away and another further still. It was a quick affair, probably a lone raider being chased by one of our fighters, time 4.57 to 5.08. Our siren did not go for the all-clear either. When I went to the Post Office later I saw a man mounted at the top of a long ladder clearing out the siren. It looked as if he were pulling out birds' nests! I suppose starlings have taken advantage of this week's lull and built there! There was no night raid.

May 26th Monday
At Inspection 5.15 in the afternoon at Oaklands the ARP and Fire Brigade members were inspected by Earl de la Warr. It was the first inspection we had. We were told to appear in our boiler suits, helmet, gas masks of course, but not in rubber boots, so we women wardens had to turn our trousers up considerably for a big length always goes into the boots. We all wore coats to Oaklands for it was a cold day and there had been many heavy showers.... The inspection was held in the forecourt and the civil defence included the fire service, first aid parties, ambulance service as well as wardens from Lindfield, Cuckfield and Haywards Heath. When passing down the line Earl de la Warr spoke to a member here and there and when he came to me I gave him a smile. 'Have you been here from the beginning?' 'Yes' I said and I added 'I come from Lindfield'. Fortunately it did not rain during our time there, threatening though the clouds were. I did not get to the Library until 6.25 but Mrs Lister spared Donald to come so all was well. It was my turn for the raid and I was glad there wasn't one.

May 27th Tuesday
We are told the *Bismarck* has been twice hit by torpedoes from the Fleet Air Arm and is still being pursued by the Navy.

May 29th Thursday
Particulars of the tea time raid last Thursday are now known. Eleven bombs were dropped at Chailey, Pelling Bridge and Newick and so on the way to the coast where our fighter in chase brought the plane down. All the bombs fell in gardens, fields or woods and no house was hit, although at Newick some were slightly damaged. The chemist at Newick was killed by a glass bottle falling on the back of his neck. He was standing in the doorway. Others with more sense lay flat and were not hurt.

June 1st Whit Sunday 92nd week

The headline in the papers this morning is 'Clothes rationed from this morning'. Information is given on garments rationed or not and how many coupons are needed for the clothes that are rationed. Tinned fruits have disappeared from the market. They have not been imported for some months because they take up too much cargo space. Lord Leconfield, Lord Lieutenant of our county, is to be in control of all civil defence along an important part of the south coast.... Raids are not long now on account of fewer dark hours.... The siren sounded this evening at 11.52, the all-clear at 1.20. The planes were going west. I do not think London was visited. We all returned and went happily to bed but at 2.55 there was a second call. I dressed quickly and Mr Parsons went out to see who else was about. He met Mr Knight but as Mr Ridgeway did not turn up we supposed he had not heard the siren. The raid was short, all-clear at 3.25.

June 6th Friday

Jock came over and we went to Hapstead Wood although the bluebells there were, like us, past their prime.

June 13th Friday

I suppose that when I wrote to Betty Paterson on June 1st for her birthday I used an envelope with a stick on patch of paper for reuse.... This morning I received a notice from the Censorship Department that for abroad this use is not permitted.... There were 2 raids today, a short one in the morning from 11.55 to 12.25 and a night raid from 1.30 to 3.30. For fully 45 minutes before the siren sounded planes were overhead, there was gun-firing in the distance and machine gun-firing nearer. It puzzles us that so often we hear all this going on and yet no siren. It seemed that London and Portsmouth were the objectives and a bright flash suggested a plane was brought down.... We were glad of Oxo when Mr Parsons and I got back to the Post, Ridgeway and Knight were there.

June 14th Saturday

There was no canteen at the Tiger this evening, the reason being that many soldiers were on manoeuvres. There was no raid warning and the traffic for several hours around midnight made me think that Lindfield itself had been invaded. All the High Street is scarred with wheel marks.

June 17th Tuesday

There was a short day raid from 12.30 to 12.53, and again I neither saw nor heard a plane. It was probably a flight over the Channel again. Soldiers were having a tug of war on the lower part of the Common. There was no night raid.

June 23rd Monday

Yesterday afternoon I was told that the news had come through the wireless that Germany had attacked Russia beginning at 4am on Sunday morning. I went next door to hear the Premier speak at 9pm before the news. He made his speech in his usual good and sturdy form and I wonder how many millions heard his denouncement of Hitler and his promise of all possible aid to Russia in their fight, which he says we shall pursue to the end. Our new RAF offensive is only the beginning. By day and by night we shall bomb Germany, dropping a growing weight of bombs in 'ever increasing measure.' No warning was given but the Premier had already warned Stalin of what was to come. 'The Russian danger is our danger and the danger of the USA because the cause of any Russian fighting for hearth and home is the cause of every free people.' He said that we had reached one of the climacterics of the war. The first was when France fell, the second when the RAF beat the Hun out of the daylight air, the third when the US passed the Lease and Lend Act and the fourth is now upon us. Hitler wants to destroy the Russian power because if he succeeds he will be able to bring his main strength to bear for an attack on this island. His mission of Russia is no more than a prelude to an attempted invasion here. Mass raids on the Soviet Baltic bases in Latvia, Estonia and Lithuania, on Russian towns in the Ukraine on the Black Sea began the battle Hitler described as 'the greatest armies ever to meet on a 1,500 mile front'. Red bombers replied immediately, attacking German forces moving through East Prussia and raiding the Finnish naval base at Alskar in the Aaland Isles. On land 150 German Divisions are supporting the Finns and Romanians in a three-fold attack. About 160 Red Divisions are said to be resisting. Hitler is said to have given Keitel 4 weeks to smash Russian resistance. The Red Army has recently been reorganized on lessons from the Finnish and Balkan campaigns. In another sweep by RAF fighters and bombers over the Channel and France yesterday 30 Nazi fighters were destroyed for 2 of ours, the pilot of one being saved. Some shot down were the new 'crack' 109 Fs. After the fall of Damascus, which is likely to be the turning point in the Syria campaign, Allied forces have made local gains everywhere. Australians have been reinforced and will now advance on Beirut. Jimma, north of Addis Ababa the last point of Italian resistance, fell yesterday. 'Mopping up' is now being done by Abyssinian patriots, led by British officers. Germany is now beginning a great propaganda drive. The chief subject is – plug the Fuehrer as the saviour of the world from Bolshevism. Specially intensive efforts are to be made in Britain and the US, the real object being to create 'peace parties' in both countries. It will fail. The German-Russian war has startled Japanese political and public opinion, but as to the effect on Japan's policy there is silence in Tokyo. The Spaniards are pleased for they are enemies to Russia with whom, in consequence of her interference on the 'Red' side in the civil war, Spain has no diplomatic relations.

June 28th Saturday
The Welsh Fusiliers left the village today and soldiers from the Staffordshire and Essex regiments arrived in their place. I went to the canteen as usual. It was a warm evening and the soldiers came rather late. We have cold suppers for them now, egg salad, sardine salad 6d each and plenty of spring onions too, paste sandwiches and cider to drink (3d a glass) as well as hot tea. The stewed fruit and custard was sold out soon after 9 o'clock.

July 3rd Thursday
There was no raid here tonight.... At 1.30 I felt a few drops of rain and as a breeze had sprung up and the glass had been falling all the pleasant summer day I thought the rain, so much needed, might continue, so I gathered up my bed, brought in the garden table and trestles and went to bed upstairs.

July 4th Friday
Householders are now limited to 1 ton of coal a month until further notice. I burn one ton a year. Again there was no raid tonight but there have been many planes overhead on and off all day.

July 5th Saturday
Nazis are nearing the Stalin line, the line fortified inside the Russian frontier. They claim to have reached the Latvian–Russian border about 200 miles from Leningrad. Reports are contradictory and one cannot believe either side, but certainly many are being killed.... Roosevelt broadcast after the 9 o'clock news last night (I heard him at Val's house) and gave the American people on their Independence Day the slogan 'Speed, Efficiency and Toil'.... This is not going to be a good fruit year. I went with Sybil Fawssett early yesterday morning to try to get a lot of gooseberries which the greengrocer King promised her, but they were not forthcoming. Lady Barton gave me some from her garden, about 2lbs. She said 'You don't mind carrying them down in the basket do you?' I told her that I thought people would be envious when they saw me. There never have been any for sale in the village. The smallest cucumbers are 1/– each, in fact all vegetables are dear.

July 7th Monday
This morning I telephoned to Mr Wilson about the Library which is going to be difficult for the rest of the war. Donald Keymer came on Saturday for the last time for he has been taken for clerical work in a NAAFI and reports today at Reigate.

July 11th Friday
On Tuesday evening Mr Merry and all the wardens in our sector including our

head Mr Fraser, met at Mr Parson's house. He spoke about many things of interest, chiefly that we must take special care of our rubber boots for they cannot now be replaced. We shall all be glad *not* to have to wear them this hot weather.

July 12th Saturday

At the canteen tonight there was not much left at 8 o'clock for the soldiers to eat, the salad and fruit were finished. I made sardine sandwiches until there was no more bread and margarine but plenty of tea and lemonade for it was a hot, close, thirsty evening. I was home at 10.05 and then watered the garden. There was no raid either day or night.

> Egypt July 12th 1941
> My dear Nina, 2 letters arrived last week, 1 written on New Year's Day and the other on January 27th. They were both hardly legible and had 'salvaged from the sea' on both. Still I've got them and you must have been thinking I was very rude not to have answered!
> I'm so glad you are busy. You never were happy unless you had lots to do were you?... I am so glad brother Jock got over his operation. What an age! Graham[19]

July 21st Monday

Already V is being chalked on our brick pavements and on gates etc. I noticed them first when I went up the village street on Sunday afternoon.

July 24th Thursday

Colonel Knox, US Navy Secretary said last night that Japan would make some move but the US Navy can do whatever is necessary to carry out the country's policy in the Far East.

July 27th Sunday 100th week

The new ration books came into use yesterday.... No extra supplies of food will be allowed at seaside and holiday places on August Bank Holiday. The siren sounded tonight, or rather early in the morning, 2.05 after a bomb had been dropped in the west and many planes had passed over. It is just 3 weeks since the last raid. We saw firing Londonwards in the SW and SE but heard only this one bomb and machine gun-fire. The all-clear was 3.45.

July 30th Wednesday

There is a fortnight's salvage drive throughout Sussex beginning July 28th. Parish Committees have been formed and here the Mid Sussex Laundry has provided a place for a dump and Mr Alce has offered a covered shed for Scaynes Hill. Paper, textiles, metal and bones are asked for with the request that newsprint be kept separate. Every week some of the WVS call here for my waste paper which I put in a sack and keep in the shed.

July 31st Thursday
At 8.30 we had a gas refresher talk at the Post, Mr Parsons and we six wardens all being there. They dressed up Jack Ward and myself in the gas protective garments and very warm they felt this close thundery evening! We went through all the gases, their presence and treatment and decided to have a refresher meeting every Thursday at 8.30. Next week it is to be bandaging. There was no raid this evening.

August 6th Wednesday
According to authoritative reports in London, Hitler has used more than 20 armoured divisions against Russia, or 20,000 front line vehicles, a record for any war.... Southport Council last night endorsed the Libraries Committee's recommendation to withdraw the novels of Wodehouse from circulation because of his broadcasts from Germany. They also decided to dispose of 90 of his books as 'waste paper.' Two spies, a German and a Swiss, came over by plane and landed on the shores of Banff in a collapsible rubber boat. Both were caught and executed today at Wandsworth. They were armed, furnished with radio, maps and sausage in their food ration. No raids.

August 7th Thursday
Milk is to be rationed. There will be plenty of condensed milk available so no one will be short of milk in the winter. From the 25th the cheese will be 3oz instead of only 2, the ration for special workers being the same, 8oz. An order is also to be made controlling the prices of chocolate and sweets.... The Premier again warns us that invasion may come in September, one reason for everyone to stay put and not take holidays.... There have been no raids today, nor yet tonight. At 8.30 wardens in our sector met at our Post and we all practised first aid and bandaging. One soon gets out of practice with First Aid as well as with gas.

August 8th Friday
A big assignment of South African oranges has arrived and will soon be on sale at 7½d a 1lb. I wonder if Lindfield will get any? No raid today nor night.

August 10th Sunday 102nd week
At 9 o'clock this evening the Queen broadcast and I went next door to hear her, and Quentin Reynolds who spoke after the news.[20] The Queen spoke for 9 minutes in a delightful manner and addressed the women of America specially. She thanked them for their help, the gifts of canteens, ambulances, and medical

supplies and added 'Hardship has only steeled our hearts and strengthened our resolution'. Quentin Reynolds addressed his talk to Hitler using his old name 'Schickelgruber' and quoted a few sentences from *Mein Kampf*.[21] I hope Hitler was listening, the home truths might have been good for him. Reynolds put a bomb under the latest Nazi 'peace offensive' which is due to start in America tomorrow (or possibly today). One of the greatest mistakes made was to awake the dead here in England. When Plymouth was bombed Drake came out of his legendary past. When lightships were machine-gunned, Nelson roused and 'today his spirit rides the bridge of every ship that flies the British flag'. It is dangerous to awake the dead, their spirits slip easily from their shrouds to walk the streets of Britain. Do you think for a moment that a man bearing the name of Winston Churchill will ever bend his knee to anyone named Schickelgruber? Really, Mr S. really? There were no raids.

August 11th Monday
I went for a walk this evening to Kenwards. All the fields of the farm and others around are bearing good crops of wheat, oats, and bearded wheat instead of only roots and pasture. The hay crop this summer has been excellent and now we have a bumper harvest. I took some snapshots of Kenwards Farm, now up for sale, and one of Miss Daisy Wood who was with me.

August 12th Tuesday
Field Marshal von Rundstedt has a million men in the furious Ukraine battles around Odessa. The Nazi reports of the fighting are unreliable and the Soviet says that battles are continuing.... I went to Brighton today to see Jock, taking with me in my gas mask case a postcard from him saying his eyes were troublesome and would I go. This for safety in case I was turned back, as many visitors to the town have been. But I had no trouble at all and no questions were asked as I passed through the station gates. There was no raid here.

August 15th Friday
At 3 o'clock yesterday afternoon there was given by radio the news in this morning's paper that Roosevelt and Churchill met on an American warship off Ireland for a 3 day discussion which explains the President's 'fishing holiday'. The chief point was how to bring about America's fullest aid to the Allies. Officers of high rank were present, both British and Americans, and a full text was cabled to Stalin. It gave their war aims and declarations for the establishment of permanent peace after the war.

August 16th Saturday
Churchill and Roosevelt have sent a message to Stalin, suggesting a meeting in

Moscow of representatives of Britain and the United States to discuss Russia's supply needs in her war. It is not likely that Stalin will lose time in taking advantage of the proposal. It is known now that the battleship they met on was the new *Prince of Wales*. As there is no library now I went to the canteen at 5 o'clock and was home soon after ten. By 9.30 there was no bread left but the tea held out until closing time. There were more planes than usual overhead and at 11.46 the siren sounded. While I was on Black Hill the all-clear rang out and no bombs were dropped in our hearing. A note has been sent to the Post warning us against leaves which may be dropped to fire crops. Wet puts them out and so they would not have much chance of firing this very showery weather.

August 17th Sunday 103rd week
This afternoon Mr Mason from East Grinstead came over to talk about taking measurements of the old houses in the village in case such was needed for reconstruction. When Mr Bottrill was out on Home Guard tonight he told me he saw what was quite new to him. One of our fighters flying had a bright searchlight attached to his machine. This will be useful in clouds and help to spot enemy machines.

August 19th Tuesday
Mrs Bevan is again organizing the Soldiers Comfort Fund and has held at Criplands Court two young people's tennis tournaments, one last Saturday and one this afternoon to which Mrs Bottrill and I went, 1/- including tea. There have been no sirens and no night raid.

August 21st Thursday
By the end of next month every man in London between 18 and 60 will have registered for compulsory fire watching. It is also to be enforced here. There are no men in my sector now who are failing to fire watch. Home Guard is not counted.

August 24th Sunday 104th week
In the evening I went to Pelham House to hear the Premier broadcast about his Atlantic meeting with President Roosevelt. He spoke for 30 minutes and said that many practical arrangements to fulfil the Anglo-American pledge for the destruction of Nazi Germany had been arranged. His chief points were that the US is negotiating with Japan for a fair settlement of their respective interests in the Pacific. That Japan's threats to Thailand, Singapore and the Philippines must stop. If the American negotiations should fail, Britain will range herself on the side of the US. We would find ways and means of giving Russia the help she needs against Hitler. Britain and the US are pledged to destroy Hitlerism and to prevent

a renewal of wars. The conquered countries could glean hope from the 'symbolic' Atlantic meeting of their coming liberation.... He ended by assuring Russia of our aid. There was no raid this evening.

August 26th Tuesday

Sanger's Circus is to close owing to the black-out, petrol difficulties, labour shortage and lack of animal feeding stuffs. The whole circus is to be auctioned at Horley next month. Mr James Sanger, whose grandfather first took the circus 'on the road' in 1821 said 'The black-out beats us'. Between 10.30 and 11.00 I went up Black Hill because lights have been showing there, so I was told. In the SE, I saw a plane with a searchlight attached to it, which has been seen every night since the first time last Sunday August 17th. It looked quite pretty, a long ray of light coming from a star, the star of course being a plane. There was no raid.

August 27th Wednesday

The Ministry of Agriculture has set a new trap for rats. Farmers are ordered to erect fences round corn ricks before they are threshed. The fences must not be less than 6ft from the rick, so that the rats can be destroyed as they run out.... From Friday the price of blackberries is controlled, 4d a pound wholesale 5½d retail. More sugar and fats are to be allowed to bakers so that more cheap cakes and biscuits will be made. It is impossible here, and I suppose at other places too, to buy cakes or buns after 11 in the morning. Unless you order a few buns or go early the supply is finished and only empty dishes and bottles ornament the shelves at Humphreys'.... In the afternoon I warned people on Black Hill about their light windows.

August 28th Thursday

'That French quisling commonly called Laval' as the Premier said in his last broadcast, was shot and wounded at an anti-communist ceremony in Versailles yesterday. The sum of £221.9.5 was collected on Tuesday 19th (for the Lord Mayor's Air Raid Distress Fund) by Cuckfield, Lindfield and Haywards Heath.

August 29th Friday

Three men were guillotined yesterday to avenge the shooting of Laval. Three more were sentenced to death and fierce sentences passed on 97 others. At 8.30 this evening we wardens had a talk at the Post with Mr Parsons about our special duties in case of invasion. We are to receive instructions from HQ about answering questions from civilians, but the chief things seem to be to use our common sense, keep people happy and house them if their homes are destroyed. In case of necessity the Congregational Hall and the Mid Sussex Laundry will be receiving stations and the Village Hall for emergency meals etc. It is impossible to give definite instructions when one does not know what may happen so much is left to each one of us. I was home at 10. There was no raid.

August 30th Saturday
Hitler and Mussolini have met again in a tent on the Russian Front.... A report stated that they were determined to carry on until victory had been won.... After 'spring cleaning' the Library this afternoon ready for Monday's reopening, I went to the canteen which was as busy as usual. I got home at 11. There was no raid to disturb the night. All this week the film of Bernard Shaw's *Major Barbara* has been shown at the Perrymount. I went to see it on Wednesday. It is a good film but I enjoyed even more the meeting of Churchill and Roosevelt in the Atlantic. There was a thrill through the whole episode.

September 2nd Tuesday
The bracken that last year grew over 6ft high in Penshurst Park is all away now and barley is growing in its place.

September 4th Thursday
News from Russia is that the Germans have been pushed back before Leningrad, Moscow and Odessa. On account of their growth and prestige the Government has decided that local ARP services will be known in future as the Civil Defence Warden's Service, the CD Ambulance Service, the CD Rescue Service and so on. A new device, the letters CD under a crown in gold colour (with the name of the town or country underneath) will appear on new uniforms, instead of the present letters ARP. The present ARP badge will continue to be worn on existing uniforms. Hostels are to be set up by the YWCA to provide shelter for girls of the ATS, WRNS and WAAF who because of trains missed at connections are stranded on stations at night. The charge will be 2/- for bed, breakfast and bath. I have spent today with Mr Mason and Mr King in some of our older village houses.

September 5th Friday
Marshal Voroshilov's army has halted the German advance on Leningrad where 'an immense and bloody battle is going on day and night.' A fine hot day. I spent it at Birchgrove picking 8lbs 3oz of blackberries and made blackberry jelly and apple jam in the evening. There was no raid.

September 6th Saturday
The defence of Leningrad, like Kiev and Odessa, has been organized with thoroughness.... The annihilation of 2 German battalions by Cossacks behind the German lines is announced. The first instalment of some 4,000ft of captured Nazi

propaganda film, destined for neutral countries, which came into the hands of the MOI will be shown in the West End tomorrow. The pictures were taken on the Eastern Front, but of course no wounded Nazi is seen. Nazi troops and planes meet with no resistance and the artillery never misses a target, no bomb ever falls short of its mark. A number of Polish political leaders have been released by Stalin and are on their way to London to help form a new Polish National Council (Government in exile) here.

September 7th Sunday 106th week

The Archbishop of Canterbury asks people to remember in prayers the armies and people of Soviet Russia.... This wet morning Miss Wood and I went by bus to Horsted Keynes and spent a long time in the Church where it was dry. About one o'clock we heard gun-firing in the porch. We watched a battle between the troops. The enemy wore tin hats. There was plenty of cover in the churchyard, tombs, bushes, tree trunks and everything well hidden. The enemy surprised and captured 3 of the others' men. It was quite an exciting battle for us looking on. The men were very wet, in fact likely conditions if we are invaded. At 8.30 we had our third gathering at the Post for a 'Refresher.' This time the subject was haemorrhage and pressure points and we had 1½ hours of it. There were no raids.... If the weather keeps good harvesters today will be busy gathering in the finest harvest of the century. The no work on Sunday tradition will be broken for every hand is needed. Students, school boys, soldiers, all are helping. For weeks it rained every day and the corn was threatened and some was spoilt, but then the change came and over 2 million workers began to bring in the grain. The response for extra help has been magnificent.... There was a full church at Matins and soldiers sat in the North Transept. The first hymn we had was all the verses of the *National Anthem* and the last *Onward Christian Soldiers*. I am sorry Drake's prayer 'O Lord God when Thou gavest to Thy servants to endeavour any great matter, grant us also to know that it is not the beginning but the continuing of the same until it be thoroughly finished which yieldeth the true glory' was not among those read.... It seems that the Germans are sending down from planes small leaves of celluloid about 4 inches square which when warmed by the sun catch fire. The special object of their use is to burn crops etc. We ask people to be on the lookout for them, to report if found and to cover them with earth if possible. I told several people about it in my special part of the sector on Black Hill. There was no raid this fine night here.

September 12th Friday

In his speech broadcast yesterday President Roosevelt ordered the US Navy and Army the policy that the German and Italian warships 'that enter American defensive waters do so at their own peril' there will be no shooting unless

Germany seeks it.... Children under 6 are to have the first call on oranges now coming into the country.... The new long-promised waterproof coats have been received for the men, the women's are not quite ready. They are fine garments, black rubber-lined cloaks and the blue oval badge with red letters on the breast, well worth waiting for. I was home at 9.45.

September 17th Wednesday
This evening I took the first lot of Christmas greeting cards to Mrs Bevan for the parcels. The WI are again sending this year the Soldiers' Comforts and many different ways of collecting the money for the presents have been devised. It was not possible to do a special card owing to lack of paper and the expense of a special block. Nor is it allowable to paste a snapshot onto a card, the reason being that messages have been written on the back of stamps and pictures. The only thing I could think of was to buy postcards of the village and write in red, 'Christmas Greeting from your Home Village, 1941' along the top of the plain side of the card. 200 are wanted this year instead of only 150 we sent last year. Tomorrow is the last day for posting Christmas mail to India and the Middle East. There was no raid.

September 19th Friday
September 19th is the date fixed when all Jews will have to wear a yellow star on the left side of the outermost coat of their dress. Jews will not be allowed to appear in public without the star.... Nazis are increasing their onslaught on Leningrad where Russian women are fighting alongside the men. Orders have been given to the Germans that Leningrad must fall before November 15th, the date they reckon winter will begin in Northern Russia.

September 22nd Monday
I finished writing the 200 Christmas greetings on the postcards for the parcels.

September 26th Friday
At 8.20 I went to the Post where we had a talk about 'incidents' that have been held at The Heath. We spoke of alternative routes if a street or road was blocked by fallen bombs. No raids.

September 27th Saturday
There has been extra army traffic in the village all day and Canadians arrived in the afternoon. They are always noisy and disturbing.

September 29th Monday
Marshal Timoshenko is back again in Smolensk, a ruined city now. Kiev has been

evacuated.... A levy of one blanket from every household in occupied France is being made by Nazis to be sent to German troops. Directions on an ARP leaflet just issued directs 'If an incendiary bomb comes through the roof, don't lose your head. Put it in a bucket and cover it with sand'.

September 30th Tuesday
I went to Brighton and although I returned by the 7 o'clock train everything was very dark. When the train stopped at a station all light was turned off which made exit difficult.

October 1st Wednesday
The Nazis are buying in Finland numbers of reindeer used for pulling heavy loads over snow. A smaller number of sledge dogs are also being acquired, proof that the High Command know that they are in for a winter campaign.

October 3rd Friday
The Ministry of Food says that oranges will be available from next Monday or Tuesday for children under six in 21 counties (including Sussex). 1lb per head may be bought for 7 days. At 8.30 we had another wardens' meeting at the Post and discussed incendiary bombs. When we left at 9.50 we watched 3 planes with their lights on pass in the way of a searchlight and when that light went off one of the planes put on its searchlight. It was a glorious moonlight night, the reflections in the Pond were very beautiful. There was no raid but we thought there would be.

October 4th Saturday
Last night a mysterious War Office telegram announced that the exchange of German and British wounded had been postponed, what a disappointment for them all on both sides!... A letter to a London woman from her parents in Jersey says 'Mother Hubbard has come to stay with us'. In the evening we had one of the busiest canteens, a full house all the time. Soon after 9 o'clock there was no more food left, so we closed at 9.30 instead of 10. The special dish was sausage on toast. There were no potatoes. I suppose the main crop has not been lifted yet. There was no raid.

October 7th Tuesday
A hen was found by the Nazis hanging by a string from a gallows opposite the Town Hall of St Maur one day last month. Scribbled on a piece of paper was 'I'd rather die than lay eggs for the Boches'.

October 8th Wednesday
In the evening Mr Parsons brought round the new winter ARP coats, long

expected, not the mackintosh coats, but good dark blue material with bright steel or composition buttons stamped in relief ARP. It may be that these coats are in place of the mackintosh ones. There was no raid. Another sunny day.

October 9th Thursday
The Germans have broken through the Russian main line and Orel has been evacuated after fierce battles. As Hitler stated the fate of the world will probably be decided by the battles on the Eastern Front. An appeal from Russia, printed in their *Red Star* asks for immediate British action in the west, saying that only 30 German Divisions were left in France. A comparatively new resident of Lindfield, Sub-Lieutenant Leslie Harper FAA, has been killed in action. He was 23 and went to the Middle East last May as a Fighter Pilot. He is in the new film *Ships with Wings* not yet released.... When I took the rest of the 200 Christmas Greetings Cards for the forces to Mrs Bevan on September 23rd I gave her all my coupons from my ration book in order to buy handkerchiefs, ties etc. for the parcels. I did not want any new clothes. When the old book is finished one gets a new supplementary book at the Post Office and the old book is surrendered there. In the new book, or rather folder, 20 of the coupons are marked x and may not be used before January 1st 1942. The Red Cross and St John's are appealing for light literature for men in hospitals in the Middle East and from now till Christmas a 'drive' is taking place for this purpose. Books etc. collected at the Post Office are for active members of the Forces, those for the sick are taken to different collectors. It is a pity that no information is given *where* to take contributions. Very British.

October 10th Friday
At our meeting at the Post tonight Mr Parsons told us that some special stunt was to take place tomorrow between 3 o'clock and 4.30 but its nature was in a sealed envelope to be opened at a certain time, so no particulars of it could be given. On Thursday morning I received from Australia a 7lb tin of tea. It was very nice to get 7lb of additional tea for 4/- and it is excellent tea. The day before I received a grand round of cheese for which I was charged no duty and Jackie had put on the same postage 4/-. Both parcels were well packed and neatly sewn up in unbleached calico which made good pudding cloths afterwards. The parcels had been dispatched from Adelaide on May 23rd received October 8th or 9th.

October 11th Saturday
The special stunt for the ARP this afternoon was at Franklands Village and our Chief Warden has passes to go to it. No doubt Mr Parsons will tell us all about it at our next Post meeting. All wardens around here have been asked to test the gas masks of all the people in their sector. There was no raid.

October 12th Sunday 111th week
Moscow says 'we retreat to new positions but inflict big losses'. While Germans are still thrusting forwards, huge Russian reinforcements with new tanks and artillery and the Red Air Force are being thrown against them.

October 14th Tuesday
A complete cut has been made in metal supplies to toy makers and by the New Year most toys will be unobtainable.

October 15th Wednesday
Mrs Roosevelt sent supplies of seeds from the US in the spring and these were distributed to various people and places. Weather has been favourable and they will help winter stores of food. The carrot seeds, also come from Mrs Roosevelt, that I am looking after grown in our WI plot are very good. There have been several 'thinning outs', and yesterday I dug up one of the 6 rows, about 20lbs. I took 14lbs after washing them to the Institute Hall and they sold for 2d per lb, the price of carrots in the market now. Some were large, weighing over 1½lb each. No raid tonight.... In the evening I wrote an article for Miss Pennethorne *A Short Introduction to Brass-rubbing....* There is little room to spare in any paper now that everything is cut and all papers and periodicals suffer. The paper she had in mind may not be able to accept it even if the editor would like to. It was 900 words. I could not cut the subject down to less.

October 17th Friday
At our wardens' Post meeting this evening we practised giving telephone messages of air raid damage, speaking through our gas masks, which deadens the voice amazingly. The Haywards Heath telephone exchange operators want to know if the voices of wardens here can be heard.... The beginning of each message is the same formula as always and my message runs 'Air raid message commences, sector 25 Warden Hall speaking. Unexploded bomb has fallen in Beckworth Lane. Please send unexploded bomb detector. Air raid damage ends.' That is a short message. There was no raid, a high wind.

October 18th Saturday
Odessa, besieged for 10 weeks, has fallen.... Odessa is described as 'a heap of ruins'. Buildings that escaped from bombs and shells have been destroyed by the Russians. This evening the canteen was as busy as usual. For the men we had sausage cakes on mashed potatoes. We were home soon after 10.30. There was no raid.

October 20th Monday
Stalin yesterday in an Order of the Day to the Russian Armies declared 'Moscow

will be defended to the last'.... The population is keeping calm and is ready to give the Soviet Army defending Moscow every possible help. Some 20,000 Jews in Berlin, Vienna and the Rhineland, between 50 and 80 years of age, were compulsorily deported to Poland at 10 minutes' notice last Friday night. They were allowed to take with them only a small handbag each and 100 marks in cash. The RAF bombing of German cities is causing a shortage of houses. Bombed out Germans are to be installed in place of the Jews who are forced to leave their homes intact, fully furnished and provided with linen and plate. The weather has been beautiful for Trafalgar Day and sunny all the time. We had lunch in the garden. I made 17lbs of chutney, just from things that I had or that was given to me.... Hitler is switching his main drive towards the Donets Basin. They want to cut off and capture Rostov where the Caucasian oil pipe ends.

October 21st Tuesday
Germans have been forced to withdraw from the Murmansk area 'leaving behind them mountains of dead'. I was told this evening that bombs were dropped at Ditchling yesterday. There was no raid tonight. In the early hours this morning I heard planes and at 3.30 a bomb which sounded at Cuckfield. The Germans have thrown more men and machines into the drive for Moscow, but Russians repulsed all attacks, even Berlin admitting the advance has been checked.

October 24th Friday
Nine of us met at Lynhatch this afternoon to arrange for the carrying on of the WI allotment. We decided what to grow, the seeds to buy and the work each one would do. The allotment has been good for its first year. We shall do even better next year we hope. I dug another lot of carrots with Mrs Robertson who brought her wheeled basket to bring them home in, a useful contrivance. There was no raid.

October 29th Wednesday.
I have spent the greater part of the day trying on the gas masks of the people in my sector, a long job.

October 30th Thursday
In the evening, I went to the last of the gas mask fittings and wrote out my report bearing 73 names in all. Most of the people readily had their masks adjusted, some needed no adjustment at all. One woman called out from the top of the stairs 'I don't want my gas mask fitted, I can't be bothered with the thing, it's quite alright'. I called out from the foot of the stairs 'I haven't the slightest intention of leaving this house until I have seen your gas mask on. I hope you will give me a nice lunch. I've no coupons'. Time was then 10.15. She came down at once and

was soon quite pleasant. A gentleman said 'I'm glad you've come to do my mask, it's never been fitted'. It was amusing because he goes to the Home Office every day and always carries his mask! It has all been a long job, I am glad it is finished. There was no raid.

October 31st Friday
20 hostages arrested in Trondheim after the shooting of 2 German officers will be executed unless the assailants are caught in 5 days.... Nazis are demanding tens of thousands of bed sheets in the occupied countries and sending them to Russia to be used for making white camouflage 'overalls' for German troops to use in the snows.

November 2nd Sunday 114th week
Only a white light is to be shown from torches and the glass must be covered by at least 2 thicknesses of paper. I went to Brighton with Phyl and Janet. For the first time I saw a policeman at the gate inspecting identity cards and asking questions. Phyl showed her aircraft Ministry card and was asked how long she was staying and why she was coming. She said 'for a few hours' and gave the reason. I wore my ARP coat and as I was getting my card out of my gas mask case the policeman said 'Alright, Madam' as he noted my badge and buttons. So we had no trouble at all. We had a very nice lunch at the Old Ship, saw the coils and coils of barbed wire along the sea front and then went to see Bertha and afterwards Jock, returning by the 7.48 train. The train and stations were dark but it was moonlight and cold, as it had been all day. There was no raid.

November 3rd Monday
Moscow defenders have been ordered by Stalin not to yield an inch.

November 5th Wednesday
Dried fruits are to be doubled this month, 12oz for each member of the family. At least 6oz will be currants, sultanas, raisins, the rest will be figs. We are saving for Christmas puddings. The Sussex Salvage Drive of last August puts the County at the head of all others. The salvage was divided into 3 classes: paper 174½ tons, metal 164, rag and bones 17½. Over 6 million books for the troops have been collected from Post Offices since the scheme began last May. A young Norwegian girl refused to dance with a German officer at a dance and was asked 'Is it because I am a German?' 'No' said the girl 'It's because I'm a Norwegian'. There was no raid.

November 8th Saturday
A further report in the *Mid Sussex Times* about the salvage collection gives the Cuckfield Rural District top of all the others in the returns of the 'drive' for East

Sussex. The symbol 'CC' Controlled Clothing will be stamped on lengths of cloth and 'ready-mades', a hallmark of quality at reasonable prices under the Government Utility Clothing Scheme!

November 9th Sunday 115th week
For economy in paper and Post Office labour the Admiralty, War Office and Air Ministry have agreed to give up exchanging official Christmas cards between units of the three Services until the war is over. Partly for the same reason I have not designed a card this year nor can I spare the time for the work.

November 12th Wednesday
Drastic new regulations for paper are issued. Christmas cards are banned for the duration in company with a lot of other paper goods, including paper bags and wrappings. Shops are not allowed to provide paper for wrapping goods in future, except foodstuffs and goods delivered. Only 10 posters are allowed to advertise a cinema or theatre programme and these must be half their usual size. After New Year's Day no one will be able to start a new shop except under licence. Nor will existing shops be allowed to sell things they have not stocked in the past. Food shops are not affected.

November 15th Saturday
Our famous aircraft carrier, *Ark Royal*, was lost yesterday, sunk more than 2 years after the Germans claimed they had destroyed her.... We were not so busy as usual at the canteen this evening, one reason being that many soldiers are having a long weekend leave. No raid.

November 18th Tuesday
Germans say another offensive aimed at the oilfields is in preparation at Kerch. On the Southern Front Cossacks have won the battle for Zuyevka, an important town in the Donets Basin, where there is now 30 degrees of frost. Three German regiments were wiped out.

November 20th Thursday
I went to Brighton about midday to see Jock and found the town more lively now the ban is lifted for a time. It was a fearfully dark night. I left Brighton by the 7.38 train and could only just find my way going very slowly from Compton Avenue to the station. What faint light there is in carriages is switched off on arrival at the station and all was dark. There was no raid.

November 21st Friday
German soldiers in occupied countries are now forcing civilians to listen to the

BBC broadcasts and pass on the news to them. They want true news of the war, not only that manufactured by Goebbels.... At Wardens' Post we talked about and arranged for our fire watchers. The only new thing is that the fire fighters on duty each time are to sign their names in a book. We wardens are to collect them, each one taking the job in turn which means one night a week each person. There will only be 3 or 4 houses to go to every time, so the task is not arduous.... Mussolini is making desperate efforts to popularize himself. Rush orders have been given in Rome for a million copies of his official 'popular' biography to be printed for distribution to the troops as autographed Christmas presents.

November 22nd Saturday
There is good news from the Libyan Front today. General Rommel the German Commander in Chief in North Africa is surrounded.... Half of Rommel's tanks have gone and their army is cut in two.... Prices for horseflesh for human consumption are fixed from Monday by a Food Ministry order, which also regulates the trade. Boneless meat is to be 1/- per lb for best ribs and other good parts, all other cuts 8d per lb. Paste, tin food, pies and so forth are not allowed for horseflesh.

November 24th Monday
The cut in milk began yesterday. I received my usual daily half pint and a tin of US preserved milk. The tin containing the milk, ½ a pint, when diluted makes a pint of milk. I have not yet tried it and shall keep it so long as I can do without it. The allowance for adults is 2 pints per week but children are allowed a pint a day. No raid.

November 26th Wednesday
The tank battle in Libya goes on furiously, Tomahawk Tank Busters playing havoc with Rommel's Panzers.... Fines are imposed for food hoarding. In a case in Harrogate yesterday it was stated that anyone storing more than a fortnight's supply of food except in special circumstances is liable to prosecution. No raid.

November 27th Thursday
At 8 o'clock this evening there was an ARP meeting in the Library. Mr Staines spoke for an hour on different sorts of bombs and the teaching of our fire spotters. Nearly all Lindfield's wardens were there. No raid.

November 28th Friday
This morning Sybil Barrow told me she had heard that her cousin Michael is a prisoner of war in Germany. He was reported over 6 months ago 'missing' from Crete. At the Post Office I bought one of the specially printed and stamped letter

forms for letters written to prisoners. I wrote to him today. I got an extra one to put in this journal…. Pétain is to publish a book under his name and it will be called *The New France*. Part will contain his speeches since 'the fall' and part the future of France in the New Order…. Results of our Poppy Day effort are given in this week's *Mid Sussex Times*. More money than ever before was collected in Mid Sussex, Lindfield being £7.4.5 more than last year £122.18.0 in all.

November 30th Sunday 118th week
Boxing Day will not be a Bank Holiday this year. Only one day's break is appealed for because of the urgent need of war production. This afternoon I went by bus with Mrs Cresswell to the Hospital to see a lonely soldier Robert Anderson from Inverness in the RA. At Paxhill Camp he had fallen 20ft and although X-rays prove no bones are broken he is in pain and not able to move in bed. He has no one to visit him and our hour cheered him, a nice clean-looking boy seemingly about 25. No raid.

December 1st Monday
Most of the last lot of Bowbells and other soldiers have left the village now and Canadian Scots have taken their place.[22] No raid.

December 2nd Tuesday
This morning the new regiment gave us a tune on bagpipes. They passed my house twice this morning and I think made a round of the village. In the afternoon I went to the Hospital and saw the Matron, Miss Learoyd who kindly allowed me to see Robert Anderson although it is not a visiting day. She said he is not badly hurt and will soon be fit again.

December 4th Thursday
Some Canadians in a lorry were in the village street this afternoon and two little boys were talking to them. One said 'How many Germans have you killed?' This evening I saw the last of my sector's fire spotters, Mr Wright. Now all the heads of the 7 parties are arranged and I will make a new list to hang on my fence so all may be reminded of their days. A mild night and no raid.

December 5th Friday
Cinema vans, showing films of Britain's war might, have been sent to our Legations in the Near East. They show films in the open air, in remote places, to the natives. In Iraq and other places the people have never seen films and are impressed…. There was a notice in a butcher's shop yesterday 'Shakespeare said "the times are out of joint" so are we'. We had our usual meeting at Wardens' Post at 8.30. Mr Parsons, Ridgeway and I were the only ones who had been to the

special meeting last Wednesday evening so Mr Parsons told what had been said and what we had learnt. Mr Ridgeway and I chipped in occasionally. It was a quiet moonlight night, not cold. No raid. The Canadians are 'all in' now. On their motor lorries both back and front they have a buff-coloured maple leaf painted on an oblong about 6x5 painted light blue. The leaf is well treated and simply drawn.

December 7th Sunday 119th week
I went to the Heath Hospital to see Robert Anderson again. He is doing well but as he had his two sisters to see him, I did not stay. It has been the brightest day we have had for a long time.... It has been suggested that church bells be rung again, beginning on Christmas Day.... Some other warning would do for an invasion warning.

December 8th Monday
At dawn yesterday Japan declared war on US and Britain and began with air strikes in the Pacific on US Army and Naval bases in Hawaii and Manila.

December 10th Wednesday
Lord Woolton said that there was to be no additional food for Christmas. Hotel restaurants will not serve turkey save on Christmas Day, to allow more in shops for the public.... I listened to the nine o'clock news which gave again the 10 o'clock report of the loss of the battleships at Singapore, *The Prince of Wales* and the *Repulse*. There are but few particulars as yet, it is a sad loss. No raid. 45° below zero in Moscow.

December 11th Thursday
Boys of 14–17 wearing battle dress are to study scouting, signalling and map reading and to attend summer and weekend camps to prepare them for the Home Guard. They will be cadets. For the children's Christmas parties extra supplies of tea, sugar, milk and margarine are to be allowed. The 11,000 children still using Tube shelters will have parties at the station. There was a short raid this afternoon from 3.35 until 3.50. Planes had been overhead in greater numbers than usual ever since 1.30 so I was not surprised when the call came. When I was out they were chiefly in the east and northeast coming up the Thames Estuary probably. This morning I went to the Guides' hut in Haywards Heath to judge competitions in various articles. For a war-time effort the results were good. Several introduced a V into their needlework. The judging took me just over 2 hours. No raid tonight.

December 12th Friday
The US is now formally at war with Germany and Italy as well as Japan.... At the

Post this evening after going through the amended fire spotters list, not yet satisfactorily arranged, we did some 'rescue exercises' carrying an unconscious victim out of the room and trying to carry a person the right way. I tried Mrs Robertson (being the smallest in the room) but hurt my back, a bone or something made a noise like a button bursting its bearings. Mr Gilbert then said 'It's not a woman's job' so we left off the carrying. No raid.

December 13th Saturday
The defeat of Germans by Russians reads similar to Napoleon's plight in 1812. This defeat is described as 'a morass of blood, ice and snow filled with the frozen carcasses of fools led into an infamous trap by the world's prize idiot.' In their flight Germans are burning villages and poisoning food they cannot take with them. I have not bought any of the tinned foods of many varieties sent from America because I don't want them. We were about as busy as usual at the canteen, the Canadian soldiers happy and chatty. I was home sometime after 10.30. There was no raid.

December 15th Monday
British crossed into Northern Thailand from Burma on Friday and have been fighting ever since around Chiang-Lai. It is thought that the thrust was carried out by Indian troops under General Wavell.... A big Waste Paper Drive begins in Westminster today. 'Give by the ton and help beat the Hun.' This morning I took to Mr Hide at the Post Office a card I wrote yesterday for Val to be displayed there. It is to advertise our Warship Week February 21–28 inclusive and it is hoped that people will set up small functions to make money for this event. I think of having a Belisha game drive for everyone enjoys that game when they come here. I bought some National Savings 6d stamps to put on cards I am giving for Christmas presents. No raid.

December 16th Tuesday
The sudden attack by the Japs on Pearl Harbour cost America 2 battleships, *Arizona* and *Oklahoma*, 3 destroyers, *Cassin*, *Downes* and *Shaw*, a minelayer *Oglala*, the target ship *Utah*. 2,729 officers and men were killed.

December 18th Thursday
The weather has suddenly turned cold. German soldiers living in the luxury of Paris last year gave fur coats to their wives. This year those wives are sending fur coats to their husbands on the Russian Front. Because of recruiting 2,000,000 fewer Germans will be at home this Christmas. The warning not to touch strange objects that appear to have dropped from the air or washed up from the sea was again given out yesterday. We have had the warning given to us at the Post some

time ago and hope we shall be informed of any 'finds'. Nothing of the kind should be kept as souvenirs. It is an offence and penalties can be imposed.

December 19th Friday
Sir Reginald Dorman Smith, Governor of Burma, said in Rangoon last night that preparations were being made to take the offensive against the Japs. A big convoy of Indian troops have arrived in Rangoon.

December 20th Saturday
As I intend going to Brighton tomorrow, I bought some point coupon cold meat for sandwiches. I have only used 4 out of the 16 available for one week. Sometime last night or early this morning a car smashed on the Common. Just past my house it missed the road, went on to the Common and crashed into a lime tree, broke it to bits and seriously damaged the car. It was a foggy night and as there are never any lights and car lights themselves are dim it is a wonder there are not more such accidents. I went to Brighton at 10.30 so have no details of the affair.... Today is Stalin's birthday. Greetings have been received from us and all over the Empire and all Allied Governments. Stalin will not take time off for any celebrations. The BBC will broadcast a special all-Russian programme at 8.38.

December 22nd Monday
Hitler has dismissed Field Marshal von Brauschitsch and assumed the role of Commander in Chief himself. The dismissal is thought to be on account of the German failure in Russia. The first group of boys from 17 to 18 register by the end of January. The 16s will follow and the girls will not get their orders till all the boys have signed up. It is a new drive to find out the nation's manpower. Those who register will join a youth organization or a junior service unit.

December 25th Thursday
No newspapers are to be published today or tomorrow and most people have spent a quiet Christmas, no buses and hardly any army lorries through the village. There was a full congregation at Matins this morning. I do not know why we did not have the *National Anthem*. Nearly all Christmas presents this year have been useful ones or something for the larder, no frills in any way. I have received envelopes, soap, eggs, darning wool and a jar of sweet orange and marrow marmalade.

December 27th Saturday
Yesterday the Prime Minister made a good speech to both houses of Congress in Washington. I listened on the wireless to his speech, one of the best. A party was given this evening by our YMCA people to the soldiers and all were invited as well as all helpers at the canteen. Captain Hood was MC and Mrs Sturdy gave prizes

for various games. The soldiers entertained us with songs, solo and chorus and all enjoyed everything. There was no siren to mar the pleasure. The hall was very full, some of the dancing couples found it difficult to manoeuvre. Refreshments were on tables in the corridor, people went in there and helped themselves to sandwiches, cakes and buns, tea and coffee was served in the usual way. The Nazis ought to have seen the spread in the corridor. But I expect they would have said 'British propaganda'. The party began at 7.30 and was over about 11.30, officially at 11.... German losses in Russia are estimated at 20,000 a day which seems high. Owing to the weather many wounded become total casualties. Russian advances continue.

December 30th Tuesday
Mr Churchill's increasing impression on the people of overrun countries is worrying Nazis so much that Goebbels 'next week is issuing a book' *I Knew Churchill* published in all European languages. It blackens the Premier in every way, charges him with being a 'monster' of wickedness and invents all manner of vices for him.

December 31st Wednesday
The Premier spoke for an hour last night in Ottawa to the Canadian Parliament headed by Mackenzie King. I went next door to hear his speech which was clear and very good. Next year's food diet is to be restricted and more vitamins are to be put in margarine. Vitamin D is to be doubled which is said to mean that 1oz of margarine will equal an ounce of fresh butter. A war-time exhibition opens at the RA tomorrow, the second United Artists' Exhibition in aid of the Red Cross and St John's Fund.

1942

—∞—

January 1st Thursday
New Year's Day and everybody wishing everyone peace. Ricardo Ling brought me an old custom New Year present, an offering, placed in a small box, of bread, coal and salt neatly arranged with bread and coal in the corners and the salt in a match box in the middle with golden coloured paper for the 'ground'. Jap troops are within 6 miles of Manila which is expected to fall very soon.

January 2nd Friday
During a daylight raid on the SE coast yesterday a Me109 diving less than 200 feet machine gunned a train striking the guard by a bullet, the only injury. I am wondering if it was the plane I saw flying yesterday afternoon at 3.15. It neither sounded nor looked like one of our planes.... British book publishers have made a voluntary agreement to cut all extravagant production 'for the duration'.... Big books will disappear.

January 3rd Saturday
Yesterday evening, instead of our usual 'practice' meeting at the Post, Mr Parsons entertained us to supper and afterwards we had two draws each from a box of 'eatables' supplied from our patrol rations but not used. I got ¼lb of tea and a tin of gelatine. At 11.15 we listened to Colonel Britton, Commander in Chief of the Continental V Army who warned his soldiers 'in Belgium, Holland, Norway and Czechoslovakia to beware of quislings whom he named'. Several he denounced by name, giving their addresses and assured them they were watched. 'A rat named de Guypere, employed by a Paymaster, at le Goute Aerodrome found two Englishmen in hiding, offered to shelter them and then turned them over to the police.' Colonel Britton urged his army to compile 'rat lists' of traitors.[23]

January 6th Tuesday
British, Indian and Chinese troops are pouring into Burma where there is to be a decisive battle.... Mr Parsons came round in the late evening with the two Fire Guards books, which now have to be signed by fire spotters every evening they are due for watching. There are two books for this sector, one for Backwoods, Meadow and Beckworth Lanes, the other for Black Hill, Pondcroft and the Common. We

wardens take it in turns to collect the signatures and this duty will occur every eighth evening. We go any time between 8 and 10pm. It's my turn tomorrow.

January 7th Tuesday
In a speech to Congress yesterday Roosevelt promised US production on a gigantic scale.... The number of planes and tanks produced must be doubled in 1943 for this war cannot be waged in a defensive spirit.

January 10th Saturday
This week the *Mid Sussex Times* is raised to 3d. Most papers have not increased their price but have reduced the size, especially magazines such as the *Sussex County Magazine*.... We had an exceptionally quiet evening at the canteen. Mrs Pellett was not there as her husband is down with flu, like many another just now. Canadians prefer coffee to tea, so we serve more coffees in consequence. It is only Camp Coffee but they like it.

January 12th Monday
Sixty German soldiers returned from the Russian Front half starved, in rags and exhausted. They ran wild, drank all they could lay their hands on and defied their military police and officers. When all leave was cancelled and they were ordered back to the Russian Front rioting broke out. Hundreds of arrests were made and 62 were shot at Besançon in occupied France.... Today has been the coldest this winter and boys were sliding on the Pond this afternoon. So soon as I got to the Library for the usual Monday session a soldier told me the room must not be used as a lecture was being held in the Hall. I protested and he referred to the CO who reported all doors must be locked, we could not have the Library and one of the Guards outside would tell the people the reason. Inconvenient, but of course the military came first. It was a cold afternoon for people to have the fruitless walk.

January 22nd Thursday
The biggest Jap threat to our troops defending Singapore is still in the Muar River area, where Japs are trying to drive a wedge into our lines.... The weather keeps very cold; seagulls were flying over the Common yesterday, children were enjoying sleighing, skating and sliding was in full swing on the Pond. It is a pleasure to see the Canadian soldiers skating, but only a few have skates.

January 23rd Friday
I went out this evening to collect the fire spotters' names. It was a terrible night, rain and sleet and the ground in lumps of slippery slush. The only safe place to walk being in the deep snow on the sides of the paths. So I had to walk very slowly

but did not fall down. My ARP blue coat is thin material and got wet through to my suit underneath. Another time I shall wear my Burberry which is still waterproof. Mr Parsons brought in Fire Guard armlets for the spotters, dark blue material with Fire Guard in block letters painted yellow, also a red card for each one to sign showing their authority for working as a fire guard.

January 28th Wednesday
The Premier made a long speech in the House yesterday. We listened to the report of it at the 9 o'clock news. The conduct of the war is to be a 3-day debate. It was a good speech... he ended by saying 'we shall have a great deal more bad news' but he saw 'the light gleaming behind the clouds'. A Food Ministry order yesterday stated that bread may not be delivered on more than 3 days in the week. But that has been the rule here for over a month now. This idea is to save man–power and petrol.

February 2nd Monday
For 24 hours Jap bombers have pounded Singapore in a non-stop bombardment.

February 5th Thursday
A letter from Mr Wilson, County Librarian, Lewes, stated that owing to difficulties in transport and loss of staff, it is necessary to have fewer exchanges of library books i.e. every three weeks to begin from March 1st.... It seems strange to me that this alteration was not made a year ago when the real difficulties began. Snow again fell this cold windy day. From Singapore comes the news that British commandos have been in action, having crossed the island to the mainland of Jahore and have harassed Japanese communications.

February 7th Saturday
I went to the canteen at 5. We were not desperately busy. The majority of the soldiers who came for supper wore 'Canadian Highlanders of Ottawa' on their shoulders. We walked home in the dark at 10.20.

February 8th Sunday 128th week
The first week of Singapore's siege is over and she has stood up well to the bombing and shelling which is increasing. Japs have begun to shell the suburbs of the city itself.... It was my turn for getting the fire guard signatures and the cold job took an hour as usual. February 21st–28th is special Warship Week. Val Bassano had a rummy tea party and 7 of us played the games. Each player put 6d in a box, the money going direct for the cause. We made 3 games a round, each player putting a penny for each round, the winner of the round having the seven pennies. Most of the winnings were put in the box so that in all about 5/6 was

taken. Today soap rationing begins, 3oz of soap flakes are allowed and the same for toilet soap, 4oz of kitchen soap.

February 10th Thursday
Japs claim 'we are within 10 miles of Singapore city'. British assure they are fighting back and 'have taken a strong line'. Let us hope all will be well for the situation looks grave at present. The trouble is lack of air support.

February 11th Wednesday
The news from Singapore is that she is facing the decisive 24 hour battle for the island. General Percival has issued the order. 'I call on all British troops to make a stand and to defend Singapore to the last man.' Japs have repaired the break made in the Causeway and are sending troops across it…. There was a concert this evening in the Village Hall in aid of our Warship Week…. The show was carried out entirely by the Canadian soldiers, some of whom were among the audience. And a very good show it was from beginning to end and lively all the time. One soldier whistled delightfully keeping in time with the music. He put fingers in his left mouth and covered all with right hand. Captain Hood was the MC announcer. The seats were 3/6 reserved and 2/- at the door but most of the 2/- ones were forms. Val Bassano, who did a good deal towards getting it up and selling tickets, wanted me to take cushions, so Mrs Bottrill and I were comfortable. I was lucky and had a chair because the form was not quite long enough. All the Canadian soldiers who sang had good voices, humour predominated.

February 12th Thursday
Yesterday Japs demanded surrender of Singapore. The answer was 'No'. Bitter fighting continues. British and Netherlands navies are getting women and children out as fast as they can…. In April comes a cut of one sixth in the petrol ration which applies to car owners only, not to motorcyclists.

February 13th Friday
News from Singapore is still very serious but our troops there are still holding on, Japs admitting fierce resistance…. Goebbels' latest fantasies being put about in neutral countries are designed to give the impression that Britain is collapsing. 1. Churchill travels in an armoured car in fear of his life. 2. Five attempts have been made to assassinate Eden in three weeks. 3. There is no milk for children over six. 4. Sand is being supplied for Londoners to wash with as there is no soap. 5. Buses are barred to civilians. Rather wonderful that G. can think of such things.

February 15th Sunday 129th week
In the evening 9 o'clock news, after I had returned from Brighton, we listened to

the Premier's speech in which he announced the fall of Singapore. He said 'We had to do our best to give substantial aid to Russia. We gave it in her darkest hour.... How then – gripped and held and battered as we were, could we have provided for the safety of the Far East against such an avalanche of fire and steel as has been hurled upon us by Japan?' Mr Churchill recalled events since his last broadcast and again offered hard adverse war for many months ahead. According to Tokyo the terms of the surrender of Singapore were signed by General Percival (Malaya) and General Yamashita at 1pm British Summer Time. Japs say Singapore will furnish an excellent base for Jap operations against Australia and the Dutch East Indies.

February 21st Saturday
Today begins the Mid Sussex Warship Week.... Last Thursday afternoon I helped Mr Fraser and Mrs Fawssett get Ellmer's shop – our HQ – ready. The coloured posters are very good, bright and attractive. It seemed a pity to stick them on dirty windows so I borrowed a pail of water from Miss Abbot, found a piece of old cloth and begged a newspaper for polishing purposes from Pollards and finally got the glass clean. I took up Union Jack and St George flags and with the violet and yellow 'draperies' Mr Fraser brought, the fish shop looked quite good.

February 23rd Monday
This evening there was a dance at the Village Hall, proceeds for our Warship Week effort. I went over at 8 o'clock to help with the refreshments which began at 9.00, the dance lasted until 11.30. The food was good and plentiful, all of it had been given, ham (real ham) sandwiches, bridge rolls spread with potted meat, sausage rolls, cakes, tea, coffee and lemonade. Soldiers paid 2/- entrance, ladies, I think, 1/- the Hall was full but not crowded and all enjoyed the evening. The peculiar modern dancing seems strange to me, all the same kind of walking jog-trot and but little grace in the movements.

February 25th Wednesday
Rangoon is carrying out the 'scorched earth' policy so it is likely soon to fall to the Japs who claim to be within 40 miles of the city. All civilians have moved.

February 26th Thursday
Rangoon is described as an 'inferno of fires.' Looters were at work and water was unobtainable. The British were destroying anything of importance.

February 28th Saturday
General Wavell is believed to be planning an offensive action against the Japs. Our bombers have bombed oil dumps and military concentrations near Palenbang and also enemy shipping near Banka Island.

March 1st Sunday 131st week
The story is published today of the paratroop landing at Bruneval, 12 miles north of Le Havre, carried out in the early hours of Saturday morning. The troops dropped in moonlight. They smashed up the radiolocation station which was their objective and also brought back prisoners. The paratroops were carried in bombers led by Wing Commander Pickard, pilot of the F for Freddie plane in *Target for Tonight*. Each was armed with an automatic gun, knife and 4 grenades. Light naval forces covered their withdrawal to the beach and from seaward came British infantry escorting landing craft. This was the first time since Dunkirk that our infantry had landed in France. No aircraft or ship was lost and our casualties were light. The Navy, Army and RAF all played important parts in this raid, all necessary to meet the German opposition. Prisoners taken were survivors of the garrison.

March 3rd Tuesday
The number of Land Army girls has gone up in East Sussex. In January 1941, 250 girls were actually working, now the number is 842. They are taking the place of men in milking sheds, in fields and in market gardens, their work varying from stock feeding and milking, farm work, tractor driving, care of pigs, threshing and thatching. In the evening from 8 o'clock onwards we heard and saw bombers going from the N to SE all heavily laden, so we know some big venture is on.

March 4th Wednesday
'Utility' clothing is to be made, our skirts are to be shorter and choice of colours and style restricted. Men are to do without double-breasted jackets, trouser turn-ups and sleeve buttons. The clothes are expected to be ready in bulk in the autumn.

March 5th Thursday
People have been 'trespassing' lately by cycling along the barred common paths, so three fresh notices have been put up in place of the customary two which were removed over a year ago. From Monday, it is an offence to throw away any waste paper. The penalties are three months in prison, or £100 fine, or both. The WVS call regularly here for waste paper, which I put from time to time in a sack and it is now to be disposed of only through a collector or a buyer. Although one is allowed to use paper for fire lighting, to burn it unnecessarily is wrong. Neither must it be thrown in a refuse bin or mixed with refuse. Since the beginning of the war, the Ministry of Supply estimates that half a million tons of paper that might have been used for munitions has been lost through being burnt, thrown away or mixed with refuse. Strange that saving it was not thought of for 2½ years.

March 7th Saturday
Britain received her invasion orders this morning. Every able-bodied man and woman will be conscripted into a People's Pioneer Corps under a new Defence Regulation if Hitler strikes. Only those essential jobs will be exempt. There will be no special travel facilities at Easter. It is to be a stay at home holiday. Yesterday women aged 20–21 received their call-up papers. The money for Warship Week, aimed at £100,000 amounted to £130,300 the last day, Saturday the 28th, bringing in the highest for any day. The Corvette for which the money was specially collected is to be HMS *Lily*. The area was Lindfield, Cuckfield, Haywards Heath and a few small neighbourhoods around. We had a busy canteen this evening but fortunately we were fully staffed.

March 13th Friday
Our troops in Burma are now withdrawn into central Burma. Rangoon flames were seen 40 miles away, the place is destroyed. A new compulsion order to strengthen the Home Guard is applied in 24 areas including Sussex. Today workmen have been digging in granite blocks at intervals along the verge of the pathway round the bend just outside my house (near the Common) in the hope of preventing the newly planted Lime trees from being knocked down by lorries or cars that come round the bend far too fast. Four trees have been broken down this last 18 months, in addition to the tree across the road that was smashed and uprooted by a car late one evening.

March 16th Monday
The Ministry of Food is soon to supply onion powder to be used in making soup powders, cubes and soups. Handy stuff to have now onions are hardly obtainable.... The siren sounded this morning but for only a short warning 11.15 to 11.45. I saw a bomber, I hope ours, cross to the south while I was on the Common. I heard no bombs drop and only a few distant planes. From today fewer copies of newspapers will be printed and we are asked to share our papers. Some people will have none. I received my *Daily Sketch* this morning and have not yet heard I shall not always have one.

March 18th Thursday
Gas, electricity and coal are all to be rationed as soon as possible. Also there are new restrictions on buying clothes.... Tins are no longer to have any tin in them. From April 14th all tin containers are to be made of steel.

March 19th Thursday
Public barter has taken place in the Channel Islands where food is scarce. Guernsey newspapers contain such advertisements as 'apples for paraffin',

'canaries all colours for rabbits', 'cigarettes for a fur coat', 'eggs for golden syrup'. A Jersey message says 'Conditions bearable, food scarcity'.... For stealing coupons from the GPO stores where he worked, sentence of 3 years penal servitude was passed on Webb and the same time for Raphman for receiving them. Far too much 'black marketing' goes on with stolen coupons and the sentences get more severe.

March 21st Saturday
The Combers of Lewes Road have been told that Alfred, RAMC is missing in Malaya, where he went in December 1940. He is 24. They do not expect to hear good news of him.

March 24th Tuesday
Our Lindfield hero, Frank Carey, is again mentioned in the paper. He has been awarded a second bar to his DFC. He has now 39 sure 'kills' to his credit and is Acting Wing Commander and has flown on every British war front. He was awarded the DFC and bar simultaneously in June 1940. He has 'displayed high qualities of leadership, and has set a high example by his courage and devotion to duty'. The village is proud of him.

March 29th Sunday 135th week
Another 'Zeebrugge' exploit has closed St Nazaire, Germany's Atlantic gate to Hitler's biggest warships.[24] St Nazaire is a U-boat and naval base. The entrance to the main dock was rammed by a destroyer filled with explosives and fitted with a fuse. Assault troops landed and carried out demolitions in the dockyard. HM *Campbeltown* rammed the dock gate, the crew were evacuated by motor launches.... This Sunday was a day of National Prayer and I listened to the King's broadcast last night in which he made a call to the nation 'We can and we must quicken the pace, for speed is the essence of modern war'. This Palm Sunday has been a lovely sunny day and we had tea in the garden for the first time. Owing to the increased shortage of paper, the *Sunday Chronicle* is one page less today and will be so every alternate week.

March 30th Monday
In New Delhi, Sir Stafford Cripps laid before India the Government's conclusions for the future of India. Britain offers her Dominion status as soon as the war is over.

March 31st Tuesday
The Chinese report Japs are using gas in the Battle of Burma.

April 1st Wednesday
India has rejected proposals. Although Indians are divided over many things they

are not divided in their abhorrence of conquest by Japan.... After Monday babies up to a year will get an extra week's soap ration.

April 2nd Thursday
Last night, beginning at 11 o'clock we heard dropping bombs, firing etc and expected the siren warning to go out. It was my night on. The 'battle' continued until between 2 and 3am but this morning I was told it was 'intensive manoeuvres'. There have been more German planes over this country the last two nights than for several months. One town on the SE coast and another on the S coast were bombed. Among the buildings hit was a hospital where the patients could not be moved until daybreak. The car of an HG company commander ran into a bomb crater where he was machine gunned by the diving plane and killed. A shelter in which 30 people were sleeping was hit and 9 were killed and several injured. After Saturday no private car owner will get a tyre of any kind unless entitled to E (essential) supplementary petrol ration. The rationing scheme applies to all vehicles running on rubber tyres except both chain bicycles and motorcycles. There has been much 'practising' lately by Home Guards.

April 4th Saturday
We were busier than usual at the canteen this evening. Just 10 minutes before closing time, 10 o'clock, 22 soldiers came in. We do not cook after 9.30 or 9.40, so they could only have tea, bread or toast. Dark wet night.... A party of 900 women and children arrived in London from Singapore last night after travelling 9 weeks. During the voyage 4 babies were born, all named after the ship.

April 5th Sunday 136th week
German High command has massed 4,000,000 on the Russian Front from the Baltic to the Black Sea. Half are concentrated on the region facing Moscow.... Condensed milk and cereal breakfast foods go on the points rations when the new rationing period begins tomorrow.

April 6th Monday
Japs wrecked Mandalay last Friday and for 3 hours, 36 bombers dropped high explosive and incendiary bombs on the city. Reports place the dead at 2 to 3,000.... Goebbels has given orders that the columns of obituary notices in German papers recording deaths of men in Russia are to be banned after May 1st. Japan claims to have prepared 20,000,000 pamphlets for Australians to be dropped by air urging them to surrender. As the population of Australia is about 7,000,000 Japs seem to be wasting an awful lot of paper.... In Lancashire food officials discovered 19cwt of tea more a week than rationing allowed was reaching the public. Retailers must cut out and keep the coupons.

April 7th Tuesday
A peculiar form of 'British propaganda' has broken out in Paris. Thousands of used British stamps are being stuck surreptitiously on wall posters, currency notes, theatre programmes and café tables. In one café used by German troops every table one morning bore a British stamp.

April 8th Wednesday
A civil servant who had been in Government employment for 24 years talked in a public house about movement of warships. Two HGs overheard him and reported him. At Bath he was fined £10 with 10s costs for 'careless talk'.

April 9th Thursday
We had an ARP wardens' meeting at the Post at 8 this evening and we discussed training our fire fighters. We decided to suggest to them a lesson at 8 on the nights they are on duty. I take Sunday's lot and Monday's and Mr Ridgeway will help me for there will be 9 spotters. Few know how to manage a sand bag and not all have used a stirrup pump. Mr Knight thought we should have 'incidents' and practices on our own account and has made some up which Mr Parsons says are good. We meet next Tuesday at 8 o'clock for the first one.

April 11th Saturday
Mr Richard Fairey, son of the aircraft manufacturer, has lost both his legs from frost bite. The ship he was in was torpedoed in the North Atlantic and he and his 12 companions took to an open boat. After 6 days they were rescued by an American destroyer. Penalties for wasting paper are severe. A motorist who kicked away a magazine he had dropped from his car was admonished in Glasgow's Sherriff's court yesterday where he was charged with throwing away paper. He was liable to a fine of £100 or 3 months imprisonment. Today we began summer time at the Library, evening sessions, instead of only afternoon ones which we have to arrange owing to the black-out. Another inconvenience of the war for we all prefer the evening times on Mondays and Saturdays.

April 12th Sunday 137th week
I went to Brighton this afternoon and Jock told me the 8 o'clock morning raid on the 10th was an attack at Salts Farm on the aerodrome between Lancing and Shoreham. There were some casualties but there were no particulars. Leaflets about people leaving Brighton in case of invasion have been left at every house. Mothers and children go first and other people not engaged in any war or special work. A little notice will probably be given. I told Jock he was to come here.

April 13th Monday
A new order came into force yesterday. Passengers waiting for buses and trains have to form a queue wherever there is no barrier rail or where more than 6 people are waiting.

April 14th Tuesday

> Time of Incident 8.24 (A practice)
> A high explosive bomb has fallen between 'Harness' and 'Elm Rock' Meadow Lane, demolishing the front corners of both houses, leaving the corner of the roof of 'Harness' suspended. The windows and doors are blown out at side and front of both houses. There are casualties in the back portion of both houses, 2 have broken legs, 2 lay under some debris, 3 others are cut and bruised and all are suffering from shock. Arrived at Post.[25]

This evening at 8 o'clock, we 7 wardens of this sector (25) met at the Post and did the exercise incidents arranged by Mr Knight and after they were over we discussed their shortcomings. Mr Ridgeway and I were the first out and on patrol down Meadow Lane found an 'incident' pinned on Mr Knight's gate. We had to decide quickly the help needed – ambulance and so forth and I hurried back with the written message. Mr Parsons said in record time. 5 minutes on the journey and the message was clear, an important point.

April 15th Wednesday
Today the most prominent news is the Budget which the Chancellor, Sir Kingsley Wood, introduced yesterday. Only luxury goods are to cost more – beer, wine and spirits. From May 10th all entertainments are to cost more. Utility clothing is to be freed of purchase tax. Cigarettes will cost 1/- instead of 9d, but all men and women in the services will be able to buy cigarettes and tobacco at pre-Budget prices at canteens.... All towns on the south coast from Rye to Littlehampton become banned areas at midnight. This order of course includes Brighton, but I expect to pass through when I go to see Jock. My ARP blue coat will help.

April 16th Thursday
Rubber is the new salvage campaign and all old rubber is wanted. It is a pity so few instructions are given about collecting it.

April 17th Friday
The King has sent a cable to General Dobbie, Governor of Malta 'To honour her brave people I award the George Cross to the Island Fortress of Malta to bear

witness to a heroism and devotion that will long be famous in history'.... At the end of March the Women's Land Army totalled 28,000. Lady Denman, Chairman of the Land Army, wants Service Authorities to open service canteens to Land Girls. It seems strange they are excluded from service canteens. Many of the girls who are lonely could meet girls of their own age if the service canteens were open to them. The siren sounded at 1.55 this morning and the all-clear at 3 o'clock. It was the first night warning since last November.... It was not my night on, so of course I did not go out.

April 19th Sunday 138th Week
Tokyo and 600 square miles of the country were bombed for 7 hours yesterday.... In the evening, 8 o'clock, we had our fire guard instruction meeting in Four Acres garden, Mr Ridgeway presiding. We went through the usual 'advice' and used Four Acres' pump and sandbags for illustrations. The rubber in the pump had become rather dry so that the spray was not so effective as it should have been. It was a quiet night here. A few minutes after midnight, there was a ring at the bell and a messenger said HG Mr Bottrill was to go at once with iron rations etc. It was for a practice. He returned about 2.00am.

April 23rd Thursday
St George's Day, so I hung out my flags.... This afternoon there was a stream of heavy tanks passing through the village, the procession lasting about 2 hours. After each tank there came a lorry, a motorcyclist and sometimes a single gun. Most of the tanks were named, so many all beginning with 'B', followed by 'C' and then 'A'. A variety of names; Boy, Brenda, Bob, Blossom, Bellicose and so forth. The noise was deafening, one wonders the drivers are not deafened for life. They passed N to S. It may be manoeuvres or they may be going abroad but I do not know where they are bound, for also early this morning there was the largest gathering of soldiers on the Common that I have yet seen. The tank drivers and soldiers were all Canadian.

April 26th Sunday 139th week
I went to Brighton this morning to see Jock and although the ban is on had no trouble at all at Brighton station gates. Every traveller had to show identity cards but the man did not even look at mine. There was a 10 minute alert in the afternoon, there are usually one or two. A village, it was said in the paper in Sussex, had been 'taken over' entirely and all the inhabitants removed. Jock thinks the village is Stanmer.

April 29th Wednesday
Last night, at 8 o'clock, all of us wardens went to a film shown at the Village Hall.

It was really for the Home Guards, but interesting to us, although I did not think it desperately good. The best of the 3 or 4 'sections' was when and when not to shoot, the examples being clearly given and understood. The film lasted 1¾ hours.

May 9th Saturday
The sale of white flour is prohibited from May 25th. The new bread we have now is very good. I like it better than the usual white bread, it keeps fresh, has a pleasant scent and is far more satisfying than white bread.

May 19th Tuesday
We were told (not in the papers) that Brighton station was hit yesterday. We saw a number of fighters going south in the afternoon, probably to Brighton.

May 22nd Friday
The terrible battle for Kharkov continues and Timoshenko is closing in on the place, having used new and heavier tanks.... Today I have seen notices on fences etc. saying all 'unnecessary' iron railings will be taken down beginning on May 22nd. I am wondering if mine will be considered necessary. Then wood must not be used to replace them. Purchase of wood is controlled, up to £1 per month. Some Irish Guards, I don't know how many, arrived in the village today. This evening they were being drilled on the Common, unusual drill. One was there stepping out slowly with knees unbent something like a low goose step. All the time their forage caps kept falling off, they are such silly caps. Bagpipes were played and sounded very good. Jock who came this afternoon for Whitsun, Michael and I went out to enjoy it all.

May 28th Thursday
Rommel's offensive in Libya has begun. Temperature is 100 degrees and tank men stripped to the waist are fighting Nazi panzers.... Heydrich 'Butcher of Moravia' was wounded yesterday when shot on the road from Prague to Berlin, but is not in any danger. A reward of £70,000 is offered for the capture of the assailants, anyone hiding or aiding them will be 'shot with his whole family'.

May 30th Saturday
A very fierce battle is taking place SW of Tobruk.... 200 hostages have been taken and will be shot if Heydrich's assailants are not forthcoming.

June 3rd Wednesday
On Monday night 1,036 planes made a raid on Essen. 35 were lost. Great buildings blazed and fires could be seen from the coast reflected onto a sheet of cloud over the Ruhr.... The Food Ministry rules that bottled soft drinks complete

in themselves are to be abolished to save transport space. Those that have water added will take their place.

June 9th Tuesday

The big tank battle in Libya goes on and General Ritchie is determined to win it. Rommel is also determined. Our radio last night asked the French to leave the coast regions warning them of the danger in 'invasion areas' which was likely to increase. But Germans forbid the leaving, intending to hold the civilian population as 'hostages' against our raiders. Lord Woolton urged people not to waste bread. It is not rationed and he does not want rationing to come. Too much is thrown into the dustbin. Last night we women wardens went to the Reading Room at 8pm to receive our shoes and winter coat.... I asked Mr Merry if I could have a new suit because mine was a disgrace to the service. He said he would try to get me one. I wonder.

June 11th Thursday

All the men of the village of Lidice near Kladno, Czech mining village, have been shot by the Gestapo as part of the German vengeance for the Heydrich shooting. The women of the village were sent to concentration camps and all the children to 'education centres'. Then all the buildings were razed to the ground and the name of the village was erased from public records. Germans give as their excuse that an illegal radio station and quantities of propaganda hostile to Germany were found in the village. Mr Fraser came for help with flags for the special United Nations parade on Muster Green next Sunday morning. I have not heard much about it but Mr Parsons wants us there before 10 on Sunday morning. I told Mr Fraser I could not do all the flags needed but we made a list of 16 which I said I would try to have ready. I cycled to Pelhams at the Heath to get the stuff, 18½ yards costing £1.13.8½d.... I asked him for a new boiler suit and showed him my old dirty one, all I have and said it was a disgrace to the service. He agreed and will do what he can.

June 14th Sunday 146th week

This morning I cycled in ARP uniform (save rubber boots) at 9.40 to Muster Green where other wardens, fire service fire guards, nurses etc were assembled. Mr Fraser conducted, Mr Thomas, vicar of St Wilfred's read a 'little prayer' from President Roosevelt, who said that June 14th was a day set apart in America for honouring their flag. This year he thought it well to honour also the flags of those nations who were fighting with us. There are 29 in all – 28 was the number given yesterday.... I kept the 16 flags I made and hope to use them for peace time celebrations.

June 18th Thursday
Every local authority in the London region is to have its own Invasion Defence Officer. Last night I went to the Post at 8.30 and we wardens talked for 2 hours, the subject being 'invasion'. Mr Parsons is our head and is organising the defence work in this village, for the Home Guard is defending at Midwyn Bridge and at Scrase Bridge and Higgs Mill, so the village itself is to be looked after by ARP and Police. There will be a lot to do in the way of preparations and on Friday we wardens are meeting at 8 o'clock at Mrs Robertson's to arrange the particular work to be done, invasion precautions and preparedness especially.

June 20th Saturday
Yesterday evening at 8 o'clock we wardens met at Mrs Robertson's house, which is to be the Post if invasion comes. We have to provide 2 wardens and 2 casualties as well as two fire parties of three fire guards, and about 6 other people for casualties all to take part in tomorrow's invasion practice. We meet at Mr Huddart's at 8 tomorrow morning and are on duty until 1 o'clock. This afternoon Mr Ridgeway and I collected our parties. It was very short notice for us, some had engagements, some were away, but we arranged the two parties in the end and 7 casualties. I myself am to be one and also Dorrie, but we have no instructions until tomorrow. I go first to the Post to Mr Parsons.

June 21st Sunday 147th week
This morning we all met at the Post and I was not a casualty after all. I was MC at the Post, staying there all the time, attending to messengers' requests, giving out incendiary bombs and getting the various 'casualties' in order. It was a grand sunny day. The Home Guard moved out early, Bob was up at 4 and left at 5. We both got back at 10 to 1. Mr Kenny and the 2 Dykes, Bob and I all enjoyed a glass of beer under the apple tree. We were all hot and felt dirty.

June 22nd Monday
Tobruk has fallen and Germans claim 25,000 prisoners besides tanks and much booty. Rommel is now in control of practically all Libya and the threat to Malta and the British sea lines in the Mediterranean is greatly increased. The siren sounded last night at 1.02 and the all-clear sounded at 1.07. I heard several planes and two bombs dropped, which sounded in a northerly direction. At the Library this afternoon I was told that Southampton was the objective. It was a lovely fine night and a pleasure to sleep out of doors.

June 24th Wednesday
Last night at 8.30 we had an ARP meeting at the Robertsons' house – all we wardens of our sector were there but not Mr Parsons. Together we decided upon

4 extra First Aid Posts. I went to see Mrs Weston of Lyngarth and she is willing for her house to be one of the Posts. The others are Four Acres, the Brown House and Commonwards, two for each part of the sector. All those I asked in the morning are willing to take a First Aid course, particulars of which will follow. Then we made notes of those who would lend oil stoves, blankets, sheets, kettles etc. Mr Gilbert and Mr Knight found which houses had wells and were usable. I have a well, used with my next door neighbour, which is workable, only the handle is broken. We went home about 10 o'clock.

June 27th Saturday
On Thursday night the RAF made a big 1,000 plane raid on Bremen leaving the place blazing, then the U-boat base. The short night, only six hours of black-out and the round trip of 1,200 miles meant that every one of the thousand planes had to be over and away from the target in 75 minutes.... On Friday, Daisy Wood and I went to Bolney and on returning at 2.30 found the blue gate and railings had been taken away. No previous notice had been given but 2 slips of paper were put through the letter box just before the men began their work. Even Dr Clarkson's good wrought iron gate has been taken and thus far most of the railings and gates in the village are lying in piles on the verges. It looks strange without them. At the canteen this evening things were quiet, the only rush time was about 10 minutes to closing time when 22 soldiers wanted tea. However I was home about 10.40. The Home Guard had a supper at the Village Hall and while at the Library from 6 to 8, it sounded as if they were enjoying the evening. I saw plates of sandwiches and cakes in the kitchen.

July 2nd Thursday
The Eighth Army is facing Rommel at El Alamein, 50 miles west of Alexandria and both are fighting furiously.... General Auchinleck has sent the Army an 'Order of the Day', a cheering one but 'the situation now calls for a supreme effort on the part of all of us'.

July 4th Saturday
Cairo reports the great battle in the El Alamein area was continued yesterday 'with unrelenting fury'.

July 5th Sunday 149th week
General Auchinleck who is personally leading the new big counter attack from his battle HQ reports that Rommel's third thrust towards the Nile has been held.

July 7th Tuesday
Yesterday evening 33 gas masks were brought in from Beckworth Hostel of God.

I loaded 12 on my cycle and took them to Mr Fraser. I asked their destination and he told me the ARP Stores Hut in Sunte Avenue. So I took them all there, 3 journeys. In the hut are all manner of ARP belongings, helmets, books, masks, biscuit tins, stirrup pumps and so forth, but I did not notice the new boiler suit I asked for!

July 8th Wednesday
Two traitors, one British, the other Belgian, were hanged as spies yesterday. Jose Key, born at Gibraltar and a British subject, spied on Gibraltar on our troop movements, Louis Zimmerman of Ostend, ex-ship's steward, came to England as a refugee, sent by the German secret service. He carried invisible ink, 475 American dollars and £97.10 in English notes. 300 tons of metal were reclaimed from the burnt out House of Commons, 20 ton tanks are being made from it. I went to see Jock this afternoon. He told me a gas holder at the far end of Kemptown had been blown up by bombs.

July 9th Thursday
The battleship *Tirpitz*, sister of the *Bismarck*, has been torpedoed and seriously damaged by a Soviet submarine in the Barento sea, near Norway, on the convoy route for Anglo-US supplies to Russia.

July 12th Sunday 150th week
Many fighters and bomber planes crossed to the south over here in the early evening. There was a field gun and instructions on the Common all the evening and a summer evening audience.

July 13th Monday
The wardens in our sector met at Mrs Robertson's at 8 this evening, Mr Ridgeway being chairman. A census of all the people is asked for and it is important to have, for supposing a house here is bombed it is well to know how many people to look for under the debris, so tomorrow I go to every house in my part of Black Hill as far as Pondcroft which Ridgeway does. Backwoods and Meadow Lane will be done by Mrs Robertson, Miss Abby and Mr Gilbert.

July 14th Tuesday
Last night I slept out as usual, the searchlights between 12.30 and 1.30 were very beautiful, criss-crossing the sky. I made the census in my sector, 135 people in all and in the evening wrote out the list for Mr Ridgeway.

July 16th Thursday
When I was sleeping out on Wednesday night I saw a beautiful sight. Planes were

crossing SE and searchlights were bright. They caught a plane and I watched its 'silvery' flight across the sky. It was fairylike. I had not seen one in the ray for a long time before, more often the plane is caught and then lost, perhaps caught again. That was at 12.45 and at 1.45 rain began so I had to hurry in.

July 17th Friday
A fierce tank battle is being fought in Egypt and the outcome is likely to affect the whole position there…. This battle… is being fought south of El Alamein where the Eighth Army the day before upset Rommel's plans in his push against the Australians at the Hill of Jesus.

July 19th Sunday 151st week
This Sunday, church collections are for the Merchant Navy, a day of thankful remembrance of their work. This afternoon the Home Guard played cricket against the AFS. The Fire Service won the match.

July 22nd Wednesday
Sweet rationing begins on Sunday and the amount will be the same for children and adults, 2oz each per week and ½ a pound every 4 week period.

July 23rd Thursday
Auchinleck's Eighth Army enters a new offensive against Rommel all along the El Alamein sector in Egypt. St Nicholas' Yarmouth, founded in 1101, the largest parish church in England, was burnt out in a recent night raid. Only the reredos was undamaged. I went to this beautiful church on my camping holiday in Norfolk in 1937 and found it very beautiful, a grand piece of work…. One thing after another comes under controlled price. Blanket prices are controlled now and all woollen blankets must comply in price and quality with a special specification. Utility blankets will carry the label 'the National Price Controlled Blanket'.

July 27th Monday
I received a small parcel from Australia this morning from Jackie McDougall, not food but a small pink and white dressing jacket.

July 29th Wednesday
I went to Brighton this afternoon and for the first time was challenged about my identity card and reason for visit. 'Is your brother over 70 etc?' After ten minutes' wait I was allowed through. Jock told me one of the recent bombs fell on Palace Pier.

July 31st Friday
It was a perfect summer's night and as I was sleeping out decided it was too

beautiful to sleep so I watched the stars, faint in the moonlight and enjoyed the slight breeze. There were many planes to and fro and at 3.17 the siren sounded. After reporting at the Post I went up Black Hill and met the fire guards for that part of the sector that night. Mr Parsons made some tea and at 3.45 the all-clear came through. It was unusual that the Burgess Hill sirens sounded 10 minutes after ours, usually we hear theirs first. The Ministry of Food yesterday said that onions would not be rationed.... Many more have been grown this year. Our crop at the allotment is very good.... An order is issued today that we are asked not to carry our gas masks about with us all the time and children need not take them to school. The chief reason to save wear and tear on the rubber, rubber being so valuable just now.

August 2nd Sunday 154th week
Fortunato Picci, formerly a waiter at the Savoy Hotel, was interned. Being English at heart he volunteered to train as a parachutist and in the raid some time ago in Italy, Picci was dropped near his old home, where knowledge of the country was useful. He was able to guide his comrades to the points they were to sabotage. He was caught, taken as a British prisoner of war, recognized and treated as a spy and on Palm Sunday shot in Rome prison yard. No honour has come his way, he made his sacrifice for a greater thing than glory.

August 5th Wednesday
Gandhi's plan for immediate negotiations with Japan 'if India were freed' is exposed today by the publication of secret documents seized during a raid on the Congress Party's offices at Allahabad.

August 6th Thursday
Last night there was much noise of planes and at 11.45 I got up imagining I heard the siren. The noise sounded like heavy bombers. The evening paper explained they were our bombers taking part in night training operations, not only aircraft crew but members of AA batteries and searchlight units. Stalingrad is now threatened.

August 8th Saturday
Danger to the Russians grows daily as Germans are near the oil fields, now only 30 miles away. Fierce fighting continues as Russians withdraw.... People caught trying to visit Brighton are to get heavier penalties. Seven people were fined from £1 to £3 but the full fines are £100 or 3 months imprisonment.

August 9th Sunday 155th week
The All India Congress have now passed their so called 'Quit India' resolution

calling on Britain to renounce the government of India at once.... Our pledge holds good that after the war Indians can and must control their own affairs.

August 10th Monday
Gandhi arrested.

August 12th Wednesday
American Marines 'Leathernecks' (on Tuesday) fought hand to hand battles in the Solomon Islands and are still holding their beach heads stormed against the Japs.... Australian airmen made most high attacks on Jap ships off Timor.... Mr Parsons brought in my new ARP shoes, stout, well made and comfortable, also a black beret to wear when on ARP work excepting in raids when we wear a helmet.... Our special incident was from 8 to 10, the first at the soldiers' bungalow at Backwoods, the second at La Casita in Meadow Lane. Nearly all the fire guards turned out and the messenger boys were quick and useful. Dorrie Robertson was at the Post timing despatches and arrivals. Afterwards we had a discussion about the whole affair and finally arrived home at 10.45. Messrs Parsons, Ridgeway and Gilbert were pleased.

August 21st Friday
Many more details of the great raid on Dieppe have come in and it is said to have been successful despite losses.[26] 91 enemy planes were destroyed and about 182 destroyed or damaged. Lord Louis Mountbatten was Chief of Combined Operations and Lord Lovat's No. 4 Commando were the first to jump ashore. Lord Lovat said 'This is the toughest job we've had. Remember that you represent the flower of the British Army'. A Commando trooper whispered to his mate 'Don't forget the other blighter is twice as scared as you'. They did not fail and the German guns were shattered, and the gunners wiped out in bayonet fighting. Owing to support from RAF and Navy the various regiments were able to land on their five appointed beaches. No German has ever been able to do that in England. The siren sounded last night at 10.30 and the warning lasted an hour. I was not on duty and heard planes but no dropped bombs or even gun-firing. At 8.30 this evening we had a wardens' meeting at the Post. Mr Fraser was there to take measurements for our battle-dresses. Afterwards Mr Parsons read through the instruction list of items for 'invasion' emergencies: instructions about water, water supplies, sanitation, billeting of homeless persons, casualties, diseases, births, deaths, the aged and infirm. We did not break up until 10.40.

August 22nd Saturday
We are losing Mr Gilbert as a warden for he has joined the Air Force. I am glad for the AF, but sorry to lose his help as warden, good and reliable. I went to the

Tiger canteen in the evening from 7 to 10.20. There was not much doing. Mr Buckingham came in to see Mr Drew as I was entering and I told him if he came upstairs I would give him a cup of tea. He came. He said ordinary soldiers were leaving Old Place, it was being done up throughout. Lady Bective was coming back to it and having a few rooms, the rest was for a special war purpose, strategic offices for Allied war arrangements, apparently something very special and posh.

August 23rd Sunday 157th week
Russians are fighting a 'back to the wall' battle to save Stalingrad.... September 3rd is to be a day of special prayer, for at 11 o'clock the war will be 3 years old.

August 26th Wednesday
From the 30th of this month till the end of October, only 3 pints of milk a week will be allowed to 'ordinary' people – mothers, invalids and children are exempt. From October 18th tins of household milk will be available on ration books, about half a pint a week.... There is a very good crop of sugar beet this year and we are likely to get our full ration this coming winter for it was wholly provided from home-grown beet.

August 28th Friday
Stalingrad has been turned from a town into a fortress.... Clothing coupons will probably have to last 18 instead of 14 months. All mine are still at Pelhams where I left them in hostage for the flag material I got for United Nations Flag day last June 14th although I asked for them several times. Always forgotten.

August 29th Saturday
Stalingrad is a City of Flames started by mass air attacks. All fit men of the city have been called out and all have answered. The central and residential quarters of the city were divided into squares by the Germans and each square is being bombed and dive bombers are over all the city. But Russians fight on.

August 30th Sunday 158th week
American troops will join our men in keeping September 3rd as the National Day of Prayer. Their Commander in Chief Eisenhower has asked all Commanders to allow as many as possible to take part in the services.... Thus we enter the 4th year of the war.

September 1st Tuesday
Japs know how to live frugally in the jungle. Their pack contains an inferior brand of dehydrated rice and soya beans of such unsavoury quality that even the New Guinea natives refuse it; also syringes of morphine for wounded, the object being

to make the jungle fighter self-contained when cut off…. A Jap trick is to advance through the jungle screaming to make Australians believe their forces are larger than they are.

September 3rd Thursday
Hitler ordered men taken at Dieppe were to be put in chains from 2pm today for reprisal. It was stated German prisoners taken at Dieppe had their hands tied by our soldiers to prevent them destroying their papers. The truth is being sought. Today is the National Day of Prayer. I went to the 7.15 Communion Service, listened to the 11 o'clock service broadcast till 11.15 and at 12 o'clock to a talk by the Roman Catholic Archbishop of Birmingham which was very good. At 6.30 in the evening there was a muster on the Common of all ARP Wardens, Fire Guards, First Aid, Ambulance Corps and the Girls' Training Corps from the Heath. Elizabeth Meales is Sergeant and the girls, fresh from school but too young to join up, in fact between 15 and 17, are trained for the Services. We all marched to church for the 7 o'clock evening service. It was packed. The Girls' Training Corps had to stand in the north aisle. Mr Buckingham gave a good address and the whole service was uplifting.

September 6th Sunday 159th week
In the afternoon I counted 23 bombers travelling SW…. On the Stalingrad Front Russian resistance is stiffening…. A German prisoner said the soldiers are all afraid of the coming cold weather but their officers are promising them that the Russian campaign will be over before winter sets in.

September 9th Wednesday
Laval has made enemies of Catholic leaders by ordering the arrest of priests who shelter Jewish children intended for deportation to Germany or concentration camps. Episcopal letters recommending every help for persecuted Jews are being read all over enemy occupied France.

September 15th Tuesday
The Nazis are getting into Stalingrad but being made to fight every foot of the ground they gain. Every house is a fortress and German losses are terrific. Germans are ransacking all Europe in preparation for the winter campaign. Clothing, skins, furs and oil stoves are being requisitioned…. Germans are concentrating on aircraft and are blasting everything out of existence.

September 22nd Tuesday
Moscow reports that during the last 24 hours no advance by the Germans has been made on the Stalingrad Front. All women and children have been removed from

the city, every house is a firing point. 5,000 Frenchmen were arrested in Paris during the weekend either for grenade throwing or other reasons. One of the 3 bombs thrown in Nice hit the HQ of the 'Riot Squad of the Legion', Laval's terrorist police. Two Germans, the Reverend Dr Kaufmann and an artist Heinrich Will have been sentenced to death for listening to English radio and 45 others have received long-term imprisonment. Germany is using women from Eire to ferret out US Army secrets in Northern Ireland. Spying is carried on by the IRA on behalf of Germany who are financing the Fifth Column. The number of women in Londonderry has increased and men have been asked questions no girl would want to know. The Soviet Government is asking the US definitely to break off relations with Finland.... Arrangements are being made for a big International Congress of newspapermen from all Allied and neutral countries to be held in London at the end of October to strengthen collaboration among all countries not on the Axis side.... The Canadian destroyer *Ottawa* has been lost in action with the enemy. Its Commanding Officer was killed and 11 officers and men are missing. This is the 3rd Navy sinking in less than a week.

September 23rd Wednesday
Timoshenko is keeping up his offensive in the NW of Stalingrad and in 2 days' fighting 3,000 Germans were killed. Yesterday evening there was a meeting of wardens at the Post, not to discuss the new explosive bombs as I thought, but to arrange in the event of invasion about first aid help and to ask certain people to look after those in a few houses near their own and see all was well with them. It is difficult to decide the best place for taking and attending to any gas infected cases should they arise and this item was hardly settled. It will be probably at the Hostel of God. The meeting was from 8 to 10, Mr Ridgeway being in charge of this particular item. We have to make another house to house visit to test gas masks.

September 24th Thursday
Timoshenko has been reinforced by regiments of Guards and Marines known as 'Black Devils' and they are slowly beating back the Germans from Stalingrad. These 'concealed' reinforcements have taken Nazis by surprise and fierce fighting went on in the city and in Mozdok.

September 25th Friday
A further advance has been made on the German left flank at Stalingrad although fighting in the street continues. Von Bock made 12 successive attacks to break into the centre of Stalingrad, supported by over 200 tanks. But he failed and 50 tanks were left blazing in the streets, their crews killed as they scrambled from the gun turrets. Germans cannot destroy the directing brain of Stalingrad. It is in an HQ

room deep underground. With the exception of Sebastopol, Stalingrad has suffered more than any other city from bombs and shells. There are few buildings left standing.

September 26th Saturday
The Russians have retaken a 'valuable position' in Stalingrad and although Germans are reinforced in the NW they have been beaten off. Russians are using every kind of weapon in the streets, guns firing down the boulevards and machine gun nests in all street approaches.

September 27th Sunday 162nd week
Germans admit Russian penetration of their main line and are cabling for reinforcements, the heavy fighting continues all along the line. The next few days are expected to turn the balance one way or the other.

September 28th Monday
Timoshenko has gained more ground in Stalingrad city but he has had to fall back in the Caucasus…. The centre of Stalingrad is outside German control, but whole sections of the town present a confused picture in which Russian and German firing points are interwoven, opposing sides holding houses in the same street.

September 29th Tuesday
The heading in today's paper is 'Stalingrad Outlook Never Graver'. Russians have had setbacks on the NW outskirts of the city, in the Mozdok area of the Eastern Caucasus and at Sinyavino, south of Leningrad.

September 30th Wednesday
A Heinkel 111 suddenly attacked 'a southern village' on Tuesday night. The village is said to be Petworth and made a direct hit on the school killing the headmaster, one of the teachers and 18 children. 28 were taken to hospital.

October 1st Thursday
Moscow reports that in the battle for the factory belt in the northwest outskirts of Stalingrad, Russians have lost ground but after another day's fighting they still bar the Nazi drive to the Volga. All day fighting went on for a height at the approach to the city but Russians kept it…. Hitler spoke in Berlin saying 'Our programme for next year is to hold on to what we have and secondly to wait to see who will be exhausted first'. He is determined to take Stalingrad and to 'mercilessly destroy every saboteur in our community.' The 'southern Sussex town' where the school was bombed last Tuesday as being Petworth has not been contradicted and more were killed than at first reported. 41 dead and missing, injured 33 are the figures

now given. All ice-cream businesses close today.... Banning of ice-cream means the saving of 30,000 tons of transport in a year. Refrigerating machinery used will be put to other uses.... Today I went to London with Bob, meeting Daisy Wood at his office. When he and I walked over London Bridge, I saw some of the blitz damage and had a good view of St Paul's from about the middle of the Bridge. I saw many, many ruins, especially churches which, however, we were able to enter. St Lawrence Jewry, close to the Guildhall is terribly wrecked, also the beautiful Temple Church and all the Inns of Court around.... After looking around ruined St James' Church Piccadilly, we walked across the Green Park, full now of various contraptions, barbed wire, deep holes and long grass, camouflages and so forth and then on to Victoria Station.

October 2nd Friday
War supplies are now being shipped in giant cargo planes to Russia and China by a globe girdling air transport system.... There was an alert this morning at 5 minutes past 2 lasting about half an hour. A good deal of gun-firing was heard overhead. I was told Flying Fortresses were fighting Nazis, but no particulars, nothing dropped here. It was all very high up.

October 3rd Saturday
Timoshenko has been reinforced with British and American tanks and made headway in his race to 'tighten the neck' on the German 'inner circle' before Stalingrad.... Things were very quiet at the canteen last night, more English than Canadian soldiers in. I returned home usual time, 10.20.

October 4th Sunday 163rd week
Yesterday was a Salvation Army Flag Day, 'Huts for Troops'. I collected in Gander Hill helping out Stella Ling who had to go to the dentist. It was a long job, both sides of the road, Wickham Way and Summerhill Close.... Four major battles are now raging round Stalingrad. Russians have recovered the ground lost on Friday. Von Hoth captured a 'populated place' on the north, probably the workers' settlement where fighting has been extra fierce. Germans lost 800 in this fight.... The Petworth headmaster who died trying to save his boys was Mr Charles Stevenson, 56, and had been head for 17 years. The death toll is now 32. He, Miss Marshall, a mistress and the 28 children were buried in a communal grave.... Fish is to be 1d a lb cheaper this week. It is hoped there will be an even distribution of onions this winter. Port and sherry have just arrived in the country, port 12/- a bottle, sherry 13/- to be released for Christmas.

October 5th Monday
Russians still hold on at Stalingrad and inside the city German attacks have been

beaten off and south of the city lost positions have been regained by Russians. Hitler is bringing in reinforcements in giant transport planes.

October 6th Tuesday
At 3am the news came that Stalingrad was holding a 'new battering-ram offensive by three German infantry divisions and 100 tanks'. All the attacks against the factory settlement in the suburb were flung back. The Germans lost 1,000 men and 14 tanks.... Enough beet sugar will be produced in our factories for war-time rations. The Fenland crop is above average and the harvest better than was thought possible.

October 7th Wednesday
Yesterday Hitler launched a fresh offensive towards Grozny oilfields. For the first time in a year those up to 18 are to have oranges, 1lb each on the ordinary ration book, allowed 5 days after children under 5 have had their share.

October 8th Thursday
Ten officers and men who carried out a raid on Sark last Saturday brought back evidence of the ill treatment of British residents in the island. Germans say that in the Sark raid a Nazi working party, an NCO and 4 men, was attacked and bound by Commandos. They said some time ago that we bound German prisoners – all proved to be a put up job. Four of these prisoners escaped and were shot while doing so. One was brought back to this country and confirmed the suspicions that males between 16 and 70 have been deported to Germany together with their families. Of 900 men conscripted from Guernsey 400 are still to go and it is expected there will be more from Jersey than from Guernsey. Eleven men from Sark were warned to go last week, but 2 committed suicide. Only 9 left. The prisoner said they were all forced labour. From midday today the German High Command has ordered all British prisoners taken at Dieppe to be put in chains until they are satisfied about the treatment of German prisoners here. 15 more Norwegians have been executed at Trondheim for carrying arms.

October 9th Friday
Germany has carried out her threat to put 2,500 British officers and men captured at Dieppe into chains and manacles at noon yesterday. Our Government replies that unless they are released an equal number of German prisoners will be so treated at noon tomorrow. 170,000 more German and Italian prisoners are in British hands than British prisoners in Axis hands. It seems like going back to the Middle Ages. Berlin boasts that Stalingrad can now be finished off by guns and dive bombers, no longer necessary to send infantry and engineers into the battle. They claim to have captured the nucleus of the city and a break through to the Volga.

October 10th Saturday
No wonder we heard many planes yesterday for the paper says the greatest day raid took place. 100 bombers, mainly four-engined Liberators and Flying Fortresses protected by 500 fighters bombed Lille steel and engineering works, one of France's most important plants. Only 4 bombers lost, crew of one is safe and all the fighters returned. At least 5 German planes were shot down.... The Stalingrad Nazi assault went on all day yesterday and twice German infantry failed to break through to the Volga. Timoshenko's relief force attacks northwest of Stalingrad have drawn German troops away from the city. Russians are using an improved model of a training plane, the U2, for bombing. It is a midget plane made of wood and canvas, capable of only 60 to 100mph. Bombs are dropped by hand. Germans called them 'Flying Boxes' until they learned to respect them. Their advantage is they can land almost anywhere, can take off in complete darkness and being slow, are excellent for precision bombing, better than dive bombers.

October 12th Monday
Just after 10.30 this morning the house shook continuously. The sky in the SE looked like thunder and I saw much smoke and heard gun-firing. Whether it was manoeuvres on the Downs or a convoy attack in the Channel Islands I do not know.... It lasted ¾ of an hour. For the black-out our library sessions started today in the afternoons, none in the evening again until the spring. Germans have dropped infantry attacks entirely at Stalingrad, they only shell and bomb the city. Many Germans were killed, 300 according to Soviet reports and 5 transports sunk in the Baltic.

October 13th Tuesday
A letter from Jock this morning tells me that Compton Avenue was blitzed yesterday morning, no doubt some of that firing I heard here. He was blown down but not hurt, much glass smashed and front door lock. No one next door was killed but there were casualties and some deaths in the road. I heard Preston Circus suffered too. Street fighting has begun again in Stalingrad. Germans making 14 tank attacks for 'a point of strategic importance' but all were beaten off. Germans lost 800 officers and men killed. Russians thinking of winter are training millions of ski troops and making thousands of skis.

October 15th Thursday
About midday I went to Brighton to make sure Jock was alright. He was in spite of the shock the blitz gave him as he was thrown across his bed. I saw a man with a notebook and an official look and asked him if he was recording damage done in the road. He said yes and soon afterwards came to no.14. The Council attend to

broken windows and roof as soon as possible, patching the windows with felt, a greyish material rather like oil cloth. No home escaped broken windows in Compton Avenue and Bath Street adjoining is wrecked. We went out and looked around and saw the tall, newish brick-built flat block that got a direct hit. It was sad to see the disturbed furniture on 3 floors, bookcase against an outer wall nearly intact, pictures adrift, clothing scattered and everything broken.

October 17th Saturday
In the main German attacks on Stalingrad have been held but one district had to be given up. The air blitz was terrible. 120 of Von Hoth's tanks have been destroyed in two days.... We were busier than usual at the canteen this evening. Soldiers enjoyed chip potatoes, Welsh rarebit, fried bread and sausage meat. ATS girls came in for supper. Many are now billeted at Compton Lea and some have joined the Library. We had an alert this morning 9.10 till 9.25 probably only passing planes.

October 21st Wednesday
There is not much change in Stalingrad positions. Germans are still trying to cross the Volga and their planes continually sow mines. On the east bank old men and women put out in rowing boats and pick their way to the opposite bank with supplies.

October 22nd Thursday
In Stalingrad mud has grounded the Luftwaffe and Russians have gained some ground.

October 23rd Friday
When Cowfold monastery was bombed, I do not know when, a number of monks asked to be released from their vows so that they might go to the war. Bombs damaged one of the finest sections of the building.

October 25th Sunday 166th week
The Eighth Army has begun its battle against Rommel for Egypt and North Africa and a fierce affair it will be.... The struggle is on a 40-mile front from El Alamein on the coast down to the edge of the Qattara Depression. Rommel's twelve divisions have a well-fortified 4 mile deep defence.... The paper says oranges are now plentiful for grown-ups as well as children. It is the first time they have been available for about two years.

October 26th Monday
We have had three warnings today: the first from 10.40 till 11, the second 11.10 till 12.30 and the third from 12.40 till 1.35. At the second warning guns sounded

Plate 1

Helena Hall.

Christmas Card
designed by
Helena Hall.

he Pond.

Plate 2

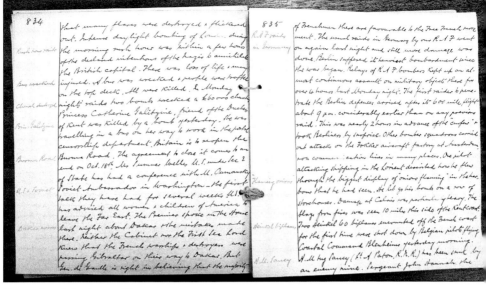

Example of the journal layout.

Example of use of pictures in the journal.

Plate 3

roup photo (see entry for December 3rd 1944). Miss Hall is believed to be seated on the ont row 5th from the right.

Believed to be Helena
Hall in gas mask and
boiler suit.

Plate 4

CUCKFIELD URBAN DISTRICT COUNCIL.

"Contex" Filters will be fitted to all the Gas Masks in your house if you bring them to:-

"THE TIGER"

HIGH STREET, LINDFIELD.

on *Saturday 20th* JULY 1940 and on *Monday 22nd* JULY 40

between the hours of 10am to 12 noon or 2 pm to 4 pm or 6 pm to 8 pm.

Bring this Form with you. It is your authority for having "Contex" fitted.

Contex filter notice (see July 15th 1940).

Tuesday April 14th 1942.

NO. 1.   Time of incident.

An H.E. bomb has fallen between "Harmers" and "Elm Rock" Meadow Lane, demolishing the front corners of both houses, leaving the corner of the roof of "Harmers" suspended. The windows and doors are blown out at side and front of both houses. There are casualties in the back portion of both houses 2 have broken legs, 2 lay under some debris, 3 others are cut and bruised and all are suffering from shock. *Arrived at Post*

Incident report (see April 14th 1942).

April 1st 1940.
no action incident   A.R.P./M.I.

WARDEN'S REPORT FORM.

Form of Report to Report Centres.

AIR RAID DAMAGE (Commence report with these words)

Designation of Reporting Agent
(e.g., Warden's Post No.   )   *25*

Position of occurrence *Old Place, main building*

Type of bombs :—HE/Incendiary/Poison Gas

Approx. No. of Casualties :—   *5. 3 Children + 2*
(If any trapped under wreckage, say so)   *adults*

If fire, say so :— *Fire on roof*

Damage to mains :—Water /Coal Gas /Overhead electric cables/Sewers

Names of Roads blocked *none*

Position of any unexploded bombs *none*

Time of occurrence (approx.) *8. a.m.*

Services already on the spot or coming :—
awaiting fire patrol.

Remarks :— *3 children trapped in wreckage. Man and woman fractured legs. Require rescue squad and ambulance.*

ORIGINAL ⎱ These words are for use with a report sent by messenger.
DUPLICATE ⎰ Delete whichever does not apply.

LINDFIELD'S SIREN GRIEVANCE.

To the Editor of THE MID-SUSSEX TIMES

Dear Sir,—May I trespass on your valuable space to air a grievance of many Lindfield residents ? Is it not possible to have a siren installed in the centre of the village, where it could be heard by all and not on the outskirts as at present. If the wind is in the wrong direction in many parts it is not heard at all. Will those responsible give it their attention and earn our gratitude that we may be forewarned, and not go out on the streets as we do now (unwittingly) causing the A.R.P. more trouble, when we all so much appreciate the service they give us out of the kindness of their heart.

Yours faithfully,
AN OLD RESIDENT.

Lindfield.   *29. Oct. 1940*

Siren grievance letter (see November 4th 1940).

Warden's report (see April 1st 1940)

Plate 5

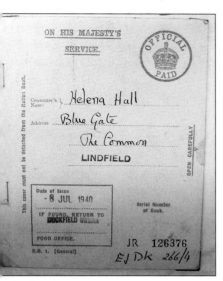

Ration book cover.

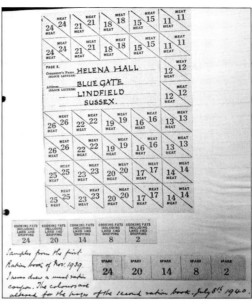

Samples from the first Ration book of Nov. 1939. I never drew a meat ration coupon. The colours are altered for the purpose of the second ration book. July 8th 1940.

Ration book stamps.

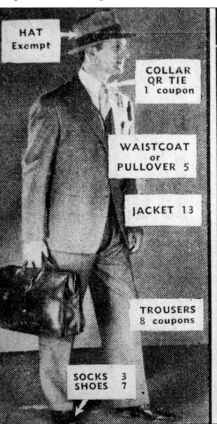

Coupons for clothing.

Plate 6

Removal of railings.

Life-line target poster.

Plate 7

THE other day, if you had been walking on a hill near the South-East Coast and had chanced to look up to the sky, you would have seen a plane in difficulties.

This is so common a sight in these parts that it would not have greatly interested you. However, it was a British plane. So if it had landed in your neighbourhood, you would probably have run to help.

It landed on a golf course. And somebody, who shall be nameless, ran to help.

* * *

Out of it stepped a young Belgian pilot. The plane was practically undamaged, but a little smoke was coming from the fuselage.

Rapidly the pilot explained that there was a danger of fire, but that if the fire brigade could be summoned at once—or at least within twenty minutes—the machine could be saved.

So the nameless one dashed to the telephone. Considering that the nearest fire brigade was only two miles away, he had not much doubt about saving that machine.

Whereupon a number of remarkable things happened. Or, rather, nothing happened at all, though a lot of astonishing questions were asked. In what part of the golf course had the machine landed? Because if it had landed at A, it was the job of X fire brigade, but if it had landed at B, it was the job of Y fire brigade.

"You see," said a placid voice, "we don't know whether it is a Rural District matter or an Urban . . ."

"Struth !", shouted the nameless one. "How do I know? All I can say is that I can see it from here. And the smoke's getting worse every minute."

They left it to burn

THERE were mutterings at the other end of the telephone. In desperation, the nameless one rang off and got through to A.R.P. headquarters at C. (He was a warden in his spare time, and knew the secret telephone number.)

"Is there an alert on?" cooed a voice at the other end.

"What has that got to do with it? All I can tell you is that the smoke . . ."

"Quite, but if there is no alert on, we shall have to ring up D. for permission to bring out an engine. You see, if we do not ring up D. . . ."

"You can ring up the devil," barked the nameless one. "You've got the facts. It's your responsibility."

* * *

Meanwhile, believe it or not, two heavily moustached policemen had arrived from the first place, on bicycles.

Needless to say, no fire engine had arrived. The knotty problem of whether it was "Rural" or "Urban" had not yet been solved.

But the plane was still intact. There was still hope. There, waiting to be saved, was a vital weapon of war . . . to say nothing of several thousand pounds. By it was the young pilot, wringing his hands.

The minutes ticked by. At least two fire brigades could have come and gone at least twice.

But, no. This is Britain. We don't hold with hustling ways. And when at last the brigade arrived, all they had to extinguish was a charred ruin.

*

An article written by Beverley Nicholls.—Cut from the Sunday Chronicle for Dec 1st 1940. His brother who lives at West Common Lindfield went to the golf links at the time of the accident

See pages 1025—26 and 886.

Letter regarding plane crashed on Haywards Heath golf course (see December 1st 1940).

Farmhouse where family sheltered during bombing

Wreckage of chicken house

May 23rd. 1940

Bomb crater

Bombed Sussex farm.

Plate 8

Crashed plane
in Lancing
cornfield (see
August 14th
1940).

Bomb damage
in a South
Coast town.

Plate 9

London barrage.

AA guns (see
September 19th 1940).

Smoke trail.

Flame lit sky (see
September 10th
1940).

Plate 10

London bomb damage.

Kiel bomb damage.

Invitation to Lindfield Spitfire fundraising event (see August 24th 1940).

Plate 11

...oops retreating to Dunkirk.

Troops returning to France in 1944.

Rubble in liberated Normandy.

'England Is Verdun To-day'

COL. CHARLES SWEENEY, famous officer in the French Foreign Legion, in a broadcast to France from London last night said:

"Frenchmen, my brothers, the truth of this war is that by words you have been led to defeat and to misery.

"We airmen of the Lafayette Squadron have rallied to the cause of England. We will fight with her, for her, for ourselves and for you. Millions will come after us, as they did in 1918.

"Britain has become the Verdun of this war. She is the rock against which barbarism will be broken as it was broken in 1916 at the gates of Verdun."

...erdun cutting.

Tank troops resting in Normandy.

Plate 12

This is a translation of an obituary notice from a Berlin newspaper.

" ' Never shall I forget thee, my darling Henry.' In faithful discharge of his duty my dearly beloved, unforgettable husband, our kind-hearted only son,
HENRY KRUGER,
Lance-corporal in a regiment of Heavy Artillery,
gave his life for his country in the hard battle against Soviet Russia on June 27, 1941.

" He was my happiness, my life, my sunshine. A Soviet bullet struck his faithful heart.

" In unspeakable grief, Margaret Krüger (née Wiepszek), Hans Krüger, Elisabeth Krüger (née Bottcher), Berlin."

Obituary.

German soldier in fur coat.

Red Army Day

Red Soldier, still we cannot believe the things we see:
It is five hundred leagues from Stalingrad to Spree!
And you, the " ragged rabble " that could not hope to win.

Have fought with faith and fury from Moscow to Berlin.
Not only now in Moscow the guns of honour roll:
All the wide world is firing a salvo from the soul.

BITTERNESS of defeat, the realisation that they have failed their Führer, utter weariness after days of constant bombardment and retreat, is shown by these Germans captured by the First Army.

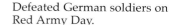
Feb. 27th 1945

Defeated German soldiers on Red Army Day.

Plate 13

Russian Army skiers.

Stalingrad.

German retreat on the Eastern Front.

Wily Russians attempt to deceive the Germans on the Eastern Front.

Plate 14

Russians return to Kursk.

Liberation, lorry in France.

Helena Hall's signature at the end of the journal.

Plate 15

—By Ian Peterson.

" I'm extremely sorry, Wilkins, but you must realise that a submarine is no place for pin-up girls."

" I'm afraid this is what comes of watching 2,000 Fortresses going over, Doctor."

" I think I'll give the hedgehog to Dad, the frogs to Mum, and the blindworms to Sister Doll."

Plate 16

" No, I can't come round to 43, 62 or 27. If you want to know, I just happen to be cleaning my own windows."

" I always think this is one of the nicest views in the village."

" I should like to have a carriage to myself because I have a nasty habit of careless-talking in my sleep."

" I had a feeling this would happen as soon as they got rid of the black-out curtains."

so near and bombs dropped that made houses shake, so I put on my mackintosh and helmet and went round to Mrs Parsons in case trouble came nearer home. I met her in the lane and we walked up and down, hearing planes but seeing nothing on account of cloud, low dull all over cloud and heavy rain. Squalls have continued all day. We both got wet and very cold and were glad to hear the all–clear. The firing was mostly in the S and SE. I met Mrs Sharpe after the library session with her sister who had come from Seaford which had been raided yesterday and today, 16 people were killed. The sister came to find a home for her daughter and 3 boys, all hit and suffering from shock. After many enquiries, the village is so full Mrs Keable said she would take the mother and 2 boys, and Mrs Sharpe the eldest boy who goes to Lewes school.

October 27th Tuesday
Thus far all Egypt gains are held.... Berlin admits 'the situation in Egypt has become extremely serious'.

October 28th Wednesday
The US Navy department announces that 2 Jap Destroyers have been sunk in the big air and naval battle off the Santa Cruz islands.... But US losses have been serious for Japs outnumber them in the South Pacific. Second-hand motor cars may no longer be sold without a permit from the Ministry of War and Transport. It will assist the Government with future requisitioning, collection of spare parts, tyres, etc. The census of cars begins today and is due to end in three weeks. Clothing restrictions must be conformed to. A tailor, Julius Goldberg, was fined £4 at Newcastle yesterday for having made a lounge suit with a double-breasted jacket and £1 for making the trousers with permanent turn-ups.... I spent yesterday afternoon trying on gas masks to the people in my sector here. We did them not so very long ago, but the order has come for them to be done again. I slipped on the wet bricks outside Pelham Place Cottages and sprained my left foot.

October 29th Thursday
The Eighth Army has won the biggest tank battle fought so far and General Montgomery's infantry have gained ground. Our air superiority surprises the Germans.

October 30th Friday
The British are keeping up their non-stop air offensive against Rommel and the heavy fighting continues.

November 1st Sunday 167th week
Eleven German raiders were shot down and many more damaged in attacks on the

SE yesterday. Canterbury was 'the main attack town'. The city streets were thronged with shoppers and in the fading light bombs dropped and many were killed before they could reach shelters. The raiders came in low under clouds. 6 were killed in a bus from blast of a bomb which fell close.... Yesterday evening I saw the film *Gone with the Wind* and after 'current events' a good long piece of Smut's speech of a few days ago. It was realistic, both he and the Premier spoke well and clearly. Applause was tremendous.

November 4th Wednesday
Extensive fighting has begun on the frontier of India and Jap occupied Burma.... The BBC last night invited the people of unoccupied France to join in a demonstration on November 11th, to assemble in front of war memorials and sing the *Marseillaise*.... Several measures against idle talk are to be made. A 21-year-old Plymouth merchant seaman was hanged yesterday for giving information to the enemy. He was bribed at Lisbon and collected information by touring pubs and pumping fellow-seamen.

November 5th Thursday
It is some time since there was such good victory news in the paper. The Eighth Army has won a great victory and one hopes Rommel will not recover from his defeat. It is known that 260 tanks were destroyed, 270 guns captured and among prisoners, the Commander of the Afrika Corps General Ritter von Thoma. General von Stumme, a senior General in command when Rommel went to Germany, has been killed. Over 9,000 prisoners have been taken and over 300 aircraft destroyed and 50,000 tons of shipping sunk carrying Axis supplies to North Africa.... There will be no Guy Fawkes celebrations today. I hope Lewes will revive hers after the war.

November 6th Friday
The war news is even more cheering this morning. The Eighth Army is widening the bulge in Rommel's lines and German anti-tank defences are broken.... The German drive against Grozny oilfields has been stopped. Stalingrad's defenders sent a message to Stalin on the 25th anniversary of the Soviet Revolution saying they would 'hold out to the death'.

November 9th Monday
American troops have landed in North Africa and Algiers, capital of Algeria, is in their hands. The French there laid down their arms last night and Admiral Darlan authorized the ceasefire and so hostilities finished less than 24 hours after Americans arrived.

November 11th Wednesday

The two minute silence was kept today here in the usual way. I went to the service at 11 and the silence was held (followed by reading the names of those who fell in the last and in this war) at the War Memorial. I was with Wilma and we thought of Dennis lost on the submarine *Seahorse*.... Mr Churchill spoke at the Mansion House yesterday and referring to the Eighth Army victory said 'Now this is not the end. It is not even the beginning of the end. But it is perhaps the end of the beginning.'

November 12th Thursday

The Premier spoke in the House yesterday. He gave a review of the war and at the end of details of the great victory in Egypt said the bells of the country will ring on Sunday in celebration. Our losses in Egypt were 13,600 compared with 59,000 on the Axis side.... Timoshenko has made fresh gains in Stalingrad where there are now 27 degrees of frost. The banks of the Volga are fringed with ice.

November 13th Friday

During the last 12 months the Allies have sent to Russia over 30,000 aircraft, 4,000 tanks and 20,000 vehicles in addition to tools, aviation spirit and accessories.

November 14th Saturday

Today many church bells are being cleaned and ropes tested for tomorrow's ringing, the first time since June 1940. Mr Merry called for the 'United Nations' flags I made last June to use for decorating tomorrow, I suppose on Muster Green where the muster is to take place tomorrow. London's chief celebration will be at St Paul's.... We were busy at the canteen this evening and all went happily.

November 15th Sunday 169th week

The Eighth Army is now threatening Benghazi. This Sunday is Civil Defence Day and commemorates the Battle of Britain 2 years ago. More than a thousand CD heroes assemble in St Paul's to hear the Archbishop of Canterbury preach and there will be processions in nearly all cities and towns. Here we all assembled in Muster Green at 9.30. I walked there after going to early service and there was a splendid attendance of all the Services, the biggest being the Home Guard.... After being inspected we all marched to Oaklands and were dismissed from there.... My flags looked well against a red background.

November 16th Monday

It is said that 75,000 Axis men have been killed, wounded or captured by the Eighth Army in the Battle of the Desert. Rommel is now in Tunis where he is expected to make a stand. He was so nearly caught by our tanks last Friday at his HQ east of Tobruk that he ran in his shirt and shorts leaving his coat and scarf.

November 18th Wednesday
General Anderson's British First Army, with Americans, have driven back Axis forces in Tunisia.... The RAF carried out another daylight raid on St Nazaire U–boat base yesterday. Six Nazi planes were destroyed, all ours returned. Seven French officers were shot yesterday for aiding Giraud's escape. From next Sunday, milk is to be cut to two pints a week for each person. Lord Woolton says green vegetables are to be controlled. Dried milk is useful, we are allowed one tin a month. Today I was allowed only ¼lb of raisins and no sultanas. They cost 4 points (1 point for every ounce) so the Christmas pudding won't be rich.

November 23rd Monday
The Germans are still short of winter clothing on the cold Russian Front in spite of the large-scale gathering of winter clothing in Norway, Finland and other occupied countries. Instead of having fur coats, fur caps, warm underwear and valenkis (felt boots), Germans are still wearing shabby overcoats with slender lining and depending for the rest on local loot: scarves, blankets, and female garments enter into the soldiers' equipment. They are less well fed too. Russians trying to close the ring round the Germans besieging Stalingrad have taken 5 more towns, 24,000 prisoners and made advances about 10 miles north and south of the Volga. General Rodimtsev's forces are also going ahead in Stalingrad itself where 1,000 Germans were killed yesterday in an all-out battle.

November 24th Tuesday
Yesterday afternoon the US Army Air Force attacked St Nazaire.... 15 enemy fighters were destroyed. We lost 4 bombers.

November 25th Wednesday
Timoshenko's relief armies have broken through to Stalingrad and joined with the defenders of the city who are now taking part in the offensive started 5 days ago. Three German Divisions and their staffs have been captured, 12 inhabited places taken and 15,000 Germans killed all in one day. Russian advances range between 4 to 25 miles.

November 26th Thursday
Russians have captured 3 more railway stations and 5 more towns, the speed of attack having thrown the Germans into disorder. Russian pincer inside the Don Elbow is now almost closed.

November 27th Friday
Some films circulated by Germany's UFA company have been recalled from Switzerland, Spain, Portugal and Sweden. The Swiss opened one of the consignments and found in it a full-length newsreel entitled *Victory in Africa*. The film was made by German newsreel men during Rommel's summer drive into Egypt. The Gestapo are trying to find out whether it was sent at this particular time by mistake or whether it was deliberate 'sabotage' in a new form.... Hitler accuses Darlan of betraying him and has told Pétain that Marshal von Rundstedt will be Dictator of all French territory. Hitler has ordered the demobilization of the whole of the French Army.

November 28th Saturday
Last Tuesday and yesterday afternoon, I helped to pack the parcels the WI members are sending to those serving who come from this village. Considering it is in the 4th year of the war, the items we have collected for the men are very good. In cardboard boxes, collapsible, given by Mr Lazell we put in writing paper, pencil, Penguin or other books (usually a detective or mystery story), shaving stick, razor blades, a new 2/6d piece in its small envelope, a game, pack of cards, a woolly, either socks or scarf with hood end and a printed letter from the Vicar.... On the parcels sent out of the country we had to write a list of contents. We worked at Mrs Bevan's Cripland Court from 2.30 until about 6 o'clock. She gave us all tea about 4.30.

November 29th Sunday 171st week
In the northern part of Stalingrad Russian forces have entirely recaptured the factory area.

December 3rd Thursday
Russians are continuing their advance on the Stalingrad and Central Fronts where fighting grows. Transport planes are reinforcing and bringing supplies to the trapped Germans. 50 of them were destroyed yesterday, 30 on the ground and 20 in the air. Moscow says the collapse of German resistance in the Stalingrad 'bottleneck' is only a matter of days.

December 9th Wednesday
The Women's Institute carries on very well under war-time conditions. We have tea at the meetings but cannot supply sugar and the ration is 2 cups of tea with milk (milk is scarce now each person is allowed only 2 pints a week), and a bun and a cake. There is no margarine and nothing to spread. We cannot have a party or a dance this year, so this afternoon we had a specially nice tea with sausage rolls and the tables were arranged in the form of a V in the middle of the room. On the

curtain in the background is a large white V. I made it on Monday and cut the V out of white paper and then pasted it onto a large sheet of brown paper supplied by Mrs Newton. All the members sang carols.

December 11th Friday
The Hostel of God at Beckworth arranged a dance for this evening at the Village Hall for the Prisoners of War Fund. I lent them flags and helped decorate the Hall with them this morning. The tickets were 1/6d single, 2/6d double. I sold 3 double tickets.... More than a third of the 313,000 Jews in Poland before the war have been killed.

December 14th Monday
Russians in Stalingrad have thrown Germans out of the southern outskirts of the city.

December 15th Tuesday
The Eighth Army is pressing hard on Rommel's retreating forces as they go down towards Tripoli.

December 18th Friday
Mr Eden made a solemn pledge in the House on behalf of the British people that the persecution of Jews in Europe will be avenged. The whole House stood for a while. Also there are Czechs, Poles, and Dutch and others. Mr James de Rothschild voiced for his people their gratitude to Britain.

December 19th Saturday
The Food Ministry has released to NAAFI a shell egg for each member of the Forces for Christmas Day breakfast.

December 20th Sunday 174th week
Last week our submarines torpedoed 17 Axis supply ships in the Mediterranean and nine were sunk. Russians have made another breakthrough on the Middle Don, thus cutting the Voronezh-Rostov railway line on which Germans relied for supplies. More than 200 inhabited places have been captured and over 10,000 prisoners taken and at least 20,000 officers and men were killed.... A plan of the Germans for exterminating the Jews in Europe is published by the Inter-allied Information Committee. The number of Jews who have died or been deported since 1939 numbers 200,000 and 5 million are in danger of extermination. The destruction is going on by shooting or by lethal gas among other methods. The cruelties are too terrible to be true.... This afternoon a four-engined bomber flew very directly over this house making a big noise. We heard later that its engine was

on fire and it was seeking a landing place. Russians in the Middle Don pushed on 16 to 20 miles yesterday and over 8,000 Germans were killed and prisoners taken numbered 3,500.

December 22nd Tuesday
German troops on the Middle Don are now retreating in disorder. Russians advanced another 12 to 16 miles capturing several places, booty and prisoners. Germans admit the position is grave.

December 27th Sunday 176th week
The papers today are full of the news. I heard it at early service on Christmas morning – the murder of Admiral Darlan. He was shot at Algiers on Thursday by a Frenchman who was executed by firing squad yesterday. His name is being kept secret for security reasons, his mother is Italian and is living in Italy. He confessed. General Giraud has been chosen Darlan's successor. He will co-operate with de Gaulle and the Fighting French. Darlan was given 'a magnificent funeral at which British and French troops were present'.

December 28th Monday
Yesterday General Giraud issued a call for unity to all Frenchmen 'Only one thing counts – France and her Empire. There is but one aim – victory'. The Eighth Army is half way to Tripoli.

1943

—∞—

January 1st Friday
A propaganda film of *Germany's Fourth Christmas at War* shows festive scenes in Berlin, with plenty of food and drink and happy faces. The film is composed of extracts from 1938 newsreels.

January 2nd Saturday
This afternoon a party of us went to the Imperial where we saw the pantomime *Dick Whittington*, an extraordinary good effort for the 4th year of a war.

January 3rd Sunday 177th week
Mr and Mrs Brooks of the Corner Shop in the village have just been told that their son, Sergeant Harry Brooks, was killed on active flying service on December 20th. He was 27.

January 4th Monday
From today the Ministry of Food will buy up one third of Britain's barley crop for flour. This will go into the National Loaf. Oats are expected to be used in National Bread at the same time. Experiments are being made with potato flour, the aim in every case being to save shipping.

January 13th Wednesday
At his weekly food conference Lord Woolton said yesterday bread would continue unrationed if the public co-operated. He wants potatoes used more than bread and the wheat stock to be conserved by using home-grown potatoes. He appeals to the women of Britain to use potato dishes whenever they can. There are 5 kinds of waste paper: 1. correspondence, 2. periodicals and catalogues, these all fetch £7 a ton, 3. ledgers £8 a ton, 4. newspapers £8.10 a ton and 5. rubbish such as cartons, cardboard and wrapping £4 a ton. There will be a demonstration of sorting at the 'Paper Goes to War' Exhibition which opens at the Royal Exchange on January 28th.

January 14th Thursday
Germans admit 3 more offensives by the Russians at Voronezh on the Upper Don and as usual make light of Russian successes. Goebbels warns Germans in *Das*

Reich 'they must bear heavier, harder and grimmer burdens'. The King signed a Royal Proclamation at a meeting of the Privy Council yesterday. Men of 18 and single women of 19 are to be mobilized for the war effort. It is thought that 150,000 young men will become available through this earlier call up and about 500,000 women. There was heavy rain all last night and many places are flooded today. The road by West View Cottages was over ankle deep and about 250 yards this side of East Mascalls bridge was not passable for anything save army lorries. Helen and I could not get to see the Cockhaise flood. The foot of Black Hill was covered, trains were brought to a standstill in Balcombe tunnel and people had to go by bus on some of their journey to town.

January 17th Sunday 179th week
This evening at 7.46 the siren sounded, the first raid for a long time. I went to the gate several times with Bob to hear better the gun-firing and watch searchlights. The all-clear sounded at 10.15.

January 18th Monday
The siren again went at 4.45 and bombs and incendiaries were dropped at 5 o'clock on Moon Hill, Cuckfield. There was a lot of gun-firing. The all-clear was at 5.55. These two raids are reprisals for our two heavy raids on Berlin.... Pitomnik aerodrome, the last link with the outside world of the 80,000 Germans trapped before Stalingrad, has been captured by Russians. The German soldiers there are hungry and cold.

January 19th Tuesday
General Dietmar, the Berlin radio commentator, told the German public last night for the first time about the plight of Von Hoth's army trapped outside Stalingrad. After a siege lasting 16 months Leningrad was relieved. After 7 days of fighting, Russians broke through the nine-mile deep enemy defences and captured Schluesburg on the shores of Lake Ladoga, 25 miles east of the city. Four German Divisions were routed, 1,300 were killed and 1,260 prisoners taken. Marshal Voroshilov and Marshal Zhukov (his promotion was announced last night) were in joint command of the operation.... Lord Halifax our Ambassador in the US said in Rochester today 'When Hitler collapses he will become desperate and have a crack at England with everything he can throw including poison gas in tremendous quantities'.... The speed of the Russian advance is on account of their tanks which have detachable armour and are used as heavy tanks for a break-through and with armour removed as light tanks for fleeing infantry. When the armour is removed it is carried on lorries at the rear. The difference is at least 10 miles an hour.

January 20th Wednesday

More accounts of the relief of Leningrad are given today. Russians put on the most intense barrage that has as yet burst on the Germans and pelted heavy shells at them for 2 hours and twenty minutes. Soviet gunners in spite of frost 36 degrees below worked stripped to the waist. Seven days of this fighting was necessary to affect the joining of the troops. Many Leningrad people died of hunger last winter. The bulk of the population was removed and the workers on the munitions and rearmament went on even when the daily ration was a ¼lb of bread. Zhukov was a directing genius. All Russia thanked him.... Yesterday evening I went to the Public Hall, Haywards Heath to see 6 films given for the benefit of CD workers. They were all good but not particularly helpful to ARP wardens. Most were of general interest especially one on the nose emphasizing the importance of sneezing into one's handkerchief. Camouflaged soldiers creeping along gingerly and firing just at the right moment was a particularly good film. I liked best the building of a Spitfire from start to finish.... Last evening there was a record warning. It lasted just 5 minutes. The siren sounded at 8.55 and I had just knocked at the door of the Post when the all-clear sounded at 9.00.... We heard the news, which was chiefly about more Russian victories, and then went home. At 12.15 there was another alert, the first night one we had had for a long time. It was a beautiful moonlight night and the rain had ceased. It was pleasant to be able to see the awful potholes in Pondcroft Lane and Backwoods. I went up Black Hill, met some fire watchers on duty and talked a while to Mr Parsons at the Post. All was quiet and all we saw was one plane and one 'mopper up'. At 1.25 the all-clear sounded, Mr Parsons made some tea and I came home at 2 o'clock. After an Allied air attack hundreds of Rommel's transports were burnt wrecks. A large part of them are leaving Tripoli and roads near the city, to the west, are blocked. The attack was made in bright moonlight and what a pilot called 'a strafer's paradise'. The Eighth Army has reached the port of Homs... and elements of the Eighth Army have penetrated into the suburbs of Tripoli which are in flames.... In the midday raid yesterday we had the strongest daylight attack since the Battle of Britain. It spread over Kent and Sussex and 6 got through to the London area. 13 raiders were destroyed and many others damaged. Two of our fighters were lost but one pilot is safe.... Mr Barrow told me about the bombing in Lewes on Wednesday. The Star was lost but there were no casualties. He said they were fortunate about their brewery, a bomb fell on each side of it, broke windows and damaged the roof. Other damage was done in the town and one little girl was killed.

January 22nd Friday

As a reprisal for the killing of two Germans the Polish village of Chlewiska was burnt down by Nazis and all inhabitants deported. Children were removed to German orphanages.

January 23rd Saturday
From North Africa comes the news that Tripoli has fallen. How pleased our soldiers must be to arrive at their goal.

January 26th Tuesday
Lord Woolton has made yet another appeal, especially to women, to eat more potatoes and less bread. We have the potatoes, and flour demands shipping, and we *can* relieve the shipping. He issued a challenge to the 300,000 members of the National Federation of WIs and said how he depended on what women do.

January 27th Wednesday
The Premier and President Roosevelt have just met near Casablanca, French North Africa and held a Council of War. The meeting, kept secret until this morning, lasted 10 days. Important decisions for the 1943 offensive were taken. One was complete Axis surrender unconditionally of Germany, Italy and Japan. The German failure to take Stalingrad has lost Hitler the cream of his army. Over 200,000 of his crack troops have been killed or captured. The last of these men have now been wiped out. Two small groups, one north of Stalingrad and one near the central part of the city, isolated from each other, number about 12,000 men but they are doomed. Over 250 – 180 men and 70 women have been shot in Marseilles. Whoever enters the forbidden zone round the old port will be shot. Thousands of poorly clad people are being forced out and marched to concentration camps and many die on the way. A group of Nazi spies has been run to earth in the US as a result of the Allies' deliberate deception about the Churchill-Roosevelt meeting at Casablanca. On January 3rd Nazi propaganda gave 'first news' from a source (they said) connected with the US Senate Foreign Affairs Committee that a meeting was planned in Washington. Europe was told all about it. Periodic information was given of the time of the meeting and the subjects discussed and as late as yesterday were giving details of what was happening to Mr Churchill in Washington. What Nazis did not know was that the 'news' had been planted to deceive and to trap certain people who were expected to pass on the false information and to give themselves away. They did. Attempts are being made by German High Command to drop tablets containing cocaine to the men trapped in Stalingrad. It is the first time Nazis have attempted to relieve war strain in this way by air.

January 28th Thursday
Germany admitted that they had suffered their first major defeat of the war of Stalingrad. 5,000 Axis troops have surrendered on the Voronezh Front and 6 towns were captured. In saying a state of emergency has arrived in Germany the spokesman Joachim Schieferdecker quoted the German law of 1689 'who deserts the colours shall be hanged without mercy: who in the midst of battle begins to

retreat shall be put to death without mercy'. Every German man from 16 to 65 and every woman between 17 and 45 shall be compelled by law to contribute by work and exertion to the war. Total war has indeed come to Germany. American airmen made their first raid on Germany yesterday with a daylight attack by Fortresses on Wilhemshaven naval base.

January 29th Friday
The Soviet is preparing an elaborate scheme for using Nazi labour to rebuild Russian cities and towns after an armistice has been signed and wants to make it a condition of the armistice terms.... It will be only fair for Germans to rebuild cities they have destroyed, particularly Stalingrad.

January 31st Sunday 181st week
The RAF again bombed Berlin, twice in daylight yesterday. The raid interrupted Germany's 'celebrations' of the 10th anniversary of Hitler's 'reign'. Goering was due to speak at 11am and at that time the bombers came and held up his talk until noon. At 4pm Goebbels was due to speak and Mosquitos came again and interrupted it.... Goering promised a new offensive to compensate for Stalingrad.... Many London buses and trams have more light. Our buses are very dim so perhaps we too will be allowed more.

February 1st Monday
Von Paulus, the Nazi General, whose 22 Divisions in Stalingrad were ordered by Hitler never to surrender, has been captured by the Russians only a few hours after Hitler promoted him to Field Marshal. Von Paulus' Chief of Staff General Schmidt, 11 other Generals and 5 Romanian Generals were also captured. Paulus repeatedly asked Hitler permission to capitulate since all resistance was now useless. Hitler would not agree. There are 330,000 men there, not the 220,000 previously reported. The haul of booty is enormous.... Germany is conscripting schoolchildren from 12 to 16 for land work this summer. Schools will be closed for 3 months.

February 2nd Tuesday
On Saturday instead of speaking to the German people, Hitler spoke to his Generals, they who have been the loudest critics of his military strategy. Naturally they are uneasy about the troops in Russia. Hitler said 'No more retreats and bickerings'.

February 4th Thursday
The last way of escape for Hitler's armies in the Caucasus falling back on Rostov has been cut off. The capture of Kuschevskaya closes the gap in the bottleneck

through which the Germans hoped to escape to the north. Yesterday Germans began 4 days mourning for the loss of Stalingrad, to be kept throughout the country.

February 17th Wednesday
Already the Victoria and Albert Museum has a collection of 'austerity clothes' period 1942 which will be preserved for posterity and will show how designers contrived to combine beauty with economy. Nearly every day there is a good deal in the paper about the Beveridge Plan and yesterday it was debated in the Commons.[27]

February 22nd Monday
Stalin sent a message thanking the British people for their praise of the Red Army. Chief celebrations were at the Albert Hall where Mr Eden spoke.

February 23rd Tuesday
If Gandhi (who is carrying out a self-imposed 3 weeks fast) should die Germany will launch an anti-British proclamation from every possible station to India.

February 25th Thursday
When I was planting shallots in the garden today there was a very short alert from 2.15 to 2.22. Several bombers flew east. In the afternoon the Fire Service were trying out something fresh and had their hosepipes all the way up the village street from the Pond to the Church. In the evening Bob and I watched searchlights making patterns in the sky. We heard droves of planes overhead and supposed the RAF were out on business. But it was a quiet night.

February 28th Sunday 185th week
Before Germans left Kharkov they staged mass murders, killing tens of thousands and hurled grenades at the children in the cellars. At least 111,000 men and women were dragged off to Germany.

March 3rd Wednesday
In Tunisia all goes well for us. Germans have retreated nearly 60 miles in the central sector.... The siren sounded this evening at 8.35 and the all-clear at 9.40.... We saw more gun-firing over London and the Thames Estuary than we have seen for many months. London therefore was getting it, a reprisal for the Berlin raid on Monday. We lost 19 planes, all bombers. Then I went to bed at 11.30 expecting a call, and we got it at 4.30 this morning. I went out first with Mrs Parsons then with Mr E. Mr Ridgeway did not turn up. He does not always hear the siren. After the all-clear at 5.40 Mrs Parsons gave us a cup of tea.

March 5th Friday
Russians are now threatening Smolensk, the main German base of the Moscow Front.... On Wednesday evening during the raid, a serious accident happened near the entrance to a London Tube shelter when 178 people were killed chiefly by suffocation and 60 sent to hospital.... Japs suffered their heaviest blow in the war when they lost 22 ships, 1,500 men and 55 planes, all wiped out by General MacArthur's men.

March 6th Saturday
A quarrel has developed between Himmler and the German High Command over the high proportion of deaths among leaders of the Storm-troopers sent to Russia. So many have been 'killed in action' that Himmler has asked for a special committee to investigate their deaths, which the High Command has refused. The late death is reported of SS General Eicke, former Inspector General of all concentration camps, who has been 'killed in action' though it has been found he had never been near the Front. Himmler thinks the military dislike for these men causes them to be 'bumped off' and that the High Command is trying to hush up the matter, so he is taking the matter to Hitler.

March 8th Monday
All Rommel's attempts against the Eighth Army have failed.... Losses both in men and material are considerable.... A great number of heavy tanks have gone through the village towards the Heath, all the same way from tea time onwards. Mr Ridgeway and I, when patrolling, watched many go by, each tank having a trailer. We heard a concentrated attack in the south, we thought Southampton, and reaching to Worthing. London got a little but not as much as the coastal towns. It was a fine starry night but cold, so a cup of tea Mrs Parsons made after the all-clear was welcome. There was a short warning at 5.30 until 5.43 this afternoon, but radio says no bombs were dropped. Of the 25 bombers that came over last night, three were destroyed.

March 9th Tuesday
For several weeks, so says the paper, we have been eating a new national loaf containing barley and in some districts loaves have contained oats and rye. No difference in the bread has been noticeable either in taste or colour, it is very good. Bread now contains more home-grown cereals than have been used in flour for many years and wheat has replaced much of that from Canada.... The coming talks between Great Britain and the US will be concerned with the need for an understanding with Russia before the war ends.... Miss A.A. Hooper, Pool Valley, Brighton was fined £1 yesterday for feeding seagulls with a slice of bread. She pleaded that the bread was 5 days old. Police said she had been feeding the birds for years.

March 10th Wednesday
Russians have been attacked by 25 German Divisions, 250,000 men at least, and have had to give up 8 towns in the Donetz Basin. Germans lost 195 planes, 650 tanks and more than 20,000 officers and men killed but failed in their main objective, the recapture of the Kharkov area.

March 13th Saturday
Germans claim to have reached Red Square in the city of Kharkov. Both sides are determined to fight on and to hold on. The situation there is critical. Germans lost more than 5,000 men in Vyasma and did as much wrecking of lines etc as they had time for when leaving.... Drastic cuts in newspapers have been made in Germany. Towns under 100,000 inhabitants have only one newspaper and outside Berlin there will be no Sunday sport papers or Monday papers. More than 100 dailies and 1,000 periodicals will stop or be merged with other publications to release manpower and materials for war purposes.

March 14th Sunday 187th week
The Kharkov fighting is furious. Russians have fallen back and Germans had big losses. Hitler is throwing everything into the battle. Timoshenko's drive west of Vyasma progresses towards Smolensk and more places have been taken.... Mr Eden, who is in Washington, summed up plans, with President Roosevelt of the United Nations, for the future of Germany and Japan. Co-operation between Britain, US, China and Russia is indispensable.... Essen is still blazing from the raid there last Friday night.... There was a warning last night at 12.20. As I walked down the garden path I saw 2 red star-like signals in the SE and they remained for fully 12 minutes, longer than any flares or signals I have seen before. The raid seemed at Newhaven, possibly Shoreham and Brighton as well, we heard a lot of gun-firing and probably bombs falling. The all-clear was at 1.32. We had some tea at the Post and I got home at 2. We had two short alerts today, 8.45 to 8.55 this morning and 3.38 to 3.55 this afternoon. I heard planes but no guns nor bombs. Germany claims capture of Kharkov by the Waffen SS, cream of Hitler's Nazi Party troops. Russians say 'heavy fighting is still going on in the Kharkov area'.... Soviet command issued 'Stalingrad orders' to the defenders of Kharkov.

March 16th Tuesday
Russians admit evacuation of Kharkov although the city held out until yesterday.

March 17th Wednesday
Russians are now 50 miles from Smolensk.... Three great battles are being fought, Kharkov, Smolensk and Staraya Russa, the last place between Leningrad and Moscow.... The Soviet Government is prepared to release all Czech prisoners if

they wish now to fight on the side of Russia. A Czech military official is leaving Britain for Russia to organize the transfer.

March 19th Friday

From the Russian Front came the news of a 25 mile advance on Smolensk and of operations 'on an unprecented scale' in the Orel area. Germans are beginning to evacuate Staraya Russa and Timoshenko is forging ahead there. Sabotage goes on all over France, German officers shot, bombs thrown, trains attacked etc. Our clothing ration is to be cut and the coupons are to last longer than stated at first. The textile industry has to make further releases of labour.

March 20th Saturday

A fake BBC radio station is being set up by the Nazis at Nevers, Central France, to be used for confusing the population and if possible the enemy when an Allied invasion begins. Announcers have been chosen already from among Germans who have lived in England and are to be trained in the BBC accent. Most have been educated at our universities. South coast towns which have suffered in raids lately are to get more protection.

March 22nd Monday

Yesterday afternoon Helen and I walked to Kenwards Farm. The fields near are all ploughed and made arable, one not yet sown, another planted with broad beans. Much, perhaps not all, of the golf course is also ploughed up.

March 23rd Tuesday

This has been a flag day, I was told throughout the country, for *Help with China*. Mr Fraser came for the flags to decorate their HQ at Oaklands and there was the usual house to house collection.

March 25th Thursday

This morning I went to London and met Daisy at the National Gallery to see the Exhibition of War Pictures there.... It is an excellent show.... One part of the gallery has plans for rebuilding London and other shattered places, with a good sprinkling of reproductions of places not to be pulled down or interfered with and thus far not 'blitzed'. In spite of the war there was a large bed of variously coloured hyacinths fully out in the Park near Pall Mall, a lovely sight it was and sweet scented. From the platform at the entrance to the National Gallery we looked down on the square where the Lancaster bomber had been for Wings for Victory Week. Coloured drawings still decorate the base of Nelson's statue, all of them planes, chiefly bombers.

March 27th Saturday
Production of goods for Britain's Home Market is to be reduced to the lowest possible level during the next few months. Fewer clothes, household goods and luxuries such as cosmetics and leather products will be made. Thousands of men and women at present working in 'home market' industries will go into war industry or the forces.

March 28th Sunday 189th week
There was a short alert from 5.55 to 6.20. On Saturday evening Mr Parsons called to collect some ARP clothing. He took my summer coat and my dirty old boiler suit, but I was not given another in place of it! In spite of washing it never looks clean. He said these clothes are all being called in for use in London for new clothes cost coupons. He says we are to wear our newly provided battledress when called out. I said I should not for it is useless as a *working* garment, one cannot put out a fire in a narrow skirt like that. I said I should wear my boiler suit with straps that was first given out, it will be better than the coat and skirt anyway. Thus far we may keep our winter and mackintosh coats.

March 30th Tuesday
I went to Brighton to see if Jock was alright after a raid on the town yesterday morning between 11 and 12. A welfare clinic on the sea front was wrecked and the chief clerk of the clinic was killed. We went to Nizells Avenue to see the wreckage there. Three houses, possibly four, were completely gone, nothing left but rubbish and pieces of wood. Houses next door lost all the windows and were vacated. Jock said there was so much gun-firing which accounted for so many roofs and windows of nearby houses being damaged. Five people were killed in the wrecked houses.

March 31st Wednesday
Changes in meat rationing and fish zoning were announced yesterday and from next Monday we are to have a proportion of corned beef in our ration for meat.

April 2nd Friday
It was reported last night that General Montgomery's Eighth Army and Americans of General Anderson's First Army have linked up. Rommel is fighting desperately but retreat is being harassed continually by the RAF. Again this year Easter is to be a 'no travel' holiday and no extra trains will be run.

April 5th Monday
Eastbourne is one of the most bombed towns on the south coast and only a third of its population remain. The siren sounded at 2.50, the all-clear 3.12. We heard, but so high up one could hardly see, a number of bombers going SE. Mr Ling told

me he counted 27. Soon after there was a fight high up in the SSE. I heard guns but saw nothing.

April 6th Tuesday
Public whistling, particularly British tunes, is barred by Nazis for in many districts the habit has grown lately of whistling such tunes as *Over There*, *Tipperary* and *The Long Trail*. German occupation authorities think they not only hearten people but may operate as some kind of signal of invasion.

April 7th Wednesday
All women between 18 and 45 not in work are to take up useful part-time work and more whole time CD workers are to go to war industry. Of course those with children of school age are exempted.

April 8th Thursday
General Montgomery's Army and the Second US Army Corps linked up yesterday. The fighting 'was as tough as anything we have seen since El Alamein' said Montgomery.

April 11th Sunday 191st week
No extra food supplies will be available at seaside places over the Easter holiday. Travelling will be reduced to a minimum.

April 12th Monday
It is said that the Governments of Britain and US will meet soon in Bermuda to plan the rescue and resettlement of refugee peoples in the light of the difficult problems of food and shipping. In the past 4 years 2,000,000 have been deported or murdered. Perhaps 500,000, one cannot be sure of the number, continue their resistance inside the Nazi fortress of Europe. Mr Buckingham gave out a notice in church yesterday that a roll will be there for anyone to sign, the petition being to the Government to expedite proposed help to the Jews to get them away from the appalling conditions they are now living in. Not an easy matter to arrange. The petition concerns the whole country. The Queen broadcast last night from a house in the country. It was addressed to the women of the Empire and to the effort they are making.

April 14th Wednesday
Today *Desert Victory* was shown in 6 cinemas in Moscow, and to packed houses. All are enthusiastic about the film. In return Stalin has sent here a film *The Story of Stalingrad* which was seen yesterday for the first time. It begins with Stalingrad in peace time and ends with pictures of the city after the German defeat. The film will be publicly shown on Friday.

April 15th Thursday
RAF and American planes made concerted attacks on Rommel's Tunis bridgehead... in an all-out bid to smash Axis air power in the Central Mediterranean. There was a 15 minute warning this afternoon, 2.25 till 2.40. I went to the Post for Mrs Parsons is not well. We heard only a few planes but there have been many about and all last night they were droning so no doubt some extra big raid was in progress.... Captain Crookshank, Postmaster General, announces a reduction in letter deliveries which will release 5,000 full time women and 2,000 full time men. The midday delivery would be abolished and in London 4 deliveries will be reduced to 3 and in the provinces, two where there are now three. For a long time we have only had two deliveries.

April 17th Saturday
Our siren sounded at 12.25 and the all-clear at 2.05am, the longest night raid we have had for a long time. It was a glorious moonlight night, no hardship to turn out. We saw flashes London way, and stop press news says high explosives were dropped in one London district, some houses were damaged and there were some casualties. Mr Ridgeway did not turn up. I went to his house, knocked and rang, disturbed neighbours on both sides but got no answer from his house and finally gave it up. There were hardly any planes over this part.... So many disturbances by young students in German universities have been found lately that a Gestapo official is to be placed in every one. There have been arrests and executions. It suggests reaction setting in among Germany's young people, for the students are under military age.

April 18th Sunday 192nd week
Some south coast beaches closed for a year will be open to bathers for a short time this summer. Details are not ready yet but in Worthing 300 yards of beach will be opened until the end of summer.... During Friday night's raid over here, 15 fighter bombers came over and four Fw 190s were destroyed, only 2 planes reached the Greater London area.

April 19th Monday
There was a 10 minute alert this afternoon 2.13 to 2.23. All quiet. There was another warning at 10.20 or as we time now 22.20, the all-clear 22.40. Another coast raid probably.

April 21st Wednesday
Germans have massed between 8 to 10 Divisions more than 100,000 men in the Taban tip of the Kuban for the great battle to save their last corner of the Caucasus. Yesterday evening we had an ARP meeting at the Post, 8–9.20, Mr

Ridgeway presiding. It was to discuss our various jobs in case of invasion or any other cause. The sector is divided into districts. We wardens have 'warden's helpers' for every few houses. The food dump is at Four Acres, although we are not telling people that. Each person receives a weekly packet costing 10/-, a liberal supply. A warning sounded at 10.50 till 11.05 or as we now record it 22.50 till 23.05. It was a coastal raid.

April 22nd Thursday
Between 7 and 8,000,000 German troops are reported massed for attack on the Eastern Front. Russians continue to bring Siberian forces and other reserves to the Front. If the clash develops the next few weeks will see 'the most terrible carnage in history'. Reports from several sources say Hitler is preparing to use poison gas against the Russian Front. We have again been warned to make sure gas masks are in good condition.

April 24th Saturday
Typed instructions have been shown us by Mr Parsons about our new ARP uniforms which although good in themselves are not so good as boiler suits for doing the jobs expected of us, such as putting out fires or helping wounded folk in bombed places. We may wear our jackets open at the neck if we like, a white blouse or shirt and a black tie, I happen to have both. The beret is to fall over the right side and the ARP badge if worn is to be on the left side.

April 25th Sunday 193rd week
From General Alexander's HQ came the news that a document has been captured indicating that Rommel has left Tunisia.... Church bells have been rung this Easter Sunday and the paper says they will ring again from today onwards.

April 27th Tuesday
Moscow announces the serious news that Russia has broken off relations with Poland. It appears that Germans started a campaign hostile to the Soviet Government concerning the Polish officers murdered by them in Smolensk which was seized on by the Polish Government and enlarged on by the Polish Press. For the investigation both Polish and Hitler Governments invited the International Red Cross to take part in the investigation. It is thought that between Hitler and the Polish Government there is contact and agreement on the campaign. Maybe the breach will be healed, perhaps by the British. The 'discovery' at Katyn of the bodies of 10,000 Polish officers alleged to have been murdered by Russians was Nazi propaganda so transparent that one took it for granted that no one would believe it. On the bodies were found sets of documents in a state of perfect preservation after 2 years internment, proving the identity of the dead. Very

suspicious. The Polish Government in Britain demanded the matter should be investigated by the Red Cross which annoyed the Russians.[28]

April 28th Wednesday
Another big batch of Italian prisoners arrived recently to work on the land, the first of the 20,000 the Minister of Agriculture promised farmers. I have seen many Italian prisoners working around here, there are some at Kenwards, others at Ardingly and West Hoathly.

April 30th Friday
I was told yesterday that the bomb that fell on Wednesday night was at Broad Street Cuckfield and it bent some blades of grass in a field!

May 1st Saturday
Fighting in Tunisia gets fiercer, von Arnim attacking with tanks and infantry but the Allies holding all key points. Goebbels confirms Rommel has left and von Arnim commands.

May 2nd Sunday 194th week
Beginning today, black-out time will be shorter, 10.07pm to 5.46am and it will last the hour after sunset and the hour before sunrise in the north and three quarters of an hour for the rest of England and Wales until August 15th when the time will return to normal, i.e. half an hour before and after. Pétain will broadcast to the French nation today at 12.40 now that Laval and Hitler have met. One of the subjects they discussed was the supply of French manpower to Germany.

May 3rd Monday
On Saturday our local Wings for Victory Week ended. Several good designs are printed for posters. I put one on my fence, which showed 5 airplanes in flight. A mobile cinema van toured the district and was on our Common on Saturday. The profits of a dance in the Village Hall were given to the RAF Benevolent Fund. I lent the flags for decorating the Hall and about £10 was made.

May 4th Tuesday
Japan made a big raid on Darwin yesterday with 57 bombers and fighters.... Nearly all the famous Jersey pedigree cattle have been removed to a special farm on Goering's estate at Karinhall. He aims to become Germany's foremost livestock breeder and his acquisition is already worth a fortune.

May 5th Wednesday
Germans are asking Dutch bulb growers to change the name of the new tulip they

are growing this spring. They name it 'Spitfire'. Mr Ernest Brown, Minister of Health, says 40,000 homes are now being repaired after bombing damage. Two and three quarter million houses have been destroyed by bombing. Yesterday afternoon Michael, Tony and I went to the Broadway cinema to see *Desert Victory* which is being shown there all this week. It is a wonderful record of the War in the Desert, the wonder is that any one of the soldiers taking part came out alive, the gunning and air battle bomb dropping was terrific, no one could imagine the scene.

May 6th Thursday
I cycled today with Tony to Chafford and saw restored to its place the first signpost, many of which have been set up again but not yet in this district. The post we saw was just before entering the village of Hartfield where a road branches off to Maresfield. Just past the Church we saw the men in a lorry finishing the next signpost indicating the road to Edenbridge.

May 7th Friday
Nazis have discovered that numbers of paintings looted from France are forgeries. Most were removed from galleries and it is assumed that when German occupation came, copies were substituted and the originals hidden. Possibly some looted personally by Goering for his palaces are also forgeries.

May 13th Thursday
Enemy resistance ended in Tunisia at 8.15 last night with the capture of Von Arnim. In order to appease the Roman Catholic world, Hitler has instructed Kerol, Nazi Minister of Ecclesiastical Affairs, to release 200 priests detained in Germany and Poland and for the reopening of a number of churches.... The *Wings for Victory Week* is ended and over £180,000 has been raised, the target being £100,000. There was a Hurricane plane in Victoria Park and the visitors' fees to it were given to the RAF Benevolent Fund. While I was at the Library the siren sounded at 6.20, the all–clear at 6.40. Two bombs were dropped, not so very far away. Later I heard a single raider flew over a town on the south coast, dropping his bombs which fell on allotments near some houses. Many were made homeless. It is thought the raider was hit. People were injured by flying glass.

May 14th Friday
Next Sunday is appointed Thanksgiving Day and it is hoped all church bells will be rung before the mid-morning service. Sunday is also Home Guard Day. Although the papers say it is hoped the public will join in the demonstrations held in honour of their work, Bob says he has not heard of any demonstrations here.... The King, as Colonel-in-Chief of the Home Guard, has sent the force a special message today, its 3rd birthday. 'It has built up a tradition of service and devotion

to duty'. We all appreciate the Home Guard and shall even more when it passes to the offensive. In the evening at 9 o'clock Bob and I listened to the Premier's broadcast from the White House. He primarily addressed the Home Guard and said 'Until Hitler and Hitlerism are beaten into unconditional surrender the danger of invasion will never pass away'. He added the time was approaching when Allied armies will invade the continent.

May 15th Saturday
The big clash in Russia is imminent. Moscow thinks Germany will strike first. She has large concentrations of men, tanks and planes ready to strike on a number of sectors. An East Anglian farmer, an HG, captured 4 German airmen yesterday bluffing them in the half light by pointing his finger at them to look like a revolver. He took their guns, they all surrendered. Several villages in East Anglia were raided yesterday but a hen was the only casualty. This evening Lindfield Home Guards were on duty at 6 o'clock and do not return until tomorrow evening. The company is testing the efficiency or otherwise of the HG 'chefs', their arrangement coinciding with Home Guard Day, Thanksgiving Sunday. Special prayers in church today gave thanks for the African victory. The Luftwaffe has left the Mediterranean and the Sicilian Straits are now free and open to every Allied ship, information given to Air Marshal Tedder yesterday.

May 16th Sunday 196th week
Special prayers in church today gave thanks for the African victory.... The Home Guard 'cook trial' went off very well, but sleeping arrangements in the Paxhill camps were not perfect and all were cold. Some of the HG soldiers were footsore.

May 17th Monday
At 0.02 last night the siren sounded after planes had been snarling for some time. I was 'sleeping out' watching the searchlights. When I returned from patrolling Black Hill, talking to one of our fire guards, Arthur Henshell, the all-clear sounded 00.15. It seemed strange because gun-firing was incessant in the northwest and up the Thames estuary. Mr and Mrs Parsons and I stood watching the reflections of the firing lighting on the Pond. I decided not to go home feeling certain there would be another call. It came at 00.41 and lasted until 4.40, the longest raid we have had for months. We heard sirens from East Grinstead, Uckfield and Burgess Hill besides our own here and at the Heath. It was a perfect moonlight night, cold but no wind and the Pond looked just beautiful.

May 18th Tuesday
One of the most shattering blows in the war has been given to Germany by the RAF who breached the gigantic Mohne and Eder dams.[29] There were 2 warnings

last night from 1.10 till 2.05 and then another from 2.40 until 3.15. There were many planes but I did not hear any bombs drop. This morning there was a short alert, 8.10 to 8.25 and this evening from 6.30 to 6.43. In the night there was another raid, again London, 2.45 till 3.40. There is a particularly powerful searchlight from the west to the southeast appearing behind the trees of Chieveley. I often see it when taking my usual prowl up Black Hill after the siren has sounded. There was gun-fire again up the Thames Estuary and some over London but things were quiet here. Mohne waters are threatening Duisburg, 5 miles away. Stockholm reports the death toll at 4,000 with 12,000 people homeless. 'Germany's biggest catastrophe of the war' was the comment of the German radio.

May 20th Thursday
Again there were two warnings in the night and after the last all-clear I heard a bomb drop. RAF photographers were again taking good photographs of the River Ruhr and the damage done. It seems that the Ruhr is completely ruined.

May 22nd Saturday
Germany is preparing *Lessons of the African Campaign. Tactics for study by Reichswehr Commanders*. Its purpose is to learn from our generals and prevent German Commanders from falling into the same trap that lost them North Africa.... Sir Archibald Sinclair says the war will end in Berlin and that the only way to do it is by paralysing German war power by Bomber Command. The RAF is now at such strength that it will cripple war industries and destroy everything set against us.

May 24th Monday
We heard that Hastings was badly hit in yesterday's midday raids. 'Two holiday coast towns received their worst bombing of the war'; the death toll is heavy.

May 25th Tuesday
Trespasses on allotments, even though no warning notices are shown, are liable to a fine of £50 unless there is a reasonable excuse. A bunch of 36 bananas arrived in a consignment of English fruit grown at Barcombe. The fruiterer did not know what to pay for them and no quotation of home-grown bananas could be discovered, so they were sold by auction and proceeds given to the Mayor of Lewes for *Wings for Victory Week*.

May 26th Wednesday
The Premier spoke of the Conference with Roosevelt but naturally gave no news or information. Brighton had a bad raid yesterday afternoon, the heaviest of the war, when about 25 raiders flew low over the sea killing at least 12 and injuring

about 60, but many are missing. I was told that Preston Park and the Viaduct were damaged and trains on the Lewes line suspended.... From July 25th all beef and pork sausages will contain the same protein content as pre-war sausages, which will be done by adding flour.

May 27th Thursday
Many more Italian prisoners will soon be in this country. Every morning we see bus loads of them being taken to work, a cheerful crowd, very brown and swarthy. The bunch of 36 bananas grown at Barcombe was to have been auctioned at Lewes and £5 had already been offered. But a notice from the Tunbridge Wells office of the Ministry of Food would not allow it as the auctioneer did not hold a retail license and also that the controlled price of bananas was 2d each. Mr Gorringe the auctioneer at once took out a license and sold the bananas at 2d each, relying on the generosity of buyers to contribute more. The bananas realized £12 for the *Wings for Victory Week* instead of at least £180. Red Tape to be sure.

May 28th Friday
This evening, our WI gave a concert ending with a play *The Way to his Heart*, which we 6 actors have lately been rehearsing. For a war-time programme it was good and the items well chosen.

May 29th Saturday
There was an alert at 2.15 today, the all-clear at 2.47. In the afternoon, hoeing on the allotment, I saw two companies of aircraft, possibly Flying Fortresses, one lot of 15 followed by another of 13, each leaving a long trail behind them and flying NW, perhaps just returned from a raid. Other planes I think fighters were going SE and 8 bombers soon after went south, much air activity about. At the canteen this evening we were busier than usual. Soldiers enjoyed drinks this hot summer's day. There were 70,000 casualties in the Eder and Mohne dams disaster. The BBC's campaign of naming the quislings of Europe warning them they have been put on the 'black list' for future punishment is having some effect already. At least one has abandoned his job, and asked for leniency at the end of the war. We had our church bells as usual yesterday.... This evening at 8 o'clock there was an ARP meeting in the Library, the speaker being Mr Merry. It was all about Fire Guards and the arrangement of sectors, there being 6, perhaps there will be more, for Lindfield.... The evening papers are full of the safe return of the Premier.... He went with Mr Eden to North Africa to confer with General Eisenhower and other Allied leaders and to tell them of his talks with Roosevelt.... There was a full church at Matins today. The north transept was filled with soldiers who overflowed into St John's Chapel, the south transept with ATS girls, officers sat in the front rows on both sides of the nave. An officer read the second lesson.

After the service was over the band of the Sussex Regiment assembled up the Welkin drive and headed the parade down the village to Hickman's Lane, soldiers and then ATS girls. I do not know who the General was who stood on the verge with two officers and took the salute. It was the best military turn out we have yet seen in the village. In the afternoon the band played on the Common.

June 9th Wednesday
This afternoon after the Library, I gave a talk to the nearest of kin to prisoners of war, that is those in the village.... Mrs Browne-Clayton is at the head of the committee and gets news through the Red Cross of Japan about the way our prisoners are treated and news generally.

June 14th Monday
This is the first anniversary of United Nations Day. I am glad I am not making 19 flags as I was this time last year.... The Board of Trade is making a new utility stocking. Stronger ones than present stock and sold at 3/- per pair are being made in large sizes as well as others.... General Sir Bernard Paget, Commander-in-Chief Home Forces, yesterday took the salute at the United Nations Day ceremony in London honouring the Flags of the Nations at war with the Axis. In the procession flags of the Dominions and India were carried in front of contingents of soldiers from all parts of the Empire, a popular holiday attraction.

June 19th Saturday
Germany now admits that she underestimated Russian strength and that all offensives have failed to break the Red Army. Russians are still holding their gains.

June 20th Sunday 201st week
There was a warning at 12.55 last night lasting just half an hour till 1.25. Raiders went over London and while I was at Black Hill, the Burgess Hill siren sounded quite 8 minutes after ours. It was a lovely full moon night, clear and no wind, not a hardship to be out. At 1.40 today I left home for the Drill ground at Bannisters where all the Services were meeting to assemble and arrange for the march to Victoria Park to take part in the tattoo for Prisoners of War Fund.[30] We wardens had to wear Battle Dress and very hot I found the coat, making the whole affair very tiring. It was very big. We walked 3 abreast from the Drill up Boltro Road, Sussex Square, Triangle Road, Sussex Road and South Road again into Victoria Park where Lady Limerick opened the tattoo and spoke about Prisoners of War and Red Cross through whom their parcels are sent. The megaphone was one of the worst I've ever heard. After speeches were finished we were dismissed and glad I was to sit down on the grass. Mr Parsons said we would not be wanted again until the final march past at 5.30. It was then quarter to four but I said I wanted to go home before this. I had

dinner to cook... there had not been time for dinner before leaving home.... Among other tattoo items was a mock battle and plenty of squibs for bombs.

June 23rd Wednesday
There is good food news today. The sugar ration for 2 weeks July 11–18 will be doubled to encourage people to make their own jam.... The plum crop is large enough for a certain quantity to go to shops instead of all to manufacturers. My tree is laden.

June 26th Saturday
This afternoon, about 5.10–5.20, four waves of Sterling bombers went from north to south, first 18, then 19, 18, 22 – seventy-seven in all. Ten minutes later, 20 fighters, I think Spitfires, passed in the same direction and there were others but they flew too high to see. Suddenly one machine twisted about and came down. I heard at the Library that the pilot bailed out in Hurstwood Park where the military hospital is. He hit a tree and broke his arm. He was taken to Haywards Heath Hospital. We were told his propeller went wrong. All were on the way to Germany. At the canteen tonight there were no cigarettes at all, the first time we have been without. Some Australians, there are many in the village now, were in but we had no rush like we so often do. I was home by 10.30.

June 27th Sunday 202nd week
I heard that the plane mishap yesterday afternoon was caused by a rear plane hitting the tail of the plane. One piece dropped in the Birch Hotel garden and another in the Mental Hospital grounds and another in Hurstwood Park. From July 4th the milk ration is to be cut from 4 pints to 3. More points are needed for biscuits, but this will not affect us in this village for usually biscuits are unobtainable.

June 28th Monday
The Red Army says 'The hour of reckoning is at hand'.

June 30th Wednesday
Another big 'Eat more potatoes' campaign is to be started next week and prices will be lowered each week.... The old potato crop is being turned into 'potato mash powder' which can be made into mashed potatoes by adding hot water. It is going to the Forces. Dried eggs are reduced in price.

July 1st Thursday
Long lists of names, 2,500 and more, are being made of Nazi criminals and quislings for post war punishment compiled in London by Governments of the

overrun countries.... German soldiers in Holland have been buying second hand civilian suits, storing the clothes. Evidently they want the garments for escape use in case of a German defeat. A number of Germans in the Afrika Korps were found with civilian clothes after the Tunisian defeat. This is Canada's Dominion Day. There is a dance in the Village Hall in the evening.

July 4th Sunday 203rd week
Today is Britain's first Farm Sunday and there is to be a rallying call from the Minister of Agriculture. Special prayers for crops and reapers will be said at services during the day. There was to have been a Home Guard church parade here but that has been called off. There will be processions in many districts. The national President of the union, Mr E.G. Gooch, said that despite losses in manpower, cultivated land had been increased by one third and in cereals alone by two thirds. There have been no strikes and no absentees. We are to have less cake and less milk and to save shipping space allowances of cakes and flour confectionery are to be cut.

July 10th Saturday
The raid was in East Grinstead where bombs were dropped, a cinema receiving a 'direct hit' and lives were lost. Shops near or along the London Road were demolished. The number of casualties is not yet given, but late last night rescue work was still going on. People were killed in the damaged shops, an ironmonger's, an outfitter's and a factory. The factory staff had left for the day. There were 10 planes in all, only two of which reached London. Two were destroyed.... Thursday night Cologne was again raided. One might think there was nothing left to bomb there, for over 1,000 tons were dropped on June 28th and July 3rd, but there are still parts of factories to be attended to.

July 13th Tuesday
A great force of RAF heavy bombers went over the Straits of Dover towards the Continent late last night. They started just after dusk and for more than ¾ of an hour afterwards there was an unbroken roar of planes going out to sea. One of the biggest night formations for some time.... There were 184 in the cinema at East Grinstead when it was bombed and it seems that most of them were killed although the actual number is not given. There will be a mass funeral service tomorrow. This morning at 7 o'clock I saw a fleet of Fortresses going south, evidently outward bound, each aircraft leaving a long exhaust stream behind it. I counted 96 and about 15 minutes later another 52 behind it. I had not seen so many as 148 together before, 9 fighters followed, there were probably more, but too high up to count.

July 15th Thursday
Those Fortresses I saw yesterday morning raided German air bases and factories in France, Bastille Day.

July 16th Friday
Of the 250,000 empty houses in Britain some will probably be requisitioned for people without homes. About 50,000 houses have already been taken over for bombed out families. Many people want accommodation in this village but it is impossible to get it. There are no empty houses here.

July 22nd Thursday
I went to the Royal Academy show yesterday, good and interesting.... On walking back to Victoria I went down St James' Street, saw the blitz there and standing near Buckingham Palace, I counted 29 barrage balloons and no doubt the trees hid some.

July 23rd Friday
Russians have captured Brekhov 30 miles north of Orel, thereby wiping out a German outpost and increased the threat to Orel. Over 6,000 prisoners have been taken and 50,000 killed. So say the Russians.

July 25th Sunday 206th week
At many of our railway stations yesterday, when a holiday rush began, thousands of people besieged the stations and, as no extra trains were run, the jam was awful. Little notice is being taken of the 'stay-at-home' advice. At Waterloo about 2,000 were left stranded and most spent the night at the station.

July 26th Monday
The great news in today's papers is that Mussolini has been dismissed. The King of Italy has assumed command of all the armed forces and Marshal Badoglio becomes Prime Minster.

July 30th Friday
It is some time since we had a night warning, but the siren sounded at 1.07am. I had just arrived at the end of my special Black Hill beat when all–clear was given at 1.25. A rocket or some other signal was sent up about 1.15. It was a coastal raid. We shall probably hear where during the day.

August 1st Sunday 207th week
The battle for Orel grows in intensity. Germans are reinforcing the 'last ditch' defences and have fallen back to prepared positions but the Red Army overcame

more counter-attacks and took more villages. Half a million men are locked in this mighty battle along a 200 mile zig-zag frontier. Fighting has flared up again in the Donetz Basin where Germans are trying to wipe out the bridge-head recently established by Russians on the west bank of the Minsk River. This month of July Germans have lost 100,000 men on the Orel and Kursk Fronts. Nearly 1,300 German tanks and over 1,300 planes have been destroyed around Orel alone. One would like to know Russia's losses.

August 6th Friday
Russians have had a double victory for in addition to Orel, Bielgorod has been captured. The gateway to Kharkov and a valuable junction is gained.

August 8th Sunday 208th week
Mr Parsons called to say that from last Sunday the fire guard party will work on their own account and we shall not have to collect signatures every evening as we wardens have been doing between us for the last 18 months or so.

August 10th Tuesday
There were many roaring planes in the early morning indicating some big raid by the RAF. When I took the chicken scraps to Mrs Parsons, she told me Manheim had been the target.

August 11th Wednesday
The procession of bombers we heard last evening lasted from 10 till 11.30, the longest time I remember and passing to the SE. The radio today said Nuremberg was attacked, we lost 16 bombers. About 4am I heard some of the planes returning.

August 12th Thursday
Brighton and other towns in a wide coastal area are to be banned again to holiday-makers and they have been warned to leave before the ban is imposed. Wednesday the 18th I am told is the day for Brighton, maybe the other places too. Notices of the extent of the ban will be at main London stations.

August 16th Monday
There was an alert last night at 12.15–12.55. I had been watching a partial eclipse of the moon and afterwards it was full and clear. I heard a distant bomb, then one nearer. During the day I learnt that bombs had been dropped on Worthing, Brighton and Portsmouth. At Brighton, Whitehawk Church had a direct hit and a warden on duty there was killed. 25 raiders came over of which 6 were shot down. 12 people were killed in one town, probably Portsmouth.... The south coast ban

begins tomorrow. All hotels etc in the areas have to cancel bookings and refuse further visitors. Barbed wire barriers will be at the boundaries.

August 18th Wednesday
In French cinemas, when a German film appears on the screen the audience 'go to sleep' en masse and wake up only when the film finishes.

August 19th Thursday
Recently a bomber crew, storm-tossed in the Mediterranean after a forced landing 50 miles from land, were saved by a pigeon released from their rubber dinghy. Although they had wirelessed their position, bad weather hampered their rescue when a pigeon came flying in from the sea, carrying a message from the dinghy giving the new position and an air-sea rescue launch found the men.

August 20th Friday
The whole German Government has left Berlin.

August 21st Saturday
Russians are now in a wide arc around Kharkov and more than 80 miles NW of the city. The Germans' escape gap has been cut to less than 13 miles. Fierce battles are being fought at Bryansk and Smolensk Fronts where Russians have made progress and the only remaining railway by which Germans could retreat is under Russian fire.... Captain Sertorious, the German radio military commentator, tried to explain in a broadcast last night how the more Germans there are on the defensive the better placed they are for winning the war. Also that the loss of North Africa and Sicily was of no real decisive importance for the war. Mrs Fawssett and Mrs Bevan with many helpers held a fete in Chievely garden for our *Christmas Parcels for Soldiers' Fund*. I made 20 coloured paper cards of flags of the Allied Nations, a competition for a two-penny entry. Being more 'thoughtful' than other attractions I made only 3/6, but the 'flags' will be useful again I expect. The weather was not too kind after this brilliant week, rain spotted but we were able to carry on. Nearly everything sold.

August 22nd Sunday 210th week
We had a busy evening at the canteen with many English soldiers now in the village. There was the usual shortage of chocolate, cigarettes and matches, no tobacco.... Russians report a new advance on Kharkov and that in the past 6 weeks Germans have lost another million men. Also they have destroyed 4,600 German planes, 3,800 guns and 20,000 lorries. One is left to wonder what Russian losses have been. They are never given. Complete destruction of men and armour takes first place in their strategy.

August 23rd Monday
Thousands more American troops reached England recently.... Among them were airmen and coloured troops.... I met Mrs Fawssett this morning, who told me on Saturday takings were £113.12.0. Very wonderful for a doubtful afternoon.

August 24th Tuesday
Stalin issued an historic Order of the Day yesterday, telling the world Kharkov had been taken from the enemy. Germans say the place is 'only a heap of ruins and was again evacuated in the course of a systematic disengagement movement'. Sertorius said Germans could have held Kharkov if they had wished. Moscow was lit up by coloured lights and the whole place jubilant, the curfew lifted until 2am. A salute was given of 20 salvos of 224 guns.... German confiscation of all radio sets in France is expected within the next week. The BBC is to give 10 commandments on how to deal with the situation with special reference to the concealment of sets. Today has been Mrs Churchill's 'Aid to Russia' flag day. Huge quantities of drugs, clothing, etc have been sent through this fund and there could hardly be a more deserving cause. Collections are being made all over the country, this district today.

August 25th Wednesday
Himmler as well as being Head of the Gestapo has been appointed Minister of the Interior. The whole of Germany now comes under the Gestapo.... It is believed 700 bombers and 5,000 airmen took part in the heaviest raid on Berlin on Monday night. 1,700 tons of bombs were dropped in 50 minutes from midnight, 34 tons a minute. The raid cost 58 bombers. At least 12 enemy fighters were destroyed. Thousands tried to leave the capital but were turned back.... Russian troops have got ahead of the retreating Germans and fighting is going on behind the new German lines (if they have any 'new' lines). CD and Fire Services along stretches of the south and southeast coasts have been strengthened the last few weeks. On arrival at the coast the men, National Fire Service and CD mobile units, were warned they were under military orders and all letters would be censored. I counted over 100 bombers going east this afternoon.

August 28th Saturday
The big bomber force I listened to yesterday evening from about 10 to 11 was one of the greatest ever to go out. There appeared to be hundreds as they crossed the southeast coast going in relays.... The big raid was on Nuremburg and described as a 'terror attack'. The journey was a thousand miles there and back.... It is now admitted that Hess flew to Britain to find quislings whom he believed were anxious to make peace with Hitler. This would have allowed Germans to concentrate on Russia. It was on May 11th that Hess' plane crashed near Glasgow

and the attack on Russia began on January 22nd 1941.... In the *Mid Sussex Times* this week a good notice is given of last Saturday's fete at Chieveley for the WI *Soldiers' Parcels Fund.* The total sum raised was £115.7.6d, rather more than at first stated.

August 29th Sunday 211th week

Nuremberg was practically wiped out by Friday night's attack when 1,500 tons of bombs were dropped in 45 minutes. Columns of smoke were seen by returning crews 150 miles away. 33 bombers are missing.

September 2nd Thursday

Germans are reinforcing Smolensk, the fortified and prized capital, the most important on the whole Russian Front. But Russians still advance, capturing towns and freeing villages and attacking both front and rear on the German lines. On Tuesday night the RAF again bombed Berlin, a desperate raid in which we lost 47 bombers. The 'cascade' attack lasted 45 minutes and about 1,800 tons of bombs were dropped. All roads to and from Berlin are now closed and only police, army and fire services are allowed on the arterial roads, 350 fires were still burning in Berlin yesterday morning.... German civil servant Koselt has been executed because he wrote to his son at the Front 'We cannot win the war. The British raids are terrible. My only hope is that you will not be killed on the Eastern Front'. Unwise things to write in letters.... To quieten Germany's 5 million foreign workers the Nazi Government has started a special newspaper for them, printed in a number of languages. The first issue is filled entirely with faked news about the Allies, descriptions of imaginary raids on London, food riots all over Britain and closing down of all Manchester.

September 3rd Friday

Air attacks on Italy continue but bad weather yesterday kept bombers grounded. This is the Day of Prayer commemorating the 4th anniversary of the War. Prayers and thanksgiving are held in all our churches. This evening at 7 o'clock there was a special service in our church, members of the Services were asked to attend. We wardens assembled outside the Red Lion at 6.30 and the Home Guard were drilling there just before marching to church. It was a full church and Mr Buckingham gave a good address, referring to Drake and Cadiz.... In factories and elsewhere, by the King's wish, the nation joined in prayer that 'we should enter the fifth year of war with undiminished constancy to give thanks for the success already granted to our cause'. Our collection was for the Soldiers' and Sailors' Family Fund, probably a good one for the Church was full and there were 6 collectors. There was a national broadcast service at 11am lasting 15 minutes.... Tremendous Russian victories on 4 Fronts stretching over 700 miles from

Smolensk to the Sea of Azov are announced. The whole Kursk region is cleared of Germans.

September 4th Saturday
British and Canadian troops have landed in Italy.... Montgomery first sent a message to the Eighth Army who are invading and ended with 'Forward to victory. Let's knock Italy out of the war. Good luck and God bless you all'.

September 6th Monday
Mr Bevin appealed for more miners for at least 20,000 must be found next year.[31] No miners are to be withdrawn from the army. We are all asked to use coal economically. The industry has been made worthwhile and given a proper status.

September 7th Tuesday
Last night bombers were overhead. London says for 2 hours, one of the biggest forces that have yet gone over. About 10 there was gun-firing which sounded near enough for us to have the siren but none came. In the night there was a 25 minute alert 2.15–3.40.

September 9th Thursday
It was at 5.30 yesterday afternoon that Italy went out of the war. Marshal Badoglio told Italians to cease war against Anglo–Americans but to oppose attacks by others.

September 10th Friday
Our landings in Italy continue. Hitler has decided 'to fight to the last man in Italy'. Spitfires, both British and Australian, have damaged or destroyed 14 out of 20 Jap fighters over Port Darwin. Russians are pushing forward to Kiev and what is happening now is not a mere battle but 'the repulsion of the enemy from the country'. Many helpers are wanted to help lift the potato crops and 10,000 of the Civil Service have given their names to the Ministry of Agriculture. Farmers in all parts of the country are appealing for helpers.

September 11th Saturday
Rommel has taken over command of the German Army in North Italy.

September 16th Thursday
Nearly 200 firms of furriers in Britain are making fur coats for Russian children in the liberated places. Already 40,000 have been completed. They are lined with rabbit skins, home produced.

September 22nd Wednesday
Germans say their withdrawal in Russia is 'a large scale retreat' caused by shortage

of reserves and the Allied landing in Italy, which Mr Churchill described yesterday as our Third Front. Kiev is being evacuated by the German Army.

September 25th Saturday
Children are allowed extra coupons and I was able yesterday to get 20 additional coupons for Michael. If children exceed a certain length of foot, 8½in for girls, 9¼in for boys, they get 20 extra clothing coupons available only for boots and shoes.

September 26th Sunday 215th week
Smolensk and nearby Roslavl are now in Russian hands.... Kiev is being stormed and the army is only about 140 miles from Poland. Smolensk and Roslavl are both blazing. A special salute from 224 guns was fired in Moscow last night to celebrate the gains.... Today is Battle of Britain Sunday. Prayers and thanksgiving services will be held throughout the country to celebrate the destruction of the Luftwaffe attacks 3 years ago. Here we had a gathering of all CD services on Muster Green. There was a good contingent of Air Force cadets but not a good number of wardens, only 3 in our sector. Mr Parsons, Knight and myself came.... The Home Guard Band, or perhaps the Heath Town Band in Home Guard uniforms, played well excepting the two hymns which were slowly dragged through, killing the spirit and time of both. We wardens dismissed at Oaklands. I walked both ways, many cycled.

September 27th Monday
Russians pushing northwest of Smolensk are less than 80 miles from the Polish frontier.... Hitler ordered the Army 'Die but do not abandon Smolensk'. A gift of £30,000 is to be made to Queen Victoria Hospital, East Grinstead by the British War Relief Society of America. Sussex Home Guards who raised £676 for presentation to the 1st Canadian Army Corps to mark their happy relationship with the Canadians, will themselves receive the benefit. The German campaign for winter clothing for the troops is now compulsory... all people must surrender the bulk of their woollen undergarments, keeping only one pair of each category for themselves.

October 6th Wednesday
Mr Hugh Dalton intends to push the making of wooden soled shoes for men as well as women and to wear them himself. They will not be made for children. (Extract from a letter dated September 22nd from Harry Newman Lieutenant Corporal):

> Lacking in news but I know you understand the reason why.... I believe the end of the war will not be far off.... I expect your war diary is becoming very interesting and should make some very good reading after the war.

October 7th Thursday
This evening the sirens sounded at 8.39 and the raid lasted until 11.08, the longest we have had for a long time. There were many searchlights and red flares were dropped at intervals... we saw at least 8 planes caught in searchlights whether our own or Germany's we could not tell. At the height of the raid, bombers and fighters were going south, probably for the Continent.

October 14th Thursday
Russians are breaking through the German lines in several places in the Crimea and on the Dnieper River and Nazis have withdrawn from Kiev. Italy declared war on Germany at 4pm yesterday.

October 18th Monday
There was a warning at 2.17 the raid lasting just an hour.... On Black Hill the gun-firing sounded louder than usual and from Brighton where defences now are strong with many guns. White flares and planes went up the Thames Estuary, so I suppose London and Brighton were the principal targets.... We had a wardens' meeting at the Post tonight, 8.30 till 9.40. Mr Parsons read several notices from HQ, most interesting I thought the one about people trapped under bomb wreckage. Seemingly they felt alright when released save for stiffness but later shock developed other troubles, often kidney trouble, and all such victims should be treated as serious cases and sent to hospital for observation.... A special Order of the Day from Hitler says 'Not a step back. On this line you are defending your families. If you want them to live you must die, but the Russians must not pass'.

October 19th Tuesday
This afternoon I went with Mrs Hollands to see at the Perrymount a film *The Silent Village* made in co-operation with Czechoslovakia and the South Wales Mining Federation. It illustrates what might have happened if the Nazis had treated this Welsh mining village, I forget its name, in the way they treated Lidice. Heydrich and the Gestapo invade the classrooms, homes, inns and shops. By the underground movement, a Gestapo on duty in the mine is killed. Then all the men of the village are shot, women sent to concentration camps, the children to the 'proper authorities' and the village razed to the ground.

October 20th Wednesday
Field Marshal Smuts addressed an Assembly at the Guildhall yesterday on the progress of the war. Next year we shall be making our dispositions for the grand assault by all arms. He said the Russian contribution has been enormous, but so also was El Alamein and Allied Strategy in the Mediterranean. The air bombing

offensive has the effect of a large scale additional Front. The siren sounded last night at 10.18, all-clear at 11.05. It was a foul night dark, windy and raining hard. On Black Hill Mr Ridgeway and I heard 3 bombs fall and later Avis telephoned through to the Post that 2 bombs fell west of Three Bridges and one at Hurstpierpoint. We have not heard yet of casualties. The searchlights were so brilliant for some 5 minutes on Black Hill that one could have seen to read and the road shone as if in a flood. We were all so wet we were glad it was not a long raid. The bombers then went on to London.

October 23rd Saturday
I heard today from several sources that the bomb said to have fallen on Hurstpierpoint was in fact at Ashington where cottages and other things were wrecked or badly damaged. All the sandbags... are being carted away from the Post. Mr Parsons is not sorry to see them go, they have killed his Virginia creeper and made the ARP telephone room damp and very dark. No doubt all sandbags will be removed; they are no protection from later missiles. Last Tuesday there was a Gift Sale for the Red Cross Agricultural Fund held at the Cattle Market. £2,500 was raised, all manner of things were auctioned. The Ministry of Supply sent out a mobile van exhibiting flax and its many uses. Flax is used for parachute harness and fire hose, for it is strong and light, and for numerous other things. None of it is wasted. The Red Army is closing the Dnieper Bend trap and the Germans' escape gap is reduced to 60 miles, nearly a million of them threatened. Local papers tell us that Roger Mead, after drifting for 11 days in a rubber dinghy, has been rescued and is in hospital. One night in September he was on operational duties, and at 10 o'clock an unfinished SOS message was picked up by another plane, but nothing more was heard until last Sunday when he was reported in hospital at Plymouth. He is 34, now Group Captain and DFC and AFC.[32]

October 24th Sunday 219th week
The warning last night was from 11.25 until 12.23. It was a starry still night, the planes flying so high they could only just be heard.... Mr Parsons said last night that the sand removed from his entrance and windows was 18 tons. One did not think it was so much. This afternoon about 5 o'clock a convoy of Red Cross ambulances and attendant cars passed by the house. There were no wounded but stretchers and plenty of men, all Red Cross soldiers. As one went by, a man seated at the back seeing me standing at the gate watching them called out 'Tea ready darling?' Soon after there was another convoy going down the Lewes Road, the tanks, I think, those stationed at Paxhill Camp.

October 25th Monday
For the first time for over a week there was no warning last night.

October 29th Friday

More than 30,000 Germans were killed in sectors of the Eastern Front last week says Moscow.... Immense quantities of equipment are being abandoned: guns, food, ammunitions, stores and whole herds of cattle which Germans try to destroy by machine-gunning.

October 30th Saturday

Germans are making desperate attempts to keep open their escape between the Dnieper and Sea of Azov.... White silk parachute material, suitable for clothes, will be on sale at reduced coupons before Christmas and moderately priced. Rejected stockings because of dyeing flaws will also be on sale. The siren sounded this evening at 7.50 and the all-clear at 8.39 while I was at the canteen. We had an average evening. Several things wanted were not in the 'shop'. It is now difficult to get black boot polish, brown has been off the market for many weeks. The usual shortage of cigarettes and chocolate – no tobacco although shop supplies are good.

October 31st Sunday 220th week

The GPO advises people not to write too often to POW, one letter a week from relatives, strangers none at all. No Christmas or New Year cards may be sent. From next Sunday the milk ration is to be reduced to 2 pints a week, the reason being poor crops of late summer grass feed. The weather has been dry. I have seldom seen the village pond so low of water. Only one tin of dried milk is allowed per ration book and the tin makes about 2½ pints.

November 1st Monday

Every Monday we pack and address soldiers' parcels for Christmas, meeting at Criplands Court. I address all the time. We are sending nearly 300 this Christmas. I finished the Christmas cards some time ago, they came out quite well and were from a design of many years ago in three colour printing made when I was at 28 Old Bond Street. One design made two cards.

November 2nd Tuesday

Russians have entered Crimea. What a triumph for them!

November 7th Sunday 221st week

Field Marshal von Rundstedt, Commander of German forces in western Germany, has told Hitler the war is lost and has called on him to resign immediately 'for the Fatherland's sake, leaving peace negotiations to people acceptable to the enemy'. Stalin told the world in a broadcast from Moscow last night that the Fascist Coalition is on the brink of catastrophe. 'The war has reached a stage when we can foresee the complete expulsion of the invaders from our land'.... Germans have lost 1,800,000 killed this year and 4 million casualties, also 25,000 tanks and 40,000 guns.... A Nazi Party conference was held, which Hitler was not informed about.

November 10th Wednesday
The Premier made a notable speech at the Lord Mayor's Banquet yesterday. We must not expect an early collapse of Germany. Hitler still has 400 Divisions under his command and a grip on the German people far stronger than the late Kaiser had. New forms of attack could be made on these islands and this is no time to relax in all our precautions nor to dream easy dreams of a brave new world.... Lady Woolton is to make 'fancy labels' illegal on food packets. They often misrepresent the contents. In future foods will have a label showing the true contents, packed name and the minimum amount of food in the package and the usual name of the food.

November 11th Thursday
The poppies are made differently this year, quite flat and attached to a flat piece of wood. No doubt wire is difficult to get. There is to be a concert this evening by the British Legion in the Albert Hall, I shall hear it on the radio.

November 12th Friday
In a May number of *Victory*, a weekly magazine issued for the Indian Command, was an appreciative article, with a portrait, of Wing Commander Frank Carey of this village. A notice of it is in this week's *Mid Sussex Times*. Carey has been mentioned before now.... He has destroyed definitely 28 enemy aircraft and a further 15 probably destroyed or damaged and he has fought in France, the Battle of Britain and in Burma. He is known as 'Chota' but to us older friends Fuzzy on account of his curly hair. The article ends 'As Carey left the mess, another pilot seemed to sum it up very well. Thank goodness Chota's on our side'. So there are two Lindfield RAF heroes, Frank Carey and Roger Mead.

November 14th Sunday 222nd week
This morning there was a special service in the Church and parade of the Home Guard, soldiers stationed in the village, wardens and other CD units. We wardens assembled in the Vicarage drive at 9.15, service 9.30, Bishop Bell of Chichester preaching. A good sermon to the packed church on the 3 chief loyalties: Home, Country, God. Our unit sat in St John's Chapel. I took my prayer book but we were given a copy of the Army Prayer Book, which we all used. The Band in the procession was the Royal Sussex. In the afternoon there was another special service for the British Legion. In the happier days before the war we used to give the men and the Band a really posh tea in the Village Hall. We cannot manage that

now, but three of us specially did not like the notion of the men having nothing. So the Army let us have the Hall, the WI cups and teapots and Mrs Mossop, Margaret Wilson and myself got 100 buns, tins of milk, tea, sugar and cigarettes and welcomed the men when they came back about 4.30, the service being at 3.30. We margarined the buns and made tea at 'Chelwood' and carried the teapots across when we heard the returning band. They were all happy, pleasant and appreciative. Then we three washed up the cups and I got home at 6.30.

November 15th Monday
A paper new to me was sent to the Library today, *The Prisoners of War*, the official journal of the Red Cross and St John's War Organization which is issued free to next of kin and is not for sale. But owing to the shortage of paper, all cannot be served with copies, therefore it is proposed to send it to all Public Libraries in future. News in it comes from prison camps – the way they produce their papers, official reports from the camps, those who were captured at St Nazaire, the workers, the hospital, their letters and so forth including fun and games.

November 16th Tuesday
Canadian soldiers left this village nearly a fortnight ago and Paxhill Camp is now empty but other Canadians are expected.

November 28th Sunday week 224th
Last night details of the Berlin bombing on Friday night were given. Correspondents of Stockholm papers wrote 'Three or more such bombings and no Berlin will be left. More than a third of the city is now in ruins, 30 to 40,000 people have been killed'. The Red Army is nearing Poland. Let us hope that when it arrives no fresh troubles will arise there. The Eighth Army goes forward and General Montgomery has sent a personal message to his men ending 'good luck to you all and good hunting as we go forward'. The Albert Hall has been placed under a black-out curfew because of the danger of shrapnel falling through its glass dome.

December 1st Wednesday
The two bridgeheads across the Sangro have now been linked together in one large penetration of German defensive positions and all attacks beaten off. The fighting has been horrific against one of the most powerfully fortified sections of the Germans 'to be held at all cost'. Nazis have retaken Korosten, important rail junction, but Russians have gained in the Pripet marshes and area. Many German groups on the left bank of the Dnieper are surrendering, being surrounded.... Double rationing of dried eggs are to be available over Christmas holidays, December 12 to January 8 when milk and fresh eggs will be scarce. Both are scarce

now. I get 2 or 2½ pints of milk every week and an egg every 3rd week.... There was an alert at 7.55 to 8.45 this evening. There was a short warning at 10.49 to 10.58. I heard planes but nothing more.

December 3rd Friday
After their Cairo talks Churchill and Roosevelt are now in Persia (Iran) for a meeting with Stalin, Tehran thought to be the place.

December 4th Saturday
The RAF made another terrific raid on Berlin last night.... Tonight the Lindfield Home Guard gave their first dance in the Village Hall and the Library was the 'bar'. The whole affair was a success, everybody enjoyed it and the Band from Brighton was not too loud, so non-dancers could hear one another speak. The Hall was gaily decorated with flags, I lent my United Nation flags, 17 in all. I made two new ones, Ethiopia and Guatemala, but had not time to finish Brazil, which I had hoped to do. But there is a lot of work in that flag. The material takes two coupons a yard, and a yard does not go far in making a flag. After the dance was over a party of us, including the concert party which owing to lack of time did not perform, went to the Barrows', who hospitably entertained all of us. Bob took me as his guest. After expenses are paid the Red Cross benefits.

December 7th Tuesday
There is published today the agreement reached between Churchill, Roosevelt and Stalin at the Conference at Tehran, a Magna Carta of 1943 arranging for war, peace and the future.

December 10th Friday
Once again people are asked not to travel this Christmas.... No late shopping will be allowed in Central London.

December 12th Sunday 226th week
For two days and nights a sea battle has been going on in the Atlantic against the 20 U-boats sent to attack convoys. Two sailors, Colin Armitage and Kenneth Cooke, lived for 50 days on a raft after being torpedoed in the South Atlantic. Aircraft failed to see them. Cooke kept a diary on a piece of sailcloth. Destroyer *Rapid* rescued them.... I went to Brighton to see Jock.

December 14th Tuesday
This afternoon I went again to Cripland Court to help address the last lot of soldiers' Christmas parcels.... Parcels for abroad were posted some time ago, today's were for those in England girls as well as the boys.

December 18th Saturday
There are 300,000 prisoners hidden by the Japanese, nine-tenths of whom are south of the Philippines.... So far Japanese have refused to let anyone know where the camps are and what the conditions are and have refused recognition to the protecting Powers. I met Mr Tanner this morning, who with myself was invited by Mr and Mrs Cobb for coffee at Pierpoint House. When at Scaynes Hill, he had had 4 evacuees from Pimlico planted on him. After arrival he suggested they wrote home and on a card provided was written 'We have got here, we do not like it at all'. But that really only meant they were not used to such a change and a carpet amazed them. (It was soon taken up.) One day scratching was heard. They were found scraping the wallpaper, 'Oh we are bug hunting but we haven't found any yet'. When their mother was informed their heads were verminous she said they had never been so before, they must have got it from the Vicarage. Russians promise this winter to hit the Germans harder than ever. Winters favour Russians.... They made several gains yesterday, some in the Kiev Bulge battle now in its 57th week.... For British post-war emigration to Canada there are already 16,000 British brides of Canadian soldiers and their 9,000 children.

December 19th Sunday 227th week
There was an alert yesterday evening but it did not last long; 10.15 to 10.40. It was a pitch dark night, rain and high SW wind, light showing up the tiniest cracks through blinds and curtains.

December 20th Monday
There were two warnings in the night the first from 2.35 to 2.56, the second 5.43 to 6.30. I heard planes but no bombs.... Stalin has begun the winter offensive and has made a big breakthrough on a 50-mile front in the Nevel area, advancing 19 miles. 2,000 Germans have been killed, 3,000 prisoners taken, 3 infantry Divisions and one tank Division routed, much equipment destroyed and still more captured. Nevel is 300 miles south of Leningrad and 60 miles from the Latvian frontier. On Saturday 4 war criminals were sentenced to death in the Kharkov trials for the terrible atrocities against Russians. They were 3 German prisoners being held, Langheld, Ritz and Retzlav and a Russian traitor Bulinov. 40,000 people witnessed their hanging in Kharkov square. Each one confessed to killing over 100 people.

December 22nd Wednesday
Nazi propaganda is saying in their Press at Christmas we are badly off for food in comparison with Germans. We have to pay: turkeys up to £50 each, chickens £2, eggs £3 a dozen, rabbits £5.... There was a warning this evening at 10 o'clock, all-clear 10.30. I went up Black Hill with Chuck Newman. There seemed only a few planes about and I saw lights in the west.

December 23rd Thursday
From here bombers were out in force and in waves for about an hour and Berlin was again off the air.

December 24th Friday
Yesterday the great force of bombers and swarms of fighters continued the non-stop 'carpet bombing' on Hitler's European fortress, the 4th day of an offensive which exceeds any previous attack against Western Europe. Today bombers have been booming overhead to and fro nearly all day in one lot going south about 12.50. For the first time targets in Northern France were named last night.

December 26th Sunday 228th week
This has been the most hopeful Christmas of any time since the war began. Few have travelled, for once people have done what they were asked to do – spend the holiday at home. In spite of the shortage I have received over 40 cards and 10 calendars and I sent 152 of my robin cards to friends. The King made his fifth war-time Christmas speech and a very good speech and message he gave.

December 28th Tuesday
The great news today is that the *Scharnhorst* has been sunk in a trap laid by the Navy off North Cape, Norway on Sunday.

December 30th Thursday
Russians have made such sweeping victories that the fate of half the German Army hangs in the balance.

December 31st Friday
The raiders last night were turned back before entering London. No one was hurt when bombs were dropped on a southeast town. Russians have made a break-through on a gap of 190 miles, routed 22 German Divisions (250,000 men) and captured more than 1,000 places.

1944

—∿—

January 1st Saturday
The New Year came in joyfully last night, the radio programme was good and this morning we read in the paper that service men and women danced in Piccadilly Circus.... Russians continue into Poland now only 40 miles away. Now two-thirds of Russia overrun by Germans has been liberated.

January 2nd Sunday 229th week
Last night Russians were only 27 miles from the old Polish border and are still pressing on. Germans have lost enormously in prisoners and booty. They are fleeing and leaving much artillery etc and are massing reserves in Poland to try to stop a complete Russian breakthrough.... Last night and in the early hours of this morning there were many planes overhead and I fully expected a warning but none came.

January 4th Tuesday
A German war reporter Friedrich Hartan broadcasting from Kirovograd said no one had any idea of the real situation. 'Our soldiers in the morning are frozen stiff. At noon we are buried in mud. In the evening, the mud begins to freeze on us. To wash, to shave, to change clothes have become unobtainable luxuries. The men are suffering untold agonies'.

January 11th Tuesday
North of Kirovograd the remnants of 5 Divisions of Germans refused to surrender and were wiped out, Russians capturing 90 tanks, 114 guns and other booty. More than 8,000 men perished.

January 13th Thursday
I met Harry Newnham this morning who came for a fortnight's leave yesterday, home with others of the Eighth Army from Italy. He showed me the Africa Star riband, buff for the desert sand, dark blue narrow stripe for the Navy, ditto light blue for the Air Force and between them a broader line red for the Army. This evening at 7.45 there was a warning till 8.05.... I went out but heard no bombs nor planes.

January 20th Thursday
General Govorov, the Russian artillery genius, has smashed a gap more than 30 miles wide and 8 to 13 miles deep in German positions on the Leningrad Front. He used a terrific artillery concentration and defeated 7 German Divisions, 80,000 men and wiped out the first group of long-range guns which have bombarded the Leningrad Front for many months. More than 20,000 Germans were killed and 1,000 captured.

January 22nd Saturday
Last night we had the biggest air raid since the blitz, 20.13 to 22.15 or as we have been used to say 8.13 to 10.15pm. We heard and saw firing on all sides. The cottage at Wivelsfield near the Plough received incendiaries but we have not heard any particulars of the damage done. The searchlights were truly amazing and new flares lasting for over 15 minutes in the SE were bigger and brighter than usual. We do not often have another warning now after a fairly long one but at 4.25am the siren again sounded, all-clear at 5.50. This time the raid seemed again on the coast. No doubt Germans are after our landing craft.

January 27th Thursday
At Leningrad and around, more Russian victories are reported and since January 14th more than 40,000 Germans have been killed and 3,000 captured and 10 Divisions routed.... A Soviet committee has proved that the 12,000 prisoners were killed in 1941 by the Nazis. On one of the bodies a letter was found dated June 20th 1941.[33].... Kesselring is calling in all available bombers as far away as Bordeaux and long-range Heinkel 177s to knock out our armada of supply ships lying off Anzio and Nettuno. Americans and French have advanced north of Cassino. The Gustav line is strong and hard fighting is in progress. Hitler has sent a message to Kesselring to hold the line at all costs.
(Letter from John Hill):[34]

'I shall hope to see you once again and see if your dandelion wine is still up to scratch.'

January 29th Saturday
Jap atrocities against British and American prisoners are now proved and all are fiercely indignant. Mr Eden has all the facts and spoke in the House last night. Their behaviour will not be forgotten. They refuse Red Cross parcels to prisoners and still do not say where prisoners are. The siren sounded this evening at 8.35, the all-clear 9.32. Things were quiet here, but some people are careless of the black-out and have not learnt to regard it seriously even after 4 years. I went on the Common with Mr Ridgeway and called on Knight who had not turned up at the Post. He was in bed with a cold. The planes went Londonwards not much gun-firing.

February 4th Friday
Over 120,000 Germans are encircled in the Dnieper Basin. In a victory Order of the Day Stalin acclaimed it only second to Stalingrad.

February 12th Saturday
The siren sounded at 19.45 last night, the all-clear at 20.18.... There was another warning this evening at 20.50, all-clear at 21.40. It was a pitch-dark night and we heard only one plane in the east. I went up Black Hill and found it difficult to keep to the path. Mr Ridgeway did not turn up, maybe he is ill. Another Lindfield boy has been killed, Fred Pearce, Gravelye Lane. Mr Buckingham has asked me to write out the names of those who are serving to hang in the church porch. At present there are 311 names but as changes are constantly occurring, I think it better to wait until the war is over. Mr B has agreed.

February 16th Friday
Today I got oranges due, 1lb per week on each book until further notice. Quite pre-war.

February 18th Friday
A special course of some kind is taking place at the Village Hall this week. The Military, who still have the Hall room itself, could not let the WI have it for their meeting on Wednesday so we had to manage with the corridor and the Library only. We postponed our charades on that account until next month. At the end of the Pond, attached to the last post, today there is a notice – Exercise 'Jill'.

February 19th Saturday
Stephen Hopkins, 18-year-old son of Harry Hopkins, has been killed in the Marshall Islands.

February 21st Monday
When the big Exercise 'Jill' was on at the Village Hall it is stated on good authority that General Montgomery came down. He was driven afterwards to the Welkin in a poor looking small car.

February 22nd Tuesday
The siren sounded in the night at 2.55, all-clear 3.30. I heard 3 bombs drop, the nearest I was told was in Broad Street, Cuckfield in the garden of a farm, and not much damage done. It rattled our windows. When I was out at midday I saw some men reinstating the signpost arms outside Masters'. Quite like old times to see it back again.... 90 million lemons arrived in the last consignment from Italy and Sicily, but none have got to this village as yet. I made pancakes today. We had jam with them. No more oranges are obtainable here either.

February 24th Thursday
The Red Army's 26th anniversary was celebrated yesterday. It is marvellous to think that 26 years ago, it did not exist and today it is millions strong, brilliantly equipped, led and brilliantly successful. The Poet Laureate, Masefield, has written an *Ode to the Red Army*. I went to Brighton today. Jock told me there had been a heavy bomb dropped at Kemp Town which shook houses severely. He had not heard of damage done. This evening the siren was at 9.32 and the all-clear 11 o'clock. I was on Black Hill and saw really wonderful sights. At first the noise overhead was loud and continuous for our planes were going out in force. We saw one plane brought down in the east and hoped it was not ours. A phosphorous bomb fell in the SW and its light continued for some long time as if a haystack was on fire. There were many flares, some ours, some German and very many searchlights which caught many a plane. I counted 14 directed at one plane.

February 25th Friday
The first report of planes brought down last night is 9 later 10 and the one we saw is said to be at Newick. Our two big forces that went out last night followed fleets of US heavies from Britain and Italy which bombed the factories producing planes for the Luftwaffe.

February 28th Monday
Today lemons have been on sale in the village, the first time for 3 years. 1lb per head is the allowance or more if there are plenty, 6d a pound.

February 29th Tuesday
This has been a great day for Lindfield. Yesterday several thousand Canadian troops from Paxhill Camp, the Welkin etc and many ATS girls assembled on the Common at 10 o'clock, and later General Worthington addressed them from a car or lorry with a loud speaker. Civilians were not allowed on the middle and lower parts of the Common. The 'incident' was a rehearsal for today's event, when even more soldiers came and General Montgomery arrived about 11.45. Bob, Michael and I happened to be standing just where his 'Priority' car drew up and he stepped out. He is exactly like his 'pictures' from time to time in the papers, a quiet pleasant smile when a big cheer greeted him. All the village seemed there.... When he had finished speaking to various officers in the units, which took 20 to 30 minutes, he went to the car and all the soldiers ran fast to gather round him while he spoke. When he had finished they all ran back again to their places. We had another good look at him when he returned to his posh car. On the car was a red shield with a broad blue St George Cross and on it two golden spears crossed. Two soldiers on motor cycles preceded his car bearing a small flag, red, white, red horizontal. Camera men were busy and as the light was good I expect they got

good results. All people living in Brest have been warned by Vichy radio to leave in the shortest possible time, if not engaged in essential war work. The evacuation of Cherbourg is to begin on Monday. Russians closing in on Pskov 'gateway' to Latvia, yesterday reached Toroshino only 7 miles from the city. Hitler has ordered his army to hold out to the last.... Three Luftwaffe Generals have been shot for cowardice and lack of enthusiasm in the Battle of Nevel where German forces were annihilated. Hitler ordered it in spite of Goering's plea for mercy.

March 1st Wednesday
7,000 are said to have assembled on the Common yesterday. The edge of the grass each side of the paths where the men stood are brown mud today. General Dietmar, most authentic of German radio commentators, warned his listeners that the Atlantic War is not insurmountable. He said the Allies have now completed all preparations for the jump into Europe from the west.

March 3rd Friday
Several pieces of 'riband' in long lengths have been picked up in many places, black on one side, silvery on the other. Dropping it interferes with radiolocation, strange as that may sound.

March 4th Saturday
The Red Army has cut off all retreat for the German garrison in Narva and is closing in on Pskov, Ostrov and Vitebsk. By the beginning of next month bread will be almost pure wheat again.

March 5th Sunday 238th week
One reads in today's papers that Germans realize they have lost the war and are basing their hopes on a third world war which they are now preparing and propose starting 25 years ahead.

March 6th Monday
A great breakthrough on a front of 112 miles was announced by Stalin last night. 12 German Divisions, 8 infantry and 4 tank, 150,000 men were routed.

March 9th Thursday
One wonders if any of Berlin is left standing. More than 360,000 bombs were dropped there in daylight yesterday by American Fortresses and Liberators, attacking for the 3rd time in 5 days. Over 350,000 incendiaries and 10,000 high explosive bombs were dropped on industrial targets in the city in a concentrated raid. This biggest daylight raid in history was carried out by over 2,000 planes....

There was a brief alert last evening 9.27 till 10 o'clock. No plane reached London, the one that came over this coast was turned back.

March 12th Sunday 239th week
Stalin is dividing and destroying Manstein's army in the Ukraine. Along the whole 400 mile front from Tarnopol to the Black Sea Germans are retreating and struggling to avoid annihilation.

March 13th Monday
Michael gave me pieces of prepared paper, long strips of which he found. They are a little different from the kind found in Meadow Lane but all answering the same purpose, interfering with radiolocation.

March 14th Tuesday
At our Post this evening Mr Parsons held a wardens' meeting pointing out the routine of procedure when a bomb dropped.... A clear cold night, many searchlights out. A short alert 12.05 to 1.25. Russians are driving on and have opened a new offensive and are out for a drive along the Black Sea coast to Odessa. Berlin admits the retreat and is applying the scorched earth tactics.... The Food Minister said yesterday food rationing will have to continue for years after the war. So many farmers in Canada, US, Australia and New Zealand as well as here have been taken off the land and it will take time to get things normal again.

March 15th Wednesday
The siren went at 10.55 last night and there was much banging and gun-firing, Londonwards chiefly, all-clear at 11.50. Another Soviet trap has cost Manstein 10,000 in killed alone. The place is east of Nikolaiev, the Black Sea naval base. Several German Divisions were trapped, more than 4,000 men taken prisoner and 300 guns captured.... Again there was a warning at 8.55 till 9.28. Very little was either seen or heard, it seemed London again. With some of the sweet oranges and the lemons we have lately had, I made 12 pots of marmalade, quite a good wartime effort and the first since the war for we have not had the fruit available before.

March 16th Thursday
Cassino has been bombed to rubble. Yesterday morning the town was wiped out by the greatest air attack against any target. More than 1,400 tons of bomb were dropped on its one square mile. Loudspeaker vans went round Chichester yesterday warning people, especially children, that any chocolates they found should be given to the police. A number believed poisoned have been scattered over streets and gardens and samples have been sent for analysis. It is thought they were dropped in Tuesday night's raid.

March 17th Friday
Police said yesterday no poison has been found in chocolates strewn over
Chichester soon after Tuesday's raid. How they got into the streets is still
unexplained. An enemy plane flew low over the city.... There was a warning this
evening at a minute to 9. I went up Black Hill. There were many planes and
searchlights and guns firing on the coast. Probably our barrage, to keep the planes
away. Also over London. All-clear 9.50. About 6 o'clock this evening many pieces
of the radiolocation interrupter came floating down, some in the garden, on the
roof and all round about. We heard no plane from which it might have descended.
Boys came across the Common with large handfuls of it, all silvery.

March 21st Tuesday
After April 1st a wide area of coastline from Newquay to the Wash will be closed
to the ordinary travelling public. No notion of how long it will last can be given
yet. The ban will be 10 miles in depth and many inland towns will be affected in
Sussex including Arundel and Chichester. The ban does not surprise any of us....
There was an alert in the night, 12.40 until 1.55, a bad raid over London where
the barrage sounded extra severe. Just before the all-clear when I was at
Beckworth Lane with Mr Parsons, we heard gunnery on the south coast. Perhaps
it was the Brighton barrage sending planes out to sea.

March 23rd Thursday
While we were rehearsing our plays for Salute the Soldier Week at the Council
School the siren sounded but it was a short raid 9.24 to 9.52. The papers this
morning say that the few who came over were on armed reconnaissance.

March 25th Saturday
There was a bad raid last night, the warning went at 11.15 all-clear 1.05. One
heavy bomb seemed to be dropped Turners Hill way. I heard in the village that a
plane was brought down at Crawley Down.... The RAF again raided Berlin 'a
large-scale terror attack' and bombs dropped on the whole town.

March 26th Sunday 241st week
The tremendous battle of Ukraine is now almost over. Two victorious armies are
racing for the Balkans. Retreating Germans it is said fling away their arms and
refuse to fight. When we were walking this afternoon by Hangman's Acre we
found many ribands.

March 27th Monday
Before the news at 9 o'clock the Premier broadcast. He gave no news but a kind of
war survey telling of victories and failures. He spoke with confidence on housing

the homeless and said the Government had a demobilization plan but before it could be told victory had to be won. 'The end is in sight.'

March 29th Wednesday
Russians have taken Nikolaiev by storm.... Nikolaiev is the biggest shipbuilding base on the Black Sea.

March 30th Thursday
Michael and I went to London today to see something of the Salute the Soldier Week celebrations. Arriving at Trafalgar Square after walking through St James' we saw many guns, three or four, 6-pounder guns each costing £1,000. There was a long American procession with troops numbering 3,000 so the papers say. There were flags of Allied nations as well as our own hung from many a house, searchlights, rocket guns, AA guns on blitzed ground near St Paul's. Bob took us to lunch at the Tiger opposite the Tower from which we had a good view now so much is down. It was sad to see the ruins of All Hallows Barking and many another church.

April 1st Saturday
It is sad to see in today's paper the death of General Wingate. He was killed in an air crash. It was he who wiped out the Arab marauders of Palestine, led Haile Selassie back to Abyssinia, the first to outwit the Japs in jungle warfare and lastly led and planned our recent airborne invasion into Burma.... On Thursday night Nuremberg was bombed and we lost 24 bombers from the 900 to 1,000 which went. Conditions favoured the Germans that night for dense cloud forced our bombers into clear moonlight where they were good targets. Coal and fuel is now becoming scarce and difficult to get. When I asked for a little coal I was told I might perhaps get a cwt and had to fill in a paper stating what fuel I had in stock.

April 6th Thursday
About two-thirds of England's coastline is included in new restrictions to be placed on coastal areas from April 8th.

April 16th Sunday 244th week
Russians are only 4 miles from Sevastopol. Tarnopol is captured, the great stronghold guarding the way to the Polish city of Lvov. 16,000 Germans were killed at Tarnopol and 37,000 captured in Crimea, Germans and Romanians. The road to Lvov is now opened. Cases of iron crosses were dropped by air to bolster up the morale of the garrison at Tarnopol. Desperate attempts were made to save the place. Germans held out for nearly two months.

April 20th Thursday
Goebbels' Ministry is training speakers to imitate Alvar Lidell, Frank Philips and Fred Grisewood so that when invasion begins false broadcasts can be sent out to Britain.

April 21st Friday
The Ministry of Aircraft Production said yesterday aluminium will be used for domestic articles again. Masters' shop now has kettles, saucepans etc in quantities but all in tin, which I do not care for. Maybe the aluminium will not reach Lindfield though.

April 23rd Sunday 245th week
This evening about 10 o'clock we saw a large motor vehicle on the Common with a gun and a tank on the top of it, and all attached to another motor lorry on the Common just opposite my gate. Mr Bottrill and I stood looking at it when one of the 3 soldiers there asked for some hot water to make some tea. I asked him to bring me the tea and I would make it and bring it out in a teapot. Afterwards they asked for a bucket of water for a 'swill'. It had been a hot sunny day and they looked tired and grimy. We put the bucket on the gas ring and when warm, Bob took it out to them. When we asked what time they were leaving they said they were sleeping under the lorry and were 'lying in'. Evidently they had not received instructions about the time of leaving so I said I would make them tea the next morning.

April 24th Monday
The three soldiers were glad of tea and another bucket of hot water about 8.30 this morning, and they moved off their heavy lorries leaving deep ruts on the Common.

April 25th Tuesday
Another ban. No one may leave Britain after midnight on Thursday except on urgent business of national importance that cannot be postponed, all to avoid any leakage about the news of forthcoming military operations. Nearly all last night planes were overhead.... The Jap thrust into Assam has received a setback by the relief of the Allied base of Kohima, 40 miles from the Burma frontier.

April 30th Sunday 246th week
Berlin has been terrifically raided again. 1,000 bombers and 1,000 long-range fighters gave it a day raid and huge fires were still burning at night. Nearly 2,000 tons of bombs, many incendiaries, were dropped. All day, bombers and fighters have been going out or coming home. I counted 63 Fortresses all silver in the

sunshine at 8.15 this morning travelling south. No doubt on their way to Germany.

May 1st Monday
May Day demonstrations yesterday were united in pledges to smash Nazism and its allies throughout the world. Thousands gathered in Trafalgar Square. All the many foreign speakers greeting this May Day as the last on which subject countries would be under the Nazi yoke.... The opening broadcast of ABSIE, the new US station for Europe, was made yesterday. Germans tried unsuccessfully to jam it.... The first broadcast: a call to the 'underground' not to be premature, the signal would be given when the hour came.

May 2nd Tuesday
A large poster for our Salute the Soldier Week has been fixed by Bank House. Our Lindfield target is £7,000. At the foot of the poster is the head and shoulders of a soldier with his right arm extended and moveable to indicate each day the amount reached. As our plays are the last item on the week's programme I hope his arm will reach the target that night.... The 5 Premiers began talks yesterday in London, and will be conducted on the principle 'nothing barred'. Not only the war will be discussed, but also post-war collaboration, education and migration.

May 3rd Wednesday
The Luftwaffe's strength is estimated to about 1,500 for the Allied aircraft have battered its factories so much.... Franco has agreed to repel all Axis spies from Spain, Spanish Morocco and Tangier.... Banned area police made a swoop yesterday in Brighton and Hove and checked road and rail passengers. Identity cards are checked only about one day in five. Too many unnecessary visitors have taken advantage and provoked a sudden swoop.

May 4th Thursday
Nazi propaganda in Turkey has been thrown into confusion because Dr Paulus, Head of Europa, the Nazi agency which operates throughout all neutral countries, has thrown up his post, refused to return to Germany, and has 'gone under cover'. One wonders if he will come over to the Allies. He knows the secrets of Berlin propaganda.

May 5th Friday
An army officer ended his lecture on thrift with 'The motto for every one of you is "Put away something for a rainy day".' Then he stepped off the platform, went into the lobby of the hall, and found his raincoat was missing. Our Salute the Soldier Week begins tomorrow. This afternoon with Mr Thompson's help I

decorated the Village Hall with flags. I have now made 27 United Nations flags and with 10 others the Hall looked gay. Many flags were put up in groups of three. Men were putting up scenery on the stage.

May 7th Sunday 247th week
Invasion fever mounts to a pitch in Europe. From Italy, from the Balkans, from listening posts all over the Continent, come reports suggesting zero hour is near. New York says all is ready for the final air offensive on Germany.

May 8th Monday
Last night after the 9 o'clock news Mr Curtin, Australian Prime Minister, broadcast to the nation. He emphasised the importance, after the defeat of Hitler, of the combined Allied effort against Japan. It might mean a prolonged war in the Pacific.

May 9th Tuesday
Yesterday evening the Home Guard gave a smashing concert as a contribution to the Soldier Week. There was plenty of drinking at tables, each taking about 6 people a side. Home Guard fellows walked about and talked asking people what they would have to drink (mostly beer) while the ladies sang their songs. A 'free and easy' concert. Tickets were sold for raffles. It lasted from 8 till just after 11. All the singers were encored.

May 10th Wednesday
The RAF's heavy bombing on the other side of the Channel rocked SE coast towns late last night and again early today. It was the heaviest ever heard and seemed in the Calais and Dunkirk areas. In daylight yesterday about 4,000 bombers and fighters were used to hit rail points, dumps and bridges.... Sevastopol was recaptured last night by Russians and with it the entire Crimea has been freed, thus ending the swiftest campaign of the Russo–German war. The Crimea has been cleared in less than a month. Today is the 4th anniversary of the German invasion of the Netherlands, Belgium and Luxembourg by land and air.

May 11th Thursday
A new League of Nations (backed by guns) is Britain's plan for world peace. It has been approved by the Dominion Premiers and will now be discussed by Allied Powers. Heaviest responsibility will be borne by the Great Powers, who must have the armament necessary to discharge those responsibilities. The smaller States will take their share in accordance with their size.... With the fall of Sevastopol the way is now clear for the Russian Balkan offensive.

May 12th Friday
Last evening at 8 o'clock on the Common the Home Guard of the village gave a demonstration of weapons, battle drill and paratroops 'dropped' on the lower part of the Common. Hitler (Mr Barrow) among them waving a swastika flag. They were surrounded by the Home Guard and captured. Hitler's get up was very good, false nose and eyebrows complete. The only unfortunate thing was, all the spectators were on the upper path and part of the Common and the 'incident' was so far away no one could hear a word of Hitler's speech nor see anything clearly of what was going on. It was a perfect evening, warm and sunny. With others I took round a collecting box.... Hitler is to visit the invasion coast of the Channel and North Sea. Two days ago at Calais, Hoffman his personal photographer arrived. The trip is intended to provide home propaganda. Russians... are preparing for another big advance. In Sevastopol what Germans could not blow up they burnt down, indeed it is a city of the dead.

May 13th Saturday
Moscow says Russians took 61,500 prisoners in the Crimea battle including two Generals.... Orders have been given for all German-held funds in Balkan countries to be withdrawn immediately, a fear that Germany may not be able to hold Balkan countries. In Holland many German officials have been exchanging Reichmarks for Dutch currency in case of collapse and now special permits must be obtained for exchange of over 200 Reichmarks.... This evening and last evening we acted our curtain raiser and 2 plays at the end of Salute the Soldier Week. All went well on both evenings and much to my delight and surprise Mr Barrow presented me with a lovely bouquet of lilac, tulips and white broom. Mrs Martin received flowers too. We finished up with a war-time 'supper' in the Library, all of us brought some contribution towards it, then dancing and games in the Hall, just the cast and those who had helped including Bob. Bernard Dickenson 'conducted' the party and thoroughly amused us all. We got home at 12pm.

May 14th Sunday 248th week
This afternoon there was a service and parade of Home Guards and Wardens on the Common. It is the Home Guard's 4th birthday. I did not join in it this time, but I saw them pass the window.

May 15th Monday
There was a warning last night, the first for over a fortnight. I heard only one plane just as I was going out, 2.20 till 3.03am and all the lights and flashes were in the SW about Portsmouth it seemed, none at all London way.... A sad thing has happened at Steyning. Shells from an RA battery practising on the Downs fell in

and around Steyning and among Home Guards at a rifle range at which one person was killed and two others injured, and also into houses, buildings and gardens. A boy digging was killed and a man with him was injured. About 12 shells over-shot their target (the anti-tank type). Norwegians are celebrating their National Day of Independence by staying indoors and keeping silent.

May 16th Tuesday
In the Steyning disaster mentioned yesterday the reason it took some time for the CD and Police to warn the Royal Artillery that shells were falling on the town on Sunday morning was that it was dangerous to cross the gunnery range. Warning reached the battery in the end by a messenger in a jeep who made a circular tour of several miles to get behind the guns. An enquiry opens tomorrow.

May 18th Thursday
We have far exceeded our target of £7,000 for our Salute the Soldier Week. The figure given up to last Saturday night, the end of the special week, was £20,584.8.0. One wonders where all the money comes from. Everybody gave something. The Empire Prime Ministers have made a Declaration and pledged lasting world peace. Churchill describes it as a 'milestone in history'.... A number of the Royal Rifle Regiment marched up the village in the early afternoon, I suppose on their way to Paxhill. Four abreast the line reached from Masters' to the Tiger.

May 19th Friday
Viscount Halifax said at a luncheon arranged by Denver University that the Axis would lose the war because of four 'irreparable and catastrophic mistakes: 1. Failure to follow up the fall of France by invasion of Britain; 2. Failure to concentrate the air blitz on military objectives instead of attempting to shatter civilian morale; 3. The attack on Russia; 4. Failure to follow up the invasion of Pearl Harbour with the invasion of Hawaii'. In spite of the ban I went to Brighton today to see Jock and had no trouble at the barrier at all. I had a letter from him asking me to go, but had no occasion to use it. I showed my identity card.

May 20th Saturday
In the evening a big assault on Northern France and Belgium was launched and last night many bombers passed overhead here.

May 22nd Monday
About 5 o'clock this afternoon the King drove through the village to Paxhill Camp, returning just after six. His car went by like a flash.

May 23rd Tuesday
There was an alert at 12.25, all-clear 1am. We heard gun-firing in the south, Brighton way I thought and even after all-clear there was still gun-firing.... People are repeatedly asked not to travel and trains may be taken off without notice. Yesterday 7 northbound trains were cancelled and hundreds of people were stranded and many were frightened to leave the queues in case they lost their places. A lot of the travelling is unnecessary.

May 24th Wednesday
News from Italy is good.... Mrs Churchill in a broadcast last night on her Aid to Russia Fund said that after the successful appeal for Stalingrad Hospital, they had been asked to equip a hospital for Rostov-on-Don. Chinese have cut the Burma Road by capturing Chefang, a town on the Irrawaddy. Chinese are advancing to the east in 3 columns and are confident of reaching Loyang in time to relieve the garrison there, besieged for ten days.

May 28th Sunday 250th week
There was much aircraft overhead here all day yesterday and at night a big force went out just before midnight until 1.15 and again at 2.30 and still more planes. This morning's paper says the RAF bombing on the other side of the Straits gave coast towns on this side one of the most severe shakings they have yet had. The attack lasted 15 minutes.... Many thousands of holiday-makers turned up at some London stations yesterday for trains that did not run. Many went to the Lord's cricket match, some to the river and others by bus to the country.

May 30th Tuesday
Thousands out of more than 2,000,000 books collected for salvage, instead of being pulped, will be sent to Europe as soon as liberation comes. The books are mainly educational, but will include war novels showing the trend of European thought, which has been barred by Nazis.

May 31st Wednesday
It is rumoured by many people in this village that Montgomery has made his HQ at Paxhill. Be that as it may Park Lane is now closed.

June 1st Thursday
May was the first whole month sirens have not sounded in London since 1942.

June 2nd Friday
38 key rail points in 'Hitler's Europe' have now been battered by our bombers.

June 5th Monday
Rome has fallen to the 5th Army, the first European capital to be liberated. Hitler ordered its evacuation after the suburbs had been reached. Outside the City, main roads were jammed for 50 miles as Germans fled.... All the city rejoiced to see the end of German tyranny, women came out to fete the troops as shrapnel still flew about them. Rome's water, gas and electricity were blown up by the enemy yesterday and there was nothing to eat. For 4 months there has been no meat, and for two months not one egg. All the leading Fascists are leaving in the confusion in the City. Again the French coast was bombed yesterday and another road bridge over the Seine, 40 miles north of Paris, was wrecked.... War against Japs is going well both in the southwest Pacific and Burma.... I went this afternoon to Trevelyan Gymnasium to hear Lady Fortescue speak about the Free French and to ask for help in forming a branch here of the AVF, the Association of Friends of the French Volunteers. It has done much for the men, their families and relatives in Great Britain.

June 6th Tuesday
Early this morning news came through on the radio that the long expected invasion had started. In the early hours our troops had landed in Normandy. Eisenhower and Montgomery were in command and thus far all had gone according to plan. Instructions from the BBC were given to patriots and later in the morning to Poland and Luxembourg. West of the Tiber Allied troops were continuing their advance pounding the German retreat and supply roads for 80 miles north of Rome.... Rome was spared the fate of becoming a battleground. In their hurried withdrawal quantities of war material were left behind. Prisoners exceeding 20,000 are still coming in.... Yesterday was the first time the RAF attacked the Channel Islands, when 8 radio stations in Jersey, Guernsey and Northern France were hit by rocket-firing and bomb carrying Typhoons. There was no fighter opposition but heavy flak at some points. Five planes were lost but pilots of two are safe. There were night raids all along the coast and here we heard planes nearly all night. All over Northern France communications were smashed. The Luftwaffe stayed on the ground. Every Thunderbolt returned and only one Marauder was lost.

June 7th Wednesday
I heard King George broadcast at 9 o'clock last evening to the world. He always interprets the mood of the people and his hope throughout the present crisis of the liberation of Europe... was inspiring to all listeners. The war news is that Montgomery is pleased with the initial landings and our losses are much less than expected. RAF pilots flying low over the fronts said 'we are doing well all along the Front. Our troops are moving inland. There is no longer any opposition on the

beaches, which are completely in our hands'. Tanks are moving towards Caen....
There was slight loss in ships, but so slight it did not affect putting the armies
ashore. The first wave of men are through and set for the land battle. The latest
news is that British, American and Canadian troops are fighting in the streets of
Caen, 10 miles up the river Orne from the Normandy Coast on which they landed
24 hours earlier. A huge air armada crossed the east coast last night, we counted
many overhead here. 10,000 tons of bombs were dropped on the French coast
early in the morning. The beaches occupied are between Cherbourg and Le
Havre. A great airborne force landed behind the enemy lines. Correspondents
send long accounts of what is going on, interesting enough but too long to quote.
Medical corps men with airborne field hospitals followed close behind the
paratroops landing in France. General de Gaulle in a broadcast to France last
night told the French they would see their own troops 'tomorrow'. He is expected
to land on French soil very soon. In Italy the 5th Army have passed beyond the
Tiber at all points and cleared Ostia harbour, at the mouth of the river. In the
Rome area 11 bridges out of 14 were intact and Allied armour was thus able to
cross rapidly and fan out 5 miles west of Rome. As one would expect Russians
were more than overjoyed at the news.... This evening for the 'Soldiers
Hospitality' we again acted our play, this time at Queen's Hall, Cuckfield.

June 8th Thursday
General Eisenhower cruised off the invasion beaches for 4½ hours in a British
warship yesterday afternoon and held conferences with Commanders, General
Montgomery and others. Rommel's first big counter-attack in Normandy with
massed tanks has been flung back by our troops in the Caen area. This is the first
engagement of any size and assumed to be a fight for the railway which runs
through Caen, and links with Cherbourg 65 miles away. Our invasion is running
to time and many of the beachheads have linked up. The RAF is believed to make
bases already in liberated territory.... Altogether between 8 and 13 Divisions out
of 80 which Eisenhower has at his disposal have been landed in France.... A
French Territorial Army is to be formed from among the population in each port
in France as it is liberated, to join up with the advancing Allies.... The Gestapo in
Germany is being denuded to half to supplement its members in France. Nazis
fear uprisings in France more than at home. British and US troops have made
another breakthrough in an offensive west of Rome and are now 10 miles past the
Capital.... June 6th is called 'D-Day' some say for Deliverance or Doomsday (for
Germans of course). But really it is just the Service abbreviation for D for Day.

June 9th Friday
The battle for Caen, 10 miles inland, which began yesterday, is developing into a
major struggle.... Montgomery went to France yesterday to take over his command

of the ground forces. Berlin radio said 'The enemy has knocked out our Atlantic Wall defences on a rather broad front'.... Fishermen who use the Atlantic Coast waters of Norway, Denmark, Holland, Belgium and France have been warned by Eisenhower that all fishing cease for 7 days beginning yesterday. Fishing boats at sea must return immediately. The capture of Bayeux is announced.... Already Nazis have opened a special radio service for the Allied invasion forces at Orleans. Unfortunately for Nazis it told the troops they were being driven back just as they were capturing Bayeux. It also offered 'safe conduct' to all who surrendered instead of being driven into the sea.... In the House the Premier again warned members against over-optimism regarding the invasion. Things are not going to be settled in a rush, and 'enormous exertions lie before us'.

June 10th Saturday
From Normandy comes news that our progress is steady. Our forces have occupied a number of towns and villages from 6 to 12 miles inland. New gains have been made in the advance from Bayeux, and Formigny, 9 miles west, on the Carentan road has been captured by Americans. Bayeux and St Mere Eglise are the only towns officially announced as captured, but others are held by Allies. The whole position is described as 'satisfactory'.... Stormy weather reduced Allied air activity.... Germany's armies north of Rome are in disorganized retreat.... The Allied Invasion film will be on the screens next week and on those of neutral countries within a few days. Nazis fear its effect on neutrals because they have nothing to put up in competition with it. No German unit was present the first two days of invasion.

June 11th Sunday 252nd week
The whole of France is rising against the enemy as the Allies continue to advance in Normandy. Every village is co-operating with our armies, sabotage and insurrection are rife. In southeast France the Maquis, led by the famous 'Blue Devils', have surrounded Grenoble and there is heavy fighting. They, the Chasseur Lapins (Blue Devils), are crack mountain troops whose uniform includes a particularly dashing type of beret. Montgomery has praised the 50th (Northumbrian) Division for the part they played in landing in France. They were one of the last British formations out of Dunkirk 4 years ago. The biggest concern of German prisoners is whether we are going to shoot them. Their biggest surprise is when they are given a cup of tea.... Montgomery has set up his HQ in France.... Finns report Russians have begun a general offensive against them in the Karelian Isthmus.... Children sent for safety to Canada and US after Dunkirk are being brought home by British warships. Whenever a warship leaving US for Britain has the opportunity, a batch of the children are taken on board and given a free trip home, but there is no regular system.

June 12th Monday
Another good day is reported from France. Bitter struggles are going on south of Bayeux and around Carentan at the base of Cherbourg Peninsula. Said a Staff Officer 'It was a very satisfactory day'.... The Interior French Force now numbers over 175,000 men.... Iceland is to seek permission to join the United Nations (I foresee another flag!).

June 13th Tuesday
Carentan has been captured after an all-night battle.... Berlin threatens North Sea fishermen with prosecution if they obey Allied orders to stay in port. Stoppage of boats would expose Nazi 'spy-boats' disguised as fishing vessels.

June 14th Wednesday
From HQ in France comes the report that Caen is held in 'a semi-circle of steel'.... British and Canadians are fighting a violent battle.... Leaders of the underground in France are sending an urgent invitation for de Gaulle to visit France so soon as possible. A recognized leader is needed to encourage the underground and they are hampered because the movement must remain secret and so they are unable to put up a figurehead of their own.... French girls married to Germans are sniping at our men from windows.

June 15th Thursday
Normandy is having the grandest battle since the landing between Caen and Tilly.... Tilly is now a no man's land of rubble, mortar and stone, still held by Germans, but under fire. De Gaulle landed in France yesterday and is visiting towns and villages in the liberated area. His relationship with the US is not to be discussed yet, Churchill will not allow it.

June 16th Friday
Last night was the most disturbed night we have had for a very long time. There were four warnings with short intervals between each and we were out all night. A misty drizzling rain fell all the time.... We heard only two bombs drop and a good way off, but many strange unusual noises unlike the general gun-fire. On the 1 o'clock radio and from the evening papers we learnt Germans used pilotless planes. A small number were used last Tuesday, early morning, but they caused only a few casualties and little damage. Last night's attacks from 11.35pm until 8.25am were more serious but particulars are not yet in either of damage done nor the number destroyed before they could explode. When the engine of the pilotless aircraft stops and the light at the end of the machine is seen to go out it may mean that the explosion will soon follow, 5 to 15 seconds. One plane about 18ft long with a total wing span of about 20ft, filled with explosive, fell in a farmyard. The only

fatal casualty was a magpie and only a few people were cut by flying glass. The force of the explosion blew up trees. The machines came in very low and were met by AA fire and rocket shells. Two other robot planes crashed in other parts of England. In one place 8 were killed and others injured. This morning there were 2 more warnings, 9.55 to 11.15 and 1.45 to 2.43 and the strange bumps again heard.... Plans for entertaining troops in France are going ahead and ENSA artists are discussing plans.

June 17th Saturday
The King arrived in Normandy yesterday.... It is 4 centuries since a King of England last landed on Norman soil to visit his fighting armies in France. There was no ceremonial and landing craft carried on. There were many cheers both by our men and French people.

June 18th Sunday 253rd week
Again there was an all-night alert, or nearly so.... We watched these new pilotless planes come up along the Thames Estuary accompanied by flares, seemingly like fireworks. Our searchlights caught them all, but made no difference to their speed.... Since D Day the French Forces of the Interior are wrecking all communications they can, destroying bridges.... It is reported in the papers this morning that many of last night's raiders, the pilotless planes, were destroyed in the air by gun-fire.

June 19th Monday
The Maquis are helping us more and more and have warned German authorities that if any of them are caught and punished as *franc-tireurs*, the patriots will deal out similar treatment to hostages they now hold.

June 20th Tuesday
Our pilots have dubbed the pilotless flying bombs 'doodlebugs'. Mustangs and Thunderbolts are shooting them down in the sea. It is said 70 were shot down yesterday, certainly we heard loud bangs at intervals all day and often our homes shook. Our pilots have achieved marked success with them. One Mustang pilot said last night 'Doodlebug hunting is a lot of fun, they cannot shoot back at you'. Their launching platforms in Pas de Calais were attacked twice yesterday.... Penicillin is doing miracle work on the French battlefield. The supply is good and it is used for all surgical cases and is particularly effective for preventing gangrene.

June 21st Wednesday
The Red Army has captured Viborg, which victory was greeted in Moscow with a

salute of 224 guns.... Sweden has informed the Finnish Foreign Office of its readiness to act as mediator in reaching peace with Russia.

June 22nd Thursday

In Cherbourg streets more Americans were fighting. The Allied command called on the German garrison to surrender by 7am today. The ultimatum was repeated throughout the night. Leaflets were dropped on Cherbourg by Allied planes.... Hundreds of tons of bombs, shells, artillery tanks and general supplies are being flown across the Channel regularly by more than 1,000 aircraft of Transport Command operated by Allied Expeditionary Air Force. Nearly 2,000 maps were sent across on one occasion. On an SOS message from the RAF or others, supplies are delivered within a few hours.... While going to my small allotment this evening the siren sounded, 6.40, and presently I heard and saw a flying bomb going by. I heard it was brought down at Turners Hill, or near there. All-clear was at 7.10. The main part of the launching sites is an oblong concrete launching platform pointed towards England and camouflaged with paint, hard to see and to hit.

June 23rd Friday

Cherbourg is getting a terrific air and land blitz.... The Luftwaffe now has its back to the wall, their reserves have been depleted. To add to Hitler's troubles a quarrel is going on in Normandy between the Nazi army and the Luftwaffe, each blaming the other for the battering they get from Allied planes.... De Gaulle is to make a speech to the French Parliament on Monday.

June 24th Saturday

Although doodlebugs flew by last night and there was plenty of gun-firing between 12.30 and 2am, we heard no warning. Russia has opened a new offensive on her central front which makes three good Fronts as it were for Hitler – France, Italy, Russia.... A Belgian sent to England to spy for Germany was executed yesterday, the 15th spy in this war.... I went to the Tiger canteen this evening after the Library. It was very full and I did not pause pouring out tea and lemon squash from 9 till 10.40. There are so many soldiers at Paxhill and elsewhere just now, no Canadians lately...all very jolly and enjoying the war-time meal.

June 25th Sunday 254th week

Flying bomb bases are being steadily bombed in the Pas de Calais area.... Three victories are announced by Stalin...and each victory saluted by 20 salvoes of Moscow's guns.... Food supplies for French refugees are being expedited. A flying bomb was brought down by a Pole at a Wivelsfield farm. His first shot missed which would have landed the bomb in a field, the second shot brought it down in a farm yard and damaged some of the farm buildings. The Pole landed and apologized to the farmer.

June 26th Monday
Over 1,000 planes yesterday attacked flying bomb bases in Pas de Calais.... Other places and railways were also hit.... A new 'Haw-Haw' is being appointed to direct German broadcasts to British and US troops in France. He will also act as chief announcer, pass as an Englishman, but is Fredk Braun, a native of Hamburg and well known in West End clubs and hotels, a friend of Ribbentrop.... I went to London today and spent most of it in the Royal Academy with Mrs Kennie, a very good war-time exhibition I thought. It was a 'sticky day' in London, the siren being on nearly all the time. Much fresh damage has been done by the new doodlebugs, but accompanied with very few casualties, plenty of wrecked homes and shattered glass.

June 27th Tuesday
In Piccadilly yesterday I saw a, to me, new sight – American Military Police.... More treasures from the Louvre are to be 'removed to safety' from the Allies. The underground will note their destination and report to London.... The War Office has recognized Women Home Guards.... They will be known as Women Home Guard Auxiliaries. The Service remains voluntary and like the men they will be entitled to meals etc when on duty.

June 28th Wednesday
London I suppose has had another 'sticky' day for we have had 4 warnings here, all of them short, as if journeying to London this way: at 9.35 to 9.55 this morning, 11.10 to 11.20 and this afternoon 1.59–2.18 and 3.04–3.15. Russia has won fresh victories.... The 3rd great Battle of Normandy, in spite of strong opposition, is going 'all in our favour', the battle for the road to Paris and Rouen. Capture of 8 villages in 24 hours and a 6 mile advance in 48 hours are announced.... German troops goose-stepped through Helsinki last night on their way to aid Finns against Russia. Germany has promised all the armed help requested to continue the war against Russia. The WAAF celebrates its 5th birthday today. The Service has expanded tremendously. The largest telephone exchange in the world is handled by WAAFs.

June 29th Thursday
It was a noisy night, with 3 warnings.... There was one loud crash and no doubt several of the flying bombs were shot down. They have now been used for a fortnight and the 'kills' are increasing by our fighters and many launching sites have been destroyed. Previous bombing has reduced the attack to less than one

quarter of what was intended. Germans meant the attack to be a powerful one and big supplies of bombs are ready, but are useless without the launching ramps. All the war news is good on our side this morning. Caen is being closed in with heavy fighting.... In Italy the 5th Army is only 30 miles from Leghorn.... Moscow announces sweeping victories.... The last main bastion of the 'Fatherland Line' in White Russia is captured. I have been trying to find the boundaries of this White Russia which is not shown on most of the maps I have, but one gives the position bordering Lithuania, Poland, Little Russia and Greater Russia, but all on a small scale. Minsk is its capital.... Russians are driving down 3 main roads to Minsk.... Philippe Henriot, Vichy Propaganda Minister, bitterly anti-British, was shot in the Paris Ministry of Information yesterday.... The French Provisional Government has appealed to Pétain from London to save French lives by preventing Germans treating French Forces as *franc-tireurs* and not as prisoners of war. This could be done if Pétain dissolved his Government and so made void the Armistice Convention Article which decrees that Frenchmen who fight Germans will be killed. One wonders what Pétain will do. There were two warnings this afternoon and each time doodlebugs were brought down...Pat Johnson and I watched two Spitfires chasing the bomb and making bursts of large puffs of smoke on their path. The first bomb was brought down at Balcombe in a field near the Viaduct, no damage to the Viaduct.

June 30th Friday
Since D-Day our armies have driven German fighter bases back 100 miles.... I went to London this morning, the train took just 2 hours on the journey.... Around Sloane Square and Sloane Avenue many houses are destroyed and a good deal of damage done by the new flying bombs. There is not much loss of life unless one is on the spot at the time, but plenty of glass broken. When we were in the bus at 5.45 one fell at Pimlico just across the street. The bus driver jumped off his seat like a grasshopper for he has glass on all sides of him and everybody in the bus ducked their heads, one fire fighter hastily pulling on his helmet. We saw the big cloud of smoke. The alerts sounded nearly all the day and some offices were badly damaged near Aldwych theatre which was closed and loose glass was everywhere.

July 1st Saturday
There were 9 flying bombs over the Sloane Avenue part of London in the night. For the nearest one Phyl and I got up and stood in the passage to be away from falling glass, which causes more injury, especially to one's eyes, than anything else.... Four German PoW's were allowed to broadcast their impressions of wartime London to their comrades on the BBC German service early today. They were taken on a trip to the West End, St Paul's and the East End of London. They

were astonished that meals, cigarettes and many other things could be bought without points or coupons.... The Soviet Government is to grant Soviet citizenship to exiled White Russians (former anti-Reds) for they have rallied to the Russian cause, casting political differences aside.

July 3rd Monday
When Cossacks broke through German lines on the Berezina River the massacre was terrible. Germans were panic stricken and few escaped alive. In December 1812 Napoleon's Army was finished at the same place and all hope abandoned.... So far 73 Americans have lost their sight in this war. A new building for them in the US will be modelled on our St Dunstan's, which US eye surgeons have visited. Doodlebugs have been over several times today and warnings given 11.23–11.24; 12.50–1.10; 3.18–3.45 and some have gone over without warning at all. The siren usually sounds *after* the bomb has passed over so it seems useless to sound it at all.

July 5th Wednesday
Gains at both ends of the Normandy battle front by 3 armies were made yesterday and are nearing Caen. US troops also advanced at La Haye. Russians sweep on and are now only 10 miles from Latvia and 110 from the German border.... Mrs Carnes and Ruth who slept here for a week or so, had their home blasted last Monday morning by a fly-bomb that descended 3 houses off. 22 people were killed, but they had just entered their Morrison shelter.

July 6th Thursday
News came last night that the most secret of all French underground movements works inside Germany itself. The organizer escaped from a German prison camp in 1942 and went from France to Algiers last month. The movement has 20,000 actual members and 250,000 active associates preparing escapes and the ultimate revolt by PoW and foreign labourers in Germany. Their HQ is in France and volunteers maintain a flow of messages in and out of Germany.... General Koenig, French Chief of Forces of the Interior, wants to move his headquarters to Normandy and organise sabotage on a big scale behind the German lines.

July 7th Friday
Mrs Carnes' house at Norbury was blasted again yesterday when three fly-bombs came over in succession.... A friend opposite her house had only the clothes she had on and together they tried to salvage some garments among the debris. To her joy Mrs Carnes found a coat but when she held it up, although it looked alright, all became like a loose fringe. That is one aspect of blast. There is no fire with these bombs and what looks like smoke when they fall is really dust and rubbish blowing high up. I heard one or two in the night but there was no call until 6.45

this morning, all-clear 6.55. The bomb that fell early Thursday morning was brought down at Cowfold. The one this evening went to the coast. I do not know if it was brought down.... Today is the 7th anniversary of China's war with Japan.... More fly-bombs have been over and we had warnings 7.40–7.55 and at 10 o'clock to 10.10. I watched a single gold star and it was steady for quite 10 minutes. Sign possibly.

July 8th Saturday
Japan had her third air raid last night.... Jap troops in Burma have been told to fight or die.

July 10th Monday
The taking of Caen by British and Canadian troops and the capture of La Haye by Americans has been received with great joy.

July 12th Wednesday
I went into the Heath this morning. The shop windows of Rice and of Terry are boarded and a good deal of smashing was done in Franklands Village, no loss of life.... Russians are advancing on East Prussia and the Baltic over the whole 400 miles of front.... Japan is trying to get submarines from Germany for the Pacific War. It is thought in defeat Germany would be likely to pass over her submarine fleet to prevent the Allies taking it over.

July 13th Thursday
Germans are retreating in Cherbourg peninsula.... Thousands of imported foreign workers in Germany, now workless as a result of Allied factory bombing, are being asked to volunteer for the armed forces instead of being sent home. They are offered special bonuses after their service to the disgust of German forces who are not offered the same terms.

July 14th Friday
We had a warning last night, after a quiet day, at 11.05 for nearly an hour, all-clear 11.55. The fly-bomb behaved in an unusual manner. It arrived in its usual place, SE, accompanied with an extra display of fireworks, the red falling stars, much gun-firing and after going north it swerved west then southwest and finally south. We supposed our airmen have found a way of diverting the course of the bomb. We did not hear it come down. In today's paper the Air Ministry says the fly-bombs now come under 3 categories: 1. Shut off and dive; 2. Shut off and glide; 3. Dive with the engine running. The first ones explode from 5 to 15 seconds after the engine has stopped. Some now go into a shallow glide for a distance before dropping, making a slight whistling noise as they fall. I read a leaflet at the Post

(specially for police and wardens telling them what to do in the event of a bomb falling in our sector). Also an illustration was given and the measurements.... Children and others are still being removed from London, 22,000 left yesterday.

July 15th Saturday
The French yesterday celebrated Bastille Day joyously, on French soil with her liberators. French girls enjoyed dances with Canadian and US soldiers.

July 16th Sunday 257th week
Soldiers' letters from Normandy and other Fronts have been long delayed. At one time 4,000 bags of mail were unopened.... Tokyo radio said last night that more captured US airmen had been executed.

July 17th Monday
Leaflets bearing forged signatures of Churchill and Roosevelt are being dropped by Germans in several ports of occupied countries calling on partisans to revolt. Germans hoped the leaflets might cause premature uprisings. They failed because there is only one official signal for uprising which is changed periodically from London.... Mr and Mrs Ellis' house was blitzed again today, a message came through about midday. It is at Wandsworth. 16 houses were downed by the doodlebug for which we had the warning at 8.38. No one was killed and most of the people crawled out from cellars and Morrisons through the debris. Wardens were helping and one woman whose home had been destroyed said 'Chronic – ain't it'. That was the spirit Hitler thinks to destroy.

July 20th Thursday
All goes well for us on Caen positions.... Moscow announces more victories.... The German Government has told householders that if they object to receiving refugees from East Prussia their houses will be confiscated till the end of the war.... There was no warning last night, but there have been two this morning.

July 21st Friday
News came through on the radio yesterday at 6 o'clock of a bomb and attempt on Hitler's life. Paper reports claim he came to the microphone this morning and blamed a clique of officers for the attempt.... Himmler has been placed in full control of Germany and all resisters will be 'exterminated'.... Japan has asked Germany to supply her with our latest war weapons that may have been captured, especially our latest tanks and anti-tank guns.... Mr Wright told me that two days ago 25 flying bombs out of 28 were brought down in the sea. We hear little of those brought down on land.

July 22nd Saturday
Last night the siren sounded at 1.20am, some minutes before the fly-bomb went over. Usually we get the warning after it has passed over. It was an awful night, the rain descending in sheets and I arrived at the post dripping. We did not hear the bomb come down, the heavy rain must have made things difficult. We enjoyed a cup of hot Oxo before returning home and were glad there were no more warnings. A local branch of the AVF Friends of French Volunteers has been lately formed, I received the notice on the 10th inst. It comprises Haywards Heath, Cuckfield, Lindfield, Scaynes Hill, Wivelsfield and Burgess Hill. Lord Cecil of Chelwood is President. Berlin is now completely in the hands of the Gestapo and SS and numbers of them patrol the streets in cars. Wholesale raids were carried out and over 1,000 people, mainly from workers' districts, were arrested. Of course many rumours are afloat and news is not allowed through. It is said leaders of the plot against Hitler had been wiped out.... In better weather our troops are advancing all along the line in Italy.... Americans who landed on Thursday on Guam are making progress.

July 23rd Sunday 258th week
Papers today are full of conflicting news of the troubles in Germany and although many reports may be untrue yet trouble there is and details will not be published. But German Generals are up against Hitler and having been beaten in this war they want to salvage something for the next.... Russians have reached the Finnish border.

July 24th Monday
Mr Parsons came round yesterday evening to tell of a new arrangement for wardens so long as the flying bombs continue, the warnings usually lasting only 10 minutes. Instead of turning out every second night, we do so every fourth night. That means there will be one of us to mind the post and two to go out. Wardens living further from the Post than I do often arrive just as the all-clear sounds. There was a warning at 2am then a loud bang and shaking, all-clear at 2.10. The robot was shot to pieces in the air on its way north and spread a bright clear, white light before falling in pieces. The bomb was well caught in searchlights. It sounded as near as Cuckfield.... New advances are announced on the whole Russian Front.... In Italy, Pisa was entered yesterday.... The leaning tower is intact and the city not badly damaged. Soviet military scientists are to visit Britain to make a special study of the flying bomb war in Southern England with the object of devising new methods of countering it. They will pool ideas with our scientists.... We have had two sirens today, both this evening at 8.02–8.13 and 9.35–9.45. From the Library we saw the earlier fly-bomb going north and a crash some miles away. The robot brought down near here and that sounded like Cuckfield was at

Ardingly. In the afternoon I cycled there to see if Mrs Musgrave and Miss Hallmark were alright passing the wreck of the fly-bomb in the ditch, a long black thing at the entrance to Berry Lane. No one was killed at Ardingly which suffered the usual damage of broken windows, scattered glass and fallen ceilings.

July 25th Tuesday
Unfortunately there are still looters about and a CD worker was sentenced to 4 years penal servitude for looting £21.19.6 while on rescue work. Two Brighton women were also sent to prison for 12 months for looting money while on rescue work.

July 26th Wednesday
Germany is ordered by Hitler to mobilize the last ounce of her waning strength in a desperate effort to avoid final catastrophe.... The Red Army is advancing so fast that already Germans are leaving Warsaw. It is even thought Russians may be there by the weekend.

July 27th Thursday
After a quiet day here there were two warnings last night at 1.05 to 1.52 and again at 2.02 to 2.23. We heard the doodles and planes but no near crashes. I went today to West Hoathly with Mr, Mrs and Ann Ellis of Wandsworth who are staying here for a time. While walking from the Cat and nearing Selsfield, we watched a doodle crossing the valley, then it went lower, swerved and crashed. We sheltered towards it and felt no blast although only a mile away. In the bus later that took us from there to East Grinstead we saw the wrecked doodle lying in a field. It had landed in farm ground opposite Moat House, killed a cow, and shattered glass but no one was killed so far as we could learn. A man dressed in a blue tunic with Seaborne on his sleeve and bearded, got off his bicycle and asked us where Moat House was. Mr Ellis said these sailor men located all fallen doodlebugs. He found this one alright.... Allied troops are only 8 miles from Florence, advancing on a 30-mile front.

July 30th Sunday 259th week
This US advance has turned the Battle of Normandy into the Battle of France.... There is a great proportion of SS troops on the Normandy Front because it is vital to Germany and Hitler does not trust the regular German Army.... When at the Library yesterday evening there was a warning at 6.30 to 6.44 and we heard the doodle go over and fall some 12 to 14 miles away. It was another noisy night. I went out 4 times: 11.24 to 11.35; 11.50 to 12.11; 12.29 to 1.13 and the last and longest 2.50 to 3.44am. In the 3rd one the doodle was brought down at Ashdown Forest where guns and barrage balloons are in force. In the last warning I watched the fly-bomb go by flying north, extra bright. I was outside the Post. It was a pleasant,

mild night, no need to complain of being out. This evening John Hannay came on his motorcycle from Groombridge. He left Malta a short time ago and says the island now is like a holiday, very different from its life before freedom.

July 31st Monday
The 2nd Army in Normandy has advanced 4½ miles on a front of 7 miles in its new attack from Caumont, east of St Lo. The British were secretly switched to take over from American troops who previously held the sector and all goes well in an unspectacular way. Americans are now so far south they can outflank Germans facing the British at Caumont.... Many reports have been received in Normandy that Rommel had died of wounds, all from German sources. All first line German forces have been withdrawn from Yugoslavia. A scheme for bringing out of the liberated areas thousands of men and women to be trained for post-war tasks within their country has been arranged.... 3 or 4,000 are to be taken monthly to Egypt where training will be given. South coast beaches were open for holiday makers and others to escape the fly-bombs and for the first time Paddington had to close for several hours on Saturday, the rush was so great. Thousands went to the West Country. Stalin has been awarded the Order of Victory. The award is 'For exceptional services in the organisation and carrying out of the offensive operations of the Red Army which have brought about the greatest defeat of the German Army and a cardinal change in the situation'.

August 1st Tuesday
From Russia comes the news that assault on Warsaw has now begun and the Red Army is within 15 miles of East Prussia. This battle of Warsaw breaks within 2 months of the 5th anniversary of its surrender to Germany, September 27th 1939, after 3 years' siege.... A German break with Turkey is in the air and for this Germans were warned yesterday by Berlin radio. Britain, Russia, US and Turkey have been engaged in talks. Many German residents, who have been ordered to return home if relations are broken off, have applied to stay on the ground they are opposed to Hitler. The Government is suspicious, probably a Nazi trick to keep spies in the country. Only a few known refugees will be allowed to stay.... Munich was again bombed yesterday by a great force from this country.... Munich is in an unrecognizable state. Rudolph Kirchener, a Czech who owned a hotel in Jersey, and now in lately freed Granville, Normandy, said the islanders have to pay a levy of a million marks every 5 weeks to cover the cost of military occupation. Clothes are impossible and people are shabbily dressed.... People live chiefly on tomatoes and potatoes and some fruit grown in the islands.

August 2nd Wednesday
Three two-second blasts on a Klaxon at two-second intervals are to be sounded in

the London area for the near approach of a fly-bomb. The danger-past signal called the release will be a continuous six-second blast. The signals will be in addition to the ordinary sirens.

August 3rd Thursday
Last night Berlin confirmed the report that Rommel is wounded, his car being hit during an air attack on July 17th. He is not in danger. Polish undergrounds led by their Commander-in-Chief General Bors are fighting Germans in Warsaw, between 10 and 25,000 of them. Street battles are going on and Poles are in touch with the Red Army outside Praga. Warsaw is like a revival of Stalingrad.... The Premier spoke in the House yesterday evening, and gave a good report, really a glowing report, of the way things are shaping for the Allies. But the flying bomb menace has not been defeated. He said our tanks are superior to the Germans' tanks. We are at least halfway through the final phase. Churchill's testimony to the men all over the world was also glowing. He said defeat of Japan will be a shorter interval than one has supposed. He takes the possibility of rocket attacks seriously and advises all who can to leave London.

August 4th Friday
1,000 German soldiers surrendering came down the main road from Rennes yesterday, part of its garrison. They threw down their arms and surrendered in a body. They were given directions to the nearest PoW camp and marched off unguarded.... In Warsaw the Polish underground army has risen against the German garrison and fighting in the streets is fierce.... In spite of the war nearly half of the 1,285 pictures in the Royal Academy have been sold, the largest sale season for 25 years.

August 5th Saturday
General Leese's troops entered Florence yesterday and were received with enthusiasm.... Far from keeping Florence an open city, much damage has been done by Germans and beauty destroyed.... Channel Islanders are looking forward to liberation and thousands are flocking down to the harbours of St Helier and St Peter Port to listen to the different guns. Somehow news is beginning to come from French families with relatives in the island.... This evening between 7 o'clock, when the siren sounded and 7.09 many people on the Common saw a fly-bomb come down in flames, just where it fell we do not know.

August 6th Sunday 260th week
Russians are now fighting on what Hitler calls 'the sacred soil of the Reich'....
Eight more German Generals have gone over to the Russians and all are named....
New miracle drugs... and flying hospitals are doing much for the wounded. It is

said only 3 in every 100 wounded in Normandy die. No time is lost at the beginning, treatment and surgery are given at once. Very different from the last war.

August 7th Monday
Mr and Mrs Ellis' house at Wandsworth was again blitzed yesterday afternoon. They went there leaving Ann with me.... 56 flying bomb storages in Northern France have been destroyed, 23 half demolished and 21 a quarter destroyed in recent air attacks. Yesterday's attacks were the heaviest yet made against these bases and continued till evening.... With the capture of the rich oil city of Drohobych in Ukraine, Russians are in a position to advance on the Balkans along a solid front of 150 miles. The Red Army now hold a string of strategic cities from which to march against Romania and Hungary, with their valuable oil and grain supplies. Gains have been made on their other fronts. Seaside places have been packed this holiday and on account of London bombing the ban removed on most if not all of them. So long as people don't ask for emergency ration cards they may stay for at least 2 days.

August 8th Tuesday
Nazis are convinced that Paris is lost. Private warnings have been sent to all non-combatant Germans to 'wind up' and be prepared to leave for Germany at short notice. French underground leaders have marked down a number of Germans who will not be allowed to get away.

August 9th Wednesday
Dogs that smell out buried enemy mines are a new development that is saving many lives on the battlefield. The risk of injury to the dogs is negligible. The dog is taught to report to his master so soon as he has smelt the mine.

August 10th Thursday
There is more good news from France this morning. German Panzers and infantry are hastily pulling out to escape pincers closing between the Orne and Laize.... All defences round Vichy are being strengthened to meet the probable attack by the Maquis as the Allies advance. It is thought the Maquis have supporters inside Vichy awaiting the signal.... Japan is withdrawing funds from Germany saying trade is now non-existent. But probably Tokyo sees Germany as defeated.... Florence is in a deplorable state.

August 11th Friday
This morning Americans are reported to be in Chartres, about 55 miles from Paris.... Germans are quitting Paris.... American Fortresses have again attacked

Jap mainland at Nagasaki.... Germany is to put a one-year ban on divorce beginning with the end of the war, applying only to men in the services and their wives. There will thus be a chance to settle down again.... An Air Force man got tired of explaining to questioners his half-wing with an S in the middle meaning he is in signals. In desperation to another enquirer he said 'I am in a jet-propeller plane. The S means I am a stoker and my job is to shovel compressed air into the engines'. I expect the inquiring friend was bewildered.

August 12th Saturday
Fortresses have blasted shipping and industrial targets severely in Nagasaki taking Japs unprepared and by surprise.... The raid has brought the war home to Japs in reality.... German radio said last night the daily average of flying bombs sent us during the past 8 weeks was 200. Their launching sites are continually attacked and many are brought down into the sea by our fighters and AA coast batteries.... The leader in the *Daily Sketch* today points at the great importance of allied attacks on German communications.

August 13th Sunday 261st week
The Allies are now in Florence and her bells are being rung.... The Polish armoured Divisions are a welcome addition to the Allied strength in France. Their reconnaissance units are magnificent and they go miles behind the enemy lines for information and prisoners. One cannot blame them for their desire to kill when pictures of Poland have been found on Germans in Normandy, wholesale massacres, hangings and machine-gunning.

August 14th Monday
Only one warning in the night, 11.00 to 11.25. Two fly-bombs went by following one another with about 5 minutes between. Sleeping out I saw them both clearly, all on fire, the first one flying lower than usual. I did not hear either bomb fall.... Russia is to send a medical mission to Britain to compare notes with our experts on countering post-war epidemics. Our scientists have observed the health in various theatres and know the trends of various ailments.... The Soviet correspondent at Lublin in Poland tells a terrible story. At Majdan, a small town near Lublin, there is a steel gate topped by barbed wire and hundreds of barracks extending nearly 10 square miles. In the middle a huge stone building with a factory chimney. It is the world's biggest crematorium. Over 500,000 men, women and children from Europe were massacred in this building.... When the Red Army arrived Germans were building more furnaces.

August 15th Tuesday
Russians are starting the great battle before Germany and fighting steadily

increases. The French Army has returned to France and is in action. Its soldiers are rejoicing. They are led by General Leclerc and some were so anxious to get ashore they jumped overboard and swam to the beach.

August 17th Thursday
Montgomery has ordered war correspondents in France to observe the strictest secrecy over Allied army movements on the Normandy Front.

August 18th Friday
A doodle was brought down this morning seemingly 8 miles or so away, the short warning being from 7.08 to 7.15. Paris radio was seized late last night by German SS officers, who broadcast to their comrades to turn against Hitler. He, a German officer, said 'We, the men of the Waffen SS have nothing in common with the gangster SS guarding concentration camps, with the Gestapo, and the home SS'. There was much more of it and the decision to fight against the Government. The Waffen SS is a police army, set up by Hitler to keep order in territory brought within the Reich.... In response to the Premiers' appeal, Mr Hutchinson the publisher is producing a million copies of 1/6 pocket thrillers and other books as a gift to members of the Forces overseas 'to commemorate their glorious successes'.

August 19th Saturday
There is good news in the papers today. The Battle of Normandy is won, German power broken. From Montgomery's HQ it was stated 'The enemy is unable to conduct anything further than strong rear guard actions. The chance of his being able to muster another first class army is remote. Now we go forward into the phase of the pursuit battle'.... There is no news about the Americans' drive on Paris. The Eiffel Tower is said to be in sight.... The French Provisional Government in Algiers last night broadcast an appeal to French people living on the Swiss, Italian and Spanish frontiers to prevent 'at all costs' the escape of collaborators and members of the Vichy Government to neutral territory.... The Vichy Government ceases effective authority in any part of France.... While I was sketching at Hartfield this afternoon I heard a fly-bomb which I was told in the evening flew over Lindfield and the Heath. I heard it brought down, some say Cuckfield way.

August 20th Sunday 262nd week
Marshal Pétain escaped when Maquis attacked the column of German cars in which he and Laval's Government were fleeing Vichy.... French Forces of the Interior now occupy Vichy.... A new anaesthetic is now used for our wounded in France, Pentothal, which has relieved thousands of sufferers. It is so important

that it is given priority on invasion craft, troop-carrying planes and gliders.... This afternoon the Lindfield Home Guard had a cricket match on the Common against Burgess Hill HG (score Lindfield 31, Burgess Hill 71) and while watching it, at 3.50 there was a warning (lasting 9 minutes) and we all watched the doodle chased by two Spitfires, one of which hit it and turned it from N to NW and the chase went on Burgess Hill way. We heard the engine stop, saw it lower down and then a crash, one wonders where it fell. Cricket proceeded.

August 21 Monday
Germans have withdrawn the bulk of their army from northern Norway and replaced it with quisling troops.

August 22nd Tuesday
The French deal drastically with collaborators, they shave off all hair on women's heads and sometimes march them in the streets.... In a special message to his troops last night Montgomery said 'The end of the war is in sight; let us finish off the business in record time'.... Several Governments of the smaller European nations are to follow Moscow's lead and ask, as part of the armistice terms, for German labour for reconstruction work in their towns.

August 23rd Wednesday
The Allies are now less than 200 miles from Germany and for all military purposes the battle of western France is finished.... A hunt for £50,000,000 has begun in France after the flight of the Vichy Government to a destination nearer Germany. French underground say the gold was removed on Sunday from the Bank of France under Nazi escort, but has not yet crossed any frontier. It is hoped to prevent the gold leaving France.... I heard tonight that Paris has fallen. I have had my flags, French and Union Jack, ready to fly when this news came through. They will fly tomorrow.

August 24th Thursday
I hung out the flags at 7 o'clock.... Naturally there are great rejoicings in Paris and indeed all over France. French patriots seized the city. We salute the French, who never gave in, and join with them in their triumph and thanksgiving. But it was Britain that kept the flag flying when all seemed lost and we stood alone. I should like to hear the bells of Westminster Abbey and St Paul's ringing today. And the news will cheer other German-occupied countries. Freedom is on the march.

August 25th Friday
The ban on the 10-mile deep coastal strip from the Wash to Lymington, Hants, is lifted from today. On account of mines, certain beaches will remain closed.

August 26th Saturday

Paris is clear of Germans save dead ones. The German Commander surrendered unconditionally yesterday. General de Gaulle re-entered his capital which went wild with joy. The crowd roared a welcome first to General Leclerc and then to de Gaulle. The noise was so terrific that the radio commentator had to scream at de Gaulle to ask him to say a word in the microphone. All he could say was '*Vive Paris. Vive la France*'. It has been the greatest day Paris can remember. The bells of Notre Dame rang out and the chorus taken up by all other churches in the city.... Southern England and London yesterday had one of the longest lulls since the fly-bombing began 10 weeks ago. Chances of using V2 weapons are decreasing as the Allied advance goes forward to where most of the sites are believed to be.

August 27th Sunday 263rd week

We had 2 warnings, each coming after the fly-bomb had gone over, the first was 1.15 to 1.25 and the second at 7.15 to 7.27. Mr Parsons made tea for Ridgeway, himself and me at 7.00 which we enjoyed and afterwards we went home to breakfast. Both robots went in a westerly direction, but we were not sure whether we heard them come down. The fly-bomb we all watched from the Common last Sunday afternoon came down at Anstye.... These robots are coming into London up the Thames Estuary and by other ways now. Those that come this way more often go westwards. Jack Mepham who is still on duty at Camber, said that one day last week 85 came over Rye way of which 72 were brought down in the sea. A good proportion.... From now on no civilian in Germany may travel, even for health reasons. The conflict between the SS and the German regular army in France is being intensified every day, so correspondents report.... The Premier has been having talks with the Pope, vital the papers say, using one of their favourite words. Next Friday the Pope proposes to speak over the Vatican radio. While in Italy Mr Churchill did good work. He assured a better working arrangement with the Italian Government.... Bing Crosby, crooner, will sing tonight (for nothing) to Service men and women at the Queensbury Club in the West End. His first singing in war-time London.

August 28th Monday

Two attempts were made to kill de Gaulle while celebrating the liberation of Paris. He was fired at in the Place de la Concorde as he rode to Notre Dame for Saturday's Thanksgiving Service and more shots were fired as he entered the Cathedral.... Leading Paris fashion experts have already designed post-war styles for export to London/New York now Paris is freed. They were designed months ago, but kept locked away so that they could not be 'borrowed' by Germans, copied and exported.

August 29th Tuesday
In France our men are pushing on fast.... Regulations are still strict about going on beaches. Sir Herbert Williams MP for Croydon South was fined £10.10.0 yesterday for going on to the beach at East Preston. He was not exempt from the law because he was an MP.

August 30th Wednesday
The BBC broadcast instructions to French workers in Germany telling them not to try to get back to France but to fight as commanded in Germany.... A swindle in pictures claimed to have been painted by Hitler, all fakes, are being offered for large sums to British and American officers. Continental artists have been employed to paint watercolours in the style of Hitler's earlier efforts, signing them A. Hitler. One clue is that they show places Hitler never visited. Hitler's *Mein Kampf* is to be useful to de Gaulle, for over 200,000 copies found in French bookshops unsold are to be pulped to produce paper for the new Paris newspapers.

September 2nd Saturday
Many places, some of familiar names in the last war – Verdun, Arras, Dieppe, Rouen have been liberated in the last 24 hours in the great march for the Rhine. Towns are falling so quickly, with scarcely a shot fired, that a full chart of progress is not possible. Allies are within 40 miles of the German frontier. Metz only 25 miles from the border is within reach of our guns. Nor are our troops far from the Belgian frontier. Germans are said to be flooding large areas in Holland and Belgium.... It has been decided that Pétain shall not be treated as a French traitor, or punished as a collaborator on the ground that he acted partly under Nazi duress, and his age and health preclude judgement of situations. It has come to light that many decrees said to have been signed by Pétain were never even submitted to him. He will go into retirement.

September 3rd Sunday 264th week
A day for special prayer and thanksgiving. Five years ago today is in everyone's thoughts and this National Day of Prayer marks the opening of the sixth year of war.... The general picture is of an Allied triumphal pursuit into Germany.... Fierce fighting is taking place only 11 miles from Germany itself and the Maginot Line pierced at Longwy, south of Sedan, and north of Verdun, and 2 miles from the Luxemburg frontier.... As they withdraw Germans are now burning down whole villages and murdering scores of French civilians and atrocity stories are coming in.... In Dieppe cemetery are graves of 850 Canadians. The padre of the Essex Scottish, Major Dolton of Ontario, said he would never forget the long hours of waiting for the regiment to come back from Dieppe. None returned. The International Red Cross has received information that about 100,000 citizens of

Warsaw, mostly women, children, and aged have been taken to a prison camp at Pruskow 15 miles from the capital and are starving. Many have died already.... This evening at 6.15 Home Guards, Wardens, AVS and others assembled in Vicarage Lane, all in uniform, and marched to evensong on this day of special prayers. Both morning and evening the Church was full.

September 4th Monday
The Maginot Line has been abandoned by Germans.... As yet there is no sign of the important radio speech Hitler was to have made yesterday. German radio gave music broadcasts nearly all day, only a few short news broadcasts.... Ten tons of maps of Germany were dropped by parachute on Saturday night to General Patton.... He made an urgent request for them. No fly-bombs have fallen in London or southern England since Friday afternoon.... At midday the news came on the radio that Brussels has been entered.

September 5th Tuesday
I hung out the Belgian flag and a Jack from my bedroom window, yesterday was too wet to fly them. Yesterday was a dramatic day, for after taking Antwerp, the Allies drove across the Dutch frontier and pushed 12 miles inland to Breda about 30 miles north of Antwerp in the middle of Northern Brabant and on the main railway line west from the German frontier to Flushing. It was at Breda that Charles II issued his Declaration before the Restoration in 1660. Over 100,000 Germans are trapped between the Somme and Scheldt rivers, with their backs to the sea. There is no Dunkirk for them. It took our armies little more than 48 hours to sweep right across Belgium into Holland. Secrecy covers the moves of General Patton's US 3rd Army. Maybe he is getting into Germany. Germans are preparing to quit Denmark. In Copenhagen they are destroying documents and all German women and children have been instructed to leave Denmark by a week on Friday.... Plans are being made in London yesterday for reorganization of the newspaper press of Germany to give German people the truth. The plan at present is that each of the Big Three shall be responsible for the Press in its own zone of occupation with a central advisory body representing Britain, US and Russia at HQ. Re-educating Germans and weaning them from Nazi principles shall be taken through their own newspapers and shall continue for an indefinite period. The whole resources of Britain's building industry have been switched to repairing fly-bombed houses in southern England. Skilled workers from all parts of the country have been drafted in and men from the Services have helped. By the end of July 60,000 men were repairing fly-bomb damage.

September 6th Wednesday
The Battle of Germany has begun.

September 7th Thursday

All along the Siegfried Line from Antwerp to Nancy an offensive is being built up.... Very heavy German fighting is going on for Antwerp where Nazis are holding out in concrete strong points, guarding the main sluices to the docks.... The Belgian Maquis, the White Brigade, are fighting a minor civil war and are of great service to our troops. They are rounding up quislings, Fascists and collaborators including Flemish people who fought for the Germans.... When double summer time ends on September 17th some of the black-out is to go and except in some coastal places will be replaced by half lighting, i.e. curtains may show light through but must not be too flimsy. One sees plenty of trouble ahead, for if the siren sounds black-out is to be completed. Considering we have blacked out for 5 years, a short time longer would not have been hard, far better wait until it can be given up altogether.... After September 10th the HG is to have no more compulsory parades, we are all proud of that force from when it began as LDV till now.

September 8th Friday

Montgomery drove into Brussels yesterday morning in pouring rain and at the Town Hall had a terrific reception, people rushing up, cheering and shouting.... It is stated that except possibly for a few last shots, the Battle of London is ended and it was won, said Sir Herbert Morrison, by the spirit of the people of southern England and the gallant work of our defence personnel, an 80-day battle. Our AA shot down 17 out of every 100 bombs which entered the gun belt in the first week. In the last week they destroyed 74 out of every 100. In those 80 days Germany launched 8,000 fly-bombs against us, about 100 a day. Only 2,300 of them got through our defences into the London region. On August 28th 97 out of 101 bombs launched were shot down, 4 only got through to London. When I was at Chafford yesterday I saw hundreds of balloons. When it was found the bombs came in consistently low, the balloons were thickened up to nearly 2,000 and extra cables were suspended. Although these balloons were the last line of defence they brought down nearly 15 per cent of the total destroyed. A great gun belt was built up stretching from Maidstone to East Grinstead. In the middle of July the entire AA belt was moved to the coast so that the guns could get an uninterrupted field of view. Though 600 heavy and 500 Bofors guns had to be moved and re-sited, they were out of action for only 2 days. The plan worked well.

September 9th Saturday

General Eisenhower last night ordered complete black-out on news of Allied thrusts against the Siegfried Line.

September 10th Sunday 265th week

All along the banks of the Albert and Ghent canals a big battle is on. Germans are defending the water lines that bar the path to their homeland.... It is remarkable that supplies have been kept up in the way they have since D-Day, for Cherbourg is the only port we have in full operation as yet.... Despite warnings to stay put, thousands of returning evacuees crammed London stations yesterday, Paddington being the worst with holiday makers as well.... Brighton beach will not be open to the public this year, many mines have to be exploded.

September 11th Monday
British and Canadian troops in Belgium have been warned that Nazis put grenades into bouquets of flowers thrown when towns are liberated. Men are busy in the village as well as in London repairing street lamps and posts ready for peace and lighted streets again. We have no more flying bombs this way now and I think none in London. It is a relief.

September 12th Tuesday
Allied troops are now fighting on German soil.... Patton's army driving through Lorraine captured many miles of the Maginot Line along the Luxemburg frontier.... Russians and our troops enter Germany at the same time.... The Belgian Government is to begin immediately to find out the loss of art treasures during German occupation and will report to the Allied organisation in London. Fire guard duties during daylight cease throughout the country from today. Fire watching during black-out hours also is suspended in a large part of Britain. In London they will remain for a while.

September 13th Wednesday
Eisenhower has warned civilians in the Ruhr and Rhineland that bombing will come. A list of special targets was given with the advice to leave them and take refuge in the countryside as far away as possible.... Evacuees are still coming back every day to London, in spite of warnings that the danger is not yet over. As the Government does not issue warnings lightly it seems foolish of them not to wait away a little longer. Unfair to CD too.

September 14th Thursday
Last night Americans were in contact with the Siegfried Line and many more are advancing to it. General Hodge's men have captured Roetgen, a Siegfried Line town 3½ miles inside Germany and 10 miles south east of Aachen, the first German town to fall to the Allies. Berlin reports that British patrols are 19 miles into Holland towards Eindhoven. Germans have withdrawn from the Albert Canal to the Escaut Canal.... Soviet troops are driving for East Prussia.... Every day trains are crossing the Channel from England on their way direct to the armies. At a southern point they are run straight off the lines into the big between-decks

space of the LSTs (Landing Ship, Tanks) which have been specially built for the job. On arrival at Cherbourg they go straight from the ship on to the French railway lines, are loaded with supplies and ammunition and sent off to the battle areas.

September 15th Friday

Yesterday US troops pushed between 7 and 8 miles into Germany, on a nine-mile wide front.... Four penetrations of the frontier have now been made and fighting is very bitter. It is reported that the further our army goes into Germany, fear or anger on the part of the German population lessens and thus far there has been no civilian resistance. Some said they had expected to be shot. The first Allied broadcasts direct from Germany were made yesterday speaking from where Hitler told his people no enemy would ever set foot.... Russians captured Praga, suburb of Warsaw, in a new blow for that city. This means Russians are just across the Vishla from the battling Poles in the old town of Warsaw.

September 16th Saturday

Evacuees are again advised to stay put until the all-clear is given. 1,025 PoW arrived yesterday at Liverpool.... Sirens and cheering was so great that music of the bands was drowned.... A fleet of ambulances took sick men to special trains on to hospital in Cheshire and Shropshire.

September 17th Sunday

Double summer time that began in April ended at 3 o'clock this morning. A new dim-out starts tonight, but most sensible people will take no notice and continue the black-out of the last five years for a little longer. The Allies are right through the Siegfried Line.... Nazis are doing their best and fighting their hardest but nothing stops our advance.... People are still streaming back to London, but flying bombs were there again and in southern England, the first since August 31st.... Today is Battle of Britain Sunday and there is to be a gathering of CD and others on Muster Green. Mr Merry called for 12 United Nations Flags for the occasion. I usually go, but today prefer to go to our own church. The Quebec talk between Churchill and Roosevelt is ended and decisions arrived at, the chief one that Japan be destroyed so soon as Europe is wrestled from Germany. Large forces in the Battle of Europe will help. There will be no over-all command in the Pacific because of the vast geographic considerations. The date cannot be fixed because the conference was not willing to set a date for Germany's surrender. The Premier's movements after today will be blacked out until his return home. It seems the Battle of Japan will be massive. Dover has had a bad time all the week and the shelling from across the Straits continues.

September 18th Monday
Montgomery spoke in a broadcast to his troops last night and said 'The Allies have removed the enemy from practically the whole of France and Belgium and we stand at the door of Germany'. He ended 'The triumphant cry now is: Forward into Germany. Good Luck to you all and good hunting in Germany'.... Russians have begun a frontal attack on Warsaw.... Meetings have been arranged by the trade officials of Chile, Peru, Columbia, Venezuela and Brazil to discuss commerce with Britain and other European countries after the war. Argentina was not invited.

September 19th Tuesday
There are believed to be 7,000 Germans in western Holland but their position is precarious.... On the Baltic Front about 750,000 men are now in action.... The Front is over 200 miles.... There was a terrible scene in Rome yesterday when a howling mob lynched Doushella Caretta, formerly Director of Regina Coeli Prison.

September 20th Wednesday
Good news comes from all the Fronts. Risings are reported in Denmark, full revolt in Copenhagen.... Russians have made a big breakthrough south of Riga and captured 2,000 places. Never before have they taken so many on one sector.... Mr Parsons brought an official leaflet this evening saying on Thursday the 21st there will be complete relaxation of fire guard duties. Wardens will bear responsibility for summoning the Fire Service.... A few days ago I was given another chevron for the end of the 5th year of the war.

September 21st Thursday
It is good news that soldiers, sailors and air-men are to have more pay, an overdue reform. The principle is length of service. Several flying bombs crashed in southern England last night for the second night in succession and an alert was sounded in London.... As well as the Fire Guard relax beginning today, big reductions in Civil Defence are to be made excepting in London, the south, south east and eastern regions.

September 22nd Friday
The Jap Government has obtained from Germany specifications for production of fly-bombs and rocket shells.

September 23rd Saturday
Billeting is becoming difficult in Croydon so heavily blitzed. 50,000 houses damaged (3 out of every 4) and although 3,800 men are employed on repairs they

will not be ready for 6 months. Many are living in garden shelters and empty shops and compulsory billeting may be necessary. Greek patriots are advancing on Athens.... Radio Luxemburg, Europe's most powerful station, has been liberated and came on the air last night.

September 24th Sunday 267th week
Yesterday afternoon children, chiefly from Trevelyan School, got up some plays and gave them in the Village Hall for the Prisoners of War Fund. Friends paid all expenses. The military lent them the use of the Hall and arranged their lighting. Many dances all this year have been given for the same object and the Red Cross has done much for PoWs. At Church this morning just before leaving, the congregation sang, kneeling, hymn no.595 'For absent friends'. It was sung on account of the extra heavy fighting in Holland, especially at Arnhem.... Germans admit the Battle of Arnhem is the key battle of the war.... Cap Gris Nez has fallen. Patrols found all the Germans had gone to the cinema. When asked if they would surrender, they said they were willing but would rather wait until the pictures were finished. There could not have been many Germans there (if the story is true) for no cinema is large.... More news comes from the Eastern Front... and the net around trapped Germans has been drawn tighter.... Through Folkestone's Town Clerk a message has been sent asking people not to go there on holiday yet awhile. They have no accommodation for visitors and won't have much until next spring. For four years Folkestone has had everything in the way of long-range shells, fly-bombs and hit-and-run raiders. Dover was again shelled yesterday, fired by Germans still holding out at Calais, the first for 76 hours.

September 25th Monday
The last fortnight or so many people as well as myself have heard distant explosions. Apparently a bomb is dropped, giving no warning, making no noise until it reaches the ground. The Government has said nothing about them nor damage done. There was one this morning at 6.40. One wonders if it is the secret weapon V2 Germans have threatened so long about. There is brighter news this morning about our trapped Arnhem men, the line that stretched 100 miles across Holland. British infantry have burst across the Lek, northern branch of the Rhine and all through Saturday night ferried food and supplies to those heroic troops on the further bank.... Life insurance companies in Germany are to ban all 'suicide indemnities' because of the increase in self-destruction.

September 26th Tuesday
Much of today's paper is taken up with charts and so forth of the Government's scheme 'to give security to all': benefits, pensions and so on.

September 27th Wednesday
Two Belgian Girl Guide sisters helped the Allies to liberate their town of Roulers, near Passchendaele, by finding out and telling the Polish Commander what German Regiments were stationed there and where the artillery was. Roulers was taken almost without bloodshed.

September 28th Thursday
M. Bidault, new Foreign Minister of the French Provisional Government, is to meet Mr Eden to press for French participation in the occupation of Germany on equal terms with the Big Three.

September 29th Friday
The Battle of Holland is flaring up and hard fighting has broken out in all the main sectors.... Although a short time ago when many people returned to London and the black-out was only 'partly dimmed' and fire guards dispensed with, many thought the war was all but over and would surely be over before Christmas. No soldier thinks that, the war seems far from over. Soldiers are annoyed with the BBC for their glowing but false reports. The affair at Arnhem bears out the feelings of the soldiers.... Mr Churchill made a long speech in the House yesterday on the war generally and said no one could guarantee that several months of 1945 may not be required to end the war with Germany. For future organization of the world for preventing war the Premier said there must be a further meeting of the Big Three, perhaps before the end of this year.

September 30th Saturday
Lord Haw-Haw began his broadcast last night. It was to be a comment on Mr Churchill's speech and was mysteriously stopped without explanation. There has been a good deal of talk about the asylums war criminals will seek when a defeat drives them from their own countries. Argentina was named for Hitler and his lot but now the Argentine Government announces they will not be allowed entry into that country, nor yet any war criminals. Rather unexpected decision for Argentina has not been friendly to Britain lately.... The Premier calls attention to the great achievements of Burma. The Allies have fought and won the biggest land battle against the Japs of this war. They have defeated utterly the Jap project for the invasion of India.

October 1st Sunday 268th week
There are great rejoicings in Dover now the guns across the Channel are silenced. The people had their first secure sleep at home for 4 years. Those battered homes are hiding scars with flags and bunting. Dover, Deal and Folkestone folk cheered and danced in the streets, thronged the cliffs and gave thanks in their churches. The Mayors went round in loud speaker vans.

October 6th Friday
American 1st Army tanks that reached Cologne Plain, north of Aachen yesterday were fighting against Panzers, the first tank battle on German soil…. The German garrison in the Channel Islands have again rejected an invitation to surrender. In the House yesterday the Premier spoke of the Polish Home Army and the civilian population of Warsaw. This nation that first stood up to the common enemy is the last to be freed. And Poland has suffered the most. Neither is the ordeal of Greece over yet, although the British have landed there and her liberation has begun.

October 7th Saturday
Last evening in the Library we had our second meeting (the first was the Friday before) about forming a discussion society and the Library was full. Soon after the meeting had begun at 8 o'clock the siren sounded, all-clear less than 10 minutes later.

October 9th Monday
Railways have withdrawn from exhibition the war-time poster 'Is your journey really necessary?' Probably more trains and buses will be provided.

October 10th Tuesday
The Premier and Mr Eden have arrived in Moscow for talks with Stalin and Molotov…. This conference coincides with the publication of the Dunbarton Oaks proposals for world security, reports on which are given today. Among the subjects to be discussed in Russia is this Security, also Polish problems, The Quebec Conference and Control of Germany. Britain, US, USSR, China and eventually France will have the prime responsibility for keeping world peace according to the Dunbarton Oaks Plan, a far bigger thing than the League of Nations…. From today towns and stations will be allowed to show their place names in letters visible from the air.

October 11th Wednesday
In today's *Mid Sussex Times* a map is given showing where fly-bombs came down in East Sussex. But it does not give nearly all of them as one can check in this district. Himmler has given a new order to all German Army officers 'Be brutal, but stop the retreat'. He has told them 'Send the most brutal officers of the Division to halt all those who stream back. As soon as you have herded them together, shoot everybody who dares to open his mouth'. Himmler's slogan is 'Hate all thought of moving back. Catch every idle dog, bind him if necessary, and throw him on to a luggage truck'. His speech was made at Metz to German Officer cadets. In it he admitted ill-feeling between the German Army and Gestapo. His speech

will surely not make better feeling.... Home Guards are to be allowed to keep their uniform boots and great coats, but are to give up weapons and ammunition.

October 12th Thursday
Stalin and Molotov with the Premier and Eden were guests of honour at the dinner given in the British Embassy in Moscow last night. It is the first time Stalin has dined at a foreign Embassy.... An offer from the Jap Government through the International Red Cross to allow PoW and internal civilians to send 10-word cables home has been accepted. Details of a scheme to allow next of kin to send similar cables in return have still to be worked out.

October 15th Sunday 270th week
Our soldiers occupied Athens yesterday and its Port Piraeus. This morning I hung out the flag of Greece alongside our Jack.... Greeks in London celebrated the good news of Athens. Last night, just before 12, a big force of bombers went out and kept on until nearly 1am. I think I have never heard so many before. They went out after a day of the greatest air assaults of the war, when more than 1,000 RAF bombers dropped 4,500 tons of high explosives and incendiaries on Duisberg in daylight.... Tonight for the first time since the war three lamps were lighted in the village, one on each side of the Pond and one by the fountain.

October 16th Monday
The first British PoWs from Jap internment camps are coming home. They are not repatriates, but have been 'recovered' from the Japs, whatever that may mean. They are coming via the US and each man may send a personal message home.... The whole 3 miles of Hastings beach was opened yesterday.

October 17th Tuesday
The British and Australian prisoners 'recovered' from the Japs were saved when a Jap transport was torpedoed in the Pacific last month. Altogether 144 were saved, but it is feared a number were killed when the ship was hit.

October 18th Wednesday
More fly-bombs came over last night, the 7th in succession. Two were blown up in the air, and others brought down at sea, but some got through our defences. Sir James Grigg, War Minister, states there are 95,000 German prisoners in this country, 17,000 are employed. 400 are doing forestry work.

October 19th Thursday
Himmler has created a Home Guard, Volkssturm, and speaking to them yesterday said the war could not last long and their only hope was a quick death. He sees no

way out, no chance for a German victory only 'To hold the enemy back from the German frontier until peace comes'. All men between 16 and 60 are called up.... Three French wine merchants brought 16,000 bottles of French wine to a British port in a French trawler with the idea of selling it to provide arms for the FFI. They are now in London to negotiate with the authorities. From today papers may publish weather news when it is 48 hours old. Since war began it has been able only to publish it after ten days.

October 20th Friday
General MacArthur has kept his promise to the Japs to return to the Phillippines which he was forced to leave in March 1942, and has returned fighting.... Washington says it will take some time to receive official news. The battle of Formosa is still going on and a Jap military spokesman said last night 'The battle for Formosa has no equal in the history of naval warfare, both in size and violence'.

October 21st Saturday
Two big victories are announced by Stalin, the liberation of Belgrade and the capture of Die Grenzen, Hungarian town 115 miles east of Budapest. Yesterday was a day of heavy rain and if it had not been so threatening today I would have hung out the Yugoslavia flag. Also the Red Army has driven deeper into East Prussia... but Moscow still keeps quiet about Prussia.... Oranges for all are on sale just now, 1lb for each ration book cost 7½ per lb. They come from South Africa and are good and sweet. According to Lord Woolton, Minister of Works and Sir A. Eve, Rehousing Chief, the repairs are going on rapidly. 40 million tiles, 20 million slates and 40 million square yards of plaster board have been brought to London. 800,000 houses are in need of immediate repair and 117,000 have been made habitable.

October 22nd Sunday 271st week
It is reported Himmler has been murdered in Budapest, shot while driving in his car through the street. Successes and advances come from all fronts. In Holland, British and Canadians have joined 2 miles from the Dutch-Belgian border. In Italy the 5th Army is driving to split Kesselring's Lombardy Army. In the Phillippines 100,000 Americans are entering Leyte Island and Japs are falling back on all sectors. General MacArthur says their position is hopeless.... The largest ocean supply convoy from North America has arrived safely at our ports, 167 ships delivering over a million tons of cargo, all sorts.

October 23rd Monday
Most of the Allied Line is in battle today.... Russians, still silent, are getting further into East Prussia and approaching Norway.... Whole-time CD services

are to be cut by half in London. Fire guards must continue night duty, but day fire watching is not necessary. Descriptions and illustrations are given today of the great prefabricated port made in Britain, towed in sections across the Channel, and set down off the Normandy coast at Arromanches. So a synthetic port as large as Gibraltar was created in less than a month, constructed at sites as far apart as Thames area, Southampton, Portsmouth, Birkenhead, Leith, Glasgow and North Wales. Blockships sailed on D-Day were sunk to make an arc-shaped breakwater around each beach. Caissons, like concrete Noah's Arks, were towed across. 146 of them were sunk to form breakwaters. Last night more lamps were lighted in the village. It seems foolish to have them when we are not sure that we shall have no more bombs and raids.

October 24th Tuesday

Germans are fiercely defending Antwerp.... Britain, US and Russia have recognized General de Gaulle as provisional Head of France.... He will have a gigantic task in reviving the old glories of the Republic.... Swedish frontier police are preventing Norwegian quislings from coming in to their country. A Belgian collaborator worked hand in glove with the Gestapo and his house was frequented by German officers, quislings and Gestapo. When Allied forces entered the town, the house was surrounded and officers who went in to arrest 'André' (but this was not his name) were greeted calmly. 'But gentlemen', he said 'come into my cellar'. Suspiciously they went. In the cellar, well looked after in a flat of their own, were refugee British airmen. It was the airmen who told the story. André was a collaborator and Gestapo agent by day and the leader of the town's Resistance movement by night.

October 28th Saturday

Goebbels spoke to the German nation last night saying 'We have every chance of winning the war'. They would go on fighting until an acceptable peace is obtained. An account comes from the 2nd Army that 67 women in the Dutch town of Vught were packed by Nazis into a cell 12ftx7ftx8ft high with only an open grill near the ceiling and were left for 13 hours.... When dragged out at 6 the next morning 12 were dead, 3 mad, 7 died later and 30 were taken to hospital. All for a reprisal against women who had attacked another woman in a concentration camp when they learnt she was put there as a spy.... British girls are marrying Canadian soldiers at the rate of 18 a day. There have been more than 23,000 such marriages and so far 2,298 wives and 1,328 children have been sent to the Dominion. Since early 1942 the Canadian Government had given free passage to Canada for all the wives and children who wanted to go there.... Yesterday the Premier gave a review in the Commons of his recent conferences with Stalin. Relations were friendly. Poland was the burning question, not yet reaching solution.

October 29th Sunday 272nd week
Many RAF and Navy men as well as artillery soldiers are being drafted into the infantry and are training at Paxhill.

October 30th Monday
General MacArthur reports all resistance in Leyte Valley has ceased and Americans are in control of two-thirds of the island. 1,500,000 Fillipinos on Leyte and Samar are liberated. Details are given of Allied armistice terms to Bulgaria. When she joined the Axis, stretches of Greece and Yugoslavia were given as a reward. Now Bulgaria has to return that land and is to send food to Greeks and Yugoslavs. She is to disarm, hand over all German troops in the country, her merchant ships are to sail for the Allies and her factories used for the Allied war effort.

November 3rd Friday
All Belgium is now freed.... Another Lindfield boy, Cyril Boston, Second Armoured Battalion Irish Guards, has been killed in action. He was a Lindfield Home Guard before joining the Guards. At our Discussion Group this evening, the 3rd meeting, Colonel Stevenson Clarke, our member, spoke on the subject of what the soldiers wanted after the war, what they wanted to come home to.

November 4th Saturday
Annihilation of Dusseldorf, administrative headquarters of the Ruhr, has started. The battle began with the raid on Thursday night (after we heard that big force going out).... Russia has received 4,000,000 tons of stores through Persia, one of the greatest supply jobs of the war. Persians and Iraqis helped with motor drivers etc.

November 5th Sunday 273rd week
London had an alert last night (the first for 10 days).

November 6th Monday
Singapore was bombed yesterday for the first time since it fell to the Japs on February 15th 1942.

November 7th Tuesday
Lancasters, we saw many going out at 6pm, gave a swift 10 minute 'saturation' attack on Koblenz last night.... The milk ration is cut to 2 pints per week each person. Canadian firemen who came over to help in London's battle against raiders are now going home again. A farewell parade was held at Canada House.

November 8th Wednesday
Between now and April enough oranges will be in the country for everyone to have 4lbs, but if you can find them. There are to be four distributions of 1lb each for everyone. Also we are promised shell eggs for Christmas. It is a long time since we had one.

November 9th Thursday
A U-boat a day was lost in the 3 months between May and August, the turning point in the war against U-boats. When their story is told no doubt we shall know what we owe to the pilots and crews of Coastal Command.

November 11th Saturday
We had the usual 11 o'clock memorial service outside the War Memorial today.... During the silence the only sound was rain pattering on our umbrellas.... A new scheme is being made in 5-inch gramophone discs bringing personal messages from soldiers to their homes. Small recording units are being sent out, and the discs, which can be played on any gramophone will take 175 words, weigh half an oz and will be flown back to Britain and sent to the people indicated. Army Welfare and ENSA work the scheme.

November 12th Sunday 274th week
France had a great day yesterday and kept Remembrance Day for the first time for 5 years.... A million Frenchmen gave Mr Churchill the greatest welcome of his life. He drove with General de Gaulle to the Arc de Triomphe and beneath it they laid wreaths on the Unknown Warrior's grave. Then they walked half a mile down delirious Champs Elysées to a saluting stand to see a mighty Allied military parade, 8,000, led by kilted pipers. One can understand the French going mad with joy, this day they have waited for so long. Then the Premier and de Gaulle went to Clemenceau's statue and laid a chrysanthemum wreath on it and another on the tomb of Marshal Foch, where he met his blind widow.... Drainpipe anti-tank guns, pikes made of kitchen knives and broomsticks, 'coshies' and other improvised Home Guard weapons of 1940 are being collected for the Imperial War Museum.

November 13th Monday
A special warning from Moscow was given last night 'The war has entered its last phase. Allied armies today stand poised for the greatest assault ever to be made against Germany'. It came after a forecast by our Premier that 'it is possible that six months hence the enemy will have been beaten'.... Hitler yesterday broke his silence by having Himmler (apparently not shot dead) read a proclamation.

November 14th Tuesday
All goes well in Burma.... The mystery of Hitler, his health and his whereabouts continues. One significant thing is the making of a new German stamp bearing the image of Himmler instead of Hitler, proof that Himmler is to reign in Hitler's stead. Reports on Hitler himself are contradictory. The first civil air route plane out of London since war began left Croydon yesterday for Liverpool. I heard today that Pat Bannatyne of White Gates has been killed in France, the only son, 23.

November 15th Wednesday
A triumvirate of Himmler, Goebbels and Ribbentrop is to rule Germany, Himmler predominating.... The siren sounded last night at 12.15, all-clear 12.29. It was a cold dark night and neither Mr Parsons nor I heard plane or bomb fall. But the paper this morning reports a number of fly-bombs were blown up in mid-air by coastal defences.... In today's *Mid Sussex Times* a short account is given of our local hero Frank Carey (Fuzzy) who is (or was recently) in India. While in a jeep he saw a leopard in the distance, stalked it and shot it, bringing his trophy back on the bonnet of the jeep. Frank fought in the Battle of Britain, shot down 28 German aircraft and probably destroyed a further 15.

November 16th Thursday
Russians have got into the southern outskirts of Budapest.... De Gaulle has accepted Stalin's invitation to visit Moscow and as de Gaulle may take part in the next Churchill-Stalin-Roosevelt talks it seems France is coming into her own again.... The Channel Islanders, over 7,000, of Jersey and Guernsey are getting terribly short of food. Details of the islands' condition are given by 4 men who recently escaped from Jersey to France and then flew to Britain. Food stocks can tide them over until the end of November. Since D-Day the food ration has been: 4lb of bread, 5lb of potatoes a week and 2oz of meat a fortnight; 2oz of butter and 3oz of sugar a week. There is no tea, but Germans issue a 4oz packet of ersatz coffee made from acorns which has to last 6 weeks. Water supply is poor, vegetables are cooked in sea water. There is no coal.

November 17th Friday
Advances are reported from all Fronts.

November 18th Saturday
Again there is all good news from all the fighting Fronts. Our troops are moving forward under 'Monty's Moonlight', their name for the artificial daylight now being used.... We read there will be turkeys for Christmas, but they will be dear.... In the House yesterday, Sir James Grigg, Secretary for War, told of Jap treatment

of British PoWs in the southern parts of the Far East. The death rate was 1 in 5. The stories are horrifying. The reports come from Allied survivors of a sunken Jap transport, prisoners who were rescued by US Naval forces.... Ice-cream is back again. It was served in London restaurants yesterday and Thursday, for the first time since its ban on October 1st 1942. But there will be no 'Stop-me-and-buy-one' for some time yet. The Premier gave a stern warning to Palestine Jews that unless they do their best to bring the present terrorism to an end, they will lose the friendship of himself and others who have supported their cause.

November 19th Sunday 275th week
Guesses about Hitler continue and more 'explanations' are rumoured. A nervous breakdown is the most probable, and perhaps preparing for his getaway.

November 20th Monday
On December 2nd the Home Guard in great numbers will arrive in London and the next day will have a great march from Hyde Park and the Army will give them 'Hotel Service'. They are going to be well looked after and catered for.

November 21st Tuesday
Germans began evacuating St Louis yesterday and when people left their houses to demonstrate their joy in the streets the Germans fired at the crowd. Crown Prince Olaf, speaking as Commander-in-Chief of the Norwegian Army, said in the north, as the result of a German forced evacuation, terrible conditions and privations are endured. Germans are burning and destroying everything and taking the population with them.... He was concerned about the reindeer flocks which are difficult to breed.... Australia, principally Melbourne, is sending 63,000 toys in 245 cases to reach here on New Year's Eve. Industrial trouble prevented the toys arriving for Christmas.... As I write now I hear another big air force going seawards. Lights are showing on most of the planes.

November 23rd Thursday
Advances are reported from the whole line in Germany.... Our street lamps are blacked all round the glass, but they give a light on the street which is better than complete darkness.

November 24th Friday
A few mornings ago at 5.25 there was a bang and shaking of windows which I thought was a V2 down. But today it was known it was a munitions ship that blew up outside Newhaven, doing much damage to all property there. Apart from the men on board, no casualties are yet given.... The Premier spoke at the Albert Hall last night at an American Thanksgiving Day and said there was a greater

Thanksgiving Day ahead.... The US Ambassador at a Thanksgiving lunch yesterday told the story of a boy evacuated from London during the fly-bomb time to the peaceful countryside. After praying one night for his father who was fighting and his mother still in the blitz port he added 'And you take care of yourself God, for if anything happens to you, we are sunk'.... This evening there was an ARP meeting at the Post and all wardens in our sector were there. HQ is reducing the number of wardens in each sector, and two of our number of seven were down for withdrawal. Mrs Parsons and Jack Ward decided to leave, so now we number five wardens.

November 25th Saturday
Spectacular news this morning is from the 7th US Army Front, for Swiss radio says American and French shock troops have crossed the Rhine east of Strasbourg.... On the Eighth Army Front a big battle is in progress, and the well German defended Cosina river bridgeheads battle has been won by our men.

November 27th Monday
Germany says northern Norway has been evacuated because the Red Army 'which is so brutal to foreign people' has appeared there.

November 28th Tuesday
The terrific bombing of Germany nearly takes one's breath away. Our bombers, especially Lancasters, have made 60 hours of non-stop attacks.... Mosquitoes bombed Berlin last night.... The secret has just been told of how Allied bombers 'see' through miles of cloud, smoke or darkness to attack their targets. The instrument is one of the finest technical achievements of the war and British scientists are responsible for it.... Hundreds of RAF crews have been saved by it. It is hoped relief will come to the Channel Islanders. The German garrison lost touch with the mainland when the last supply port St Malo fell to Americans this August. Two British relief ships are waiting in Lisbon for the end of arrangements between Germany and Britain before setting forth. Their cargoes are Red Cross parcels, clothes, food and so forth.

November 29th Wednesday
In a small bleak house near Holland, Eisenhower and Montgomery are designing the final plans to crush Germany.... The Government's White Paper on the UK war effort has been an eye-opener to us, as well as to Americans and others. It gives in detail an account of the achievements of a nation mobilized for war in every sense. Our contribution to the war far exceeds that of any other country. In the newspapers are full pages of statistics. The comparison of output from 1940 onwards is interesting. 4,500,000 men are in the armed forces and 7,000,000

women mobilized. Yesterday's and Sunday's papers gave particulars of our help and lease-lend to America which many thought was only the other way. More than one and a quarter million food parcels and a ton of medical supplies are to be sent to the Channel Islands for civilians by the International Red Cross.

November 30th Thursday
In the House last night Mr Churchill, who is 70 today, warned the nation against 'any indulgence in the feeling that the war might soon be over'. He suggested it might last until the summer.... Captain Maurice Gill made an Atlantic speed record last Tuesday. In a Mosquito he left Goose Bay, Labrador at 10am and landed in Britain at 4.08pm, 2,188 miles in 6 hours 8 minutes.

December 1st Friday
Nazi women are fighting with troops opposing the US 3rd Army.... German maps giving routes to cities and towns if they invaded us have been captured by the British in Brussels, their blue-print of the invasion which they thought so sure. Everything was detailed, its thoroughness a characteristic of the maps. It is expected that 1,000 temporary 'demountable' houses will arrive in this country from the US each month until our needs are met. This new lend-lease agreement is that the houses are for war workers.

December 2nd Saturday
Keitel has ordered all German soldiers retreating without arms to be shot.

December 3rd Sunday 277th week
Today, a damp sunless Sunday, is the 'Stand Down' of the Home Guard. Our Lindfield section is going to East Grinstead, their HQ. In London 7,000 are taking part and representatives from all over the country and from Ulster have arrived. Many are staying at Wellington Barracks where their welcome surprised them. Sergeants and other COs were their 'nippies' at meals and much sightseeing has been enjoyed. The King sent a message thanking them for 4 years service. The Guards' share in defence was indeed an important one. This afternoon at 3.30 all the wardens of our contingent assembled in and outside the Village Hall for Marchant to take our photograph.[35] It was dull weather, the taking was outside. All we women wardens were seated on chairs along the front, those men in the back row stood on forms.... Japs are using themselves as human bombs with no hope of survival. With explosions tied round their bodies... they fling themselves against installations blowing up both themselves and their objectives.... 37,000 turkeys from Iceland reached London yesterday. One household in 10 will be able to have a turkey for Christmas. The ration of milk, 2 pints a week, is not likely to be cut. Fortunately.

December 4th Monday
De Gaulle is visiting Stalin in Moscow, hoping 'to heighten and clarify French-Soviet friendship'.... Soldiers from Burma are on their way home for leave, a month.... There is much in the papers today of the Home Guard march in London yesterday.

December 5th Tuesday
Belgian children are sending thousands of toys to our children this Christmas. One wonders how and where they get material from.

December 7th Thursday
Yesterday the Queen spoke to a gathering of women workers of all Services assembled in the County Hall, Westminster. She told them the war could not have been won without their help.

December 8th Friday
Australia has decided to admit 17,000 children into the country every year until further notice and is sending a mission to Britain to pick the first quota. Children are to be between 6 and 14 if British or 6 and 12 if of other European countries. Complete black-out during alerts will end after tonight. Nor need public service vehicles reduce inside lighting during alerts.

December 9th Saturday
Mr Wright told me last evening that a rocket bomb, V2, fell just behind Selfridges, destroying a hotel and killing 9 people.... Every day one or more of the rockets fall on the city or nearby. In today's papers an illustration is given of the mechanism of a V2.... Hat makers are set to produce 6 million utility women's hats for which prices will be controlled.

December 10th Sunday 278th week
From tomorrow (for Christmas only) we are to have extra fat and sugar and children (under 18) more sweets.

December 11th Monday
A treaty of alliance between France and Russia was signed in Moscow yesterday. Stalin and de Gaulle agree that Germany must be disarmed. No details of the pact are yet received. It will fall into place as part of the whole Allied Security system in Western Europe.

December 12th Tuesday
Budapest is burning furiously and Russians closing in.... Moscow says the

fighting is ferocious.... The whole Burma Front is now in action.... Those people evacuated from 'Hell-fire Corner' when invasion seemed likely are invited to return at Government expense. Deal, Dover, Folkestone, Margate, Ramsgate and Sandwich are the chief places.

December 13th Wednesday
This week a Swedish ship is to leave Lisbon for Jersey and Guernsey with food supply for the Islanders. The German Government has granted safe conduct. Germans on the Islands will have some of the supplies. Red Cross messages, held up since D-Day, will be delivered and two Swiss Red Cross representatives will be on the ship.

December 14th Thursday
A Red Cross mercy ship will soon leave Lisbon for occupied Holland with food and medicine supplies.... The Ranger Movement, older section of Girl Guides, is to train girls for jobs as civil airways pilots and ground staff. Girls between 16 and 21 are being enrolled throughout the country and will be known as Flying Rangers.

December 17th Sunday 279th week
The thousands of toys given by Belgian children to our children will start being given on Tuesday next.... All toys here are dear, so also are books for children.... Two Alsatian dogs, Jet and Thorn, have traced 25 buried people in the London area. They come from the Ministry of Air Production Dog School and have been lent by their owners for war work. The Franco–Soviet treaty agrees to a 20 year assistance pact designed to prevent any German aggression. If either is attacked by the Reich they go to each other's assistance. The Treaty, in eight articles, also allows France to take part in the military occupation of Germany in agreement with Britain and the US.... In the afternoon Mr Parsons brought for me to read and pass on a copy of the Queen's speech made on the 6th December to all women workers of the Civil Defence. It was a speech appreciating all we have so willingly done.

December 19th Tuesday
A French girl Marguerite Demanges and an FFI comrade Henriette Durand risked death for 4 years to help the RAF bomb targets in France and have just come to England bringing with them a red, white and blue silk cross which bears the inscription 'Offered to English mothers in memory of their dear sons fallen for the liberation of France – from the mothers of Viroflay'. They laid the cross on the RAF Memorial on the Embankment. They acted as spies, saboteurs and propagandists for the Allies.

December 20th Wednesday
Stockholm newspapers say another attempt on Hitler's life has been made. A fire broke out at night recently at the castle where Hitler was staying but it is not known whether he was injured. Sir James Grigg (Secretary for War) said that prisoners in Siam forced to build a road and railway between Siam and Burma were withdrawn to rear camps in Siam when the roads were completed in 1943. Here conditions improved. In the camps around Bampong huts were weatherproof, cooking arrangements hygienic, also space for exercise.

December 23rd Saturday
25,000 men are to be called up for a big new army, a large part of which will be from civil life. Still further efforts are needed to ensure victory.... Lights are to be allowed brighter on motors and cycles, but are to be put out on the direction of a police officer.

December 24th Sunday 280th week
News from the west is better this morning and so is the weather, the greatest help to our Army. Yesterday's sunshine and today's make all the difference to their advance. They have advanced several miles to the north of the Luxembourg-Arlon sector.... The first German spies captured in US uniforms were executed yesterday. They were captured by US military police, and were driving a jeep and were armed with American weapons.

December 27th Wednesday
There were no newspapers yesterday or on Christmas Day. The news today is that Germans reached to within 4 miles of the Meuse near Dinant on Christmas Eve. Losses have been high. Washington gives prisoners taken up to the 24th as 13,273. Berlin claims American total losses, killed wounded or prisoner, 30,000. The better weekend weather gave our air forces a chance to launch the greatest assault on the enemy.... The King broadcast a Christmas message on Monday and emphasized his belief in the birth of a new freedom for all mankind.

December 30th Saturday
A generous London banker has given £5,000 to provide houses for disabled RAF and FAA pilots and widows of pilots who have children.

1945

—ᶆᶆ—

January 1st Monday
The news this morning is that General Patton's offensive, which began two days ago, has made some progress.... Yesterday morning Hitler broke his long silence and broadcast to his people saying 'The end of the war will not come before 1946, unless by a German victory, and never by capitulation'.... A very cold ending for the Old Year and the beginning of the New, skating general and on our pond today, 20 degrees last night.

January 2nd Tuesday
Two German agents who landed from a U-boat at Maine, US on November 29th have been captured. They had £12,000 with them, lived in good hotels in Boston and New York, listened to conversations, brought short-wave radio parts and had ink for invisible writing. There are 2 million civilians in burning Budapest living in terrible conditions as Germans fight their last battle against Russians. The normal population is about one million, but as Russians advanced more came in never thinking it would become the last great battlefield in Hungary. Probably the first time a great capital has not been evacuated, but increased by refugees. There is no water, no electricity and very little bread, but their sufferings are ignored by Germans. All hope of preserving the city is gone, it is ravaged by fire. Major Lloyd George, Minister of Fuel and Power, asks the public to be careful in the use of electricity and gas today, particularly between 8 and 10am owing to the heavy strain on them. But it is the breakfast time of most people. Guernsey people hung out flags a few days ago when the first supply ship berthed at St Peter Port, carrying 1,000 tons of food parcels, medical supplies, salt and soap.

January 3rd Wednesday
Admiral Sir Bertram Ramsey was killed in a plane crash in France yesterday while on his way to a conference in Belgium. His planning launched the D-Day invasion. He is the 4th Allied leader to die in an air accident.

January 4th Thursday
A report is just issued on the atrocities committed at Breendonck concentration

camp in Belgium. It reads like another Spanish Inquisition and is too terrible to quote. Nearly all died.

January 7th Sunday 282nd week

Last night President Roosevelt gave a serious warning against the poisonous effects of Nazi propaganda in trying to split the Allied nations and prominence is given to it in all the papers. He said the wedge Germans have attempted in western Europe is less dangerous than the wedges they are continually attempting to drive between us and our Allies. All the baseless remarks bear the trade mark 'Made in Germany'.... Last night was the 11th in succession of Bomber Command raids on Germany. I heard bombers on and off all day, and then read that 1,000 planes crossed over to Germany.

January 8th Monday

Nazi Commissar for the Netherlands told the Dutch in a broadcast last night they must starve, blaming it on Dutch resistance and lack of co-operation. Rations will not even approach the minimum a human being needs.... The War Office paid tribute to the Pioneer Corps last night, the most international unit in our Army. Africans, Indians, Mauritians and Cypriots are among the many nationalities who have been Pioneers since 1939. It is with the Eighth Army that they have done their most valuable work, sometimes in places where even mules failed to find a footing.

January 9th Tuesday

A great tank battle is raging near Budapest.... Troops in Burma are now only 56 miles from Mandalay.... Every day one reads of victims of V bombs, although the places are not named, most are in London and suburbs, and nearly always some are killed.

January 11th Thursday

There was an accident this morning on the Common verge just opposite this house. An army lorry skidded on the slippery snowy road and knocked down a lime tree. Another lorry came to the rescue, but could do nothing so finally a tarpaulin was put over it and left. There have been several snow showers today, winter with a vengeance.... Russian scouts in white overalls walked under the ice of a frozen river to make a raid on Germans. There was a dam across the river and Soviet artillery damaged the dam so that the water under the ice above the dam flowed out, leaving a good space between the ice and the water level. When the men entered the river they held on to each other, water often waist deep. They climbed out on to the ice through one of the holes previously made by Soviet shells.

January 12th Friday
Last evening from about 10 to 11 two big armoured vehicles came to try to get away the skidded lorry off the Common, but did not succeed in moving it. Today at 3pm it is still there, guarded either by policemen or soldiers.

January 13th Saturday
This morning at 8.30 a large carrier attached to a big lorry came to haul on board the armoured vehicle stranded on the Common. They finally got it away at 10.40, leaving behind the broken down tree and ravaged grass, a terrible mess. Allied troops have closed in on Houffalize road junction, key to the whole Ardennes battle. Nearly all opposition has been wiped out west of the St Hubert-Laroche road. The country is more difficult to cope with than Germans: craters, demolitions, road blocks, mines, snow and slush. The Alsace threat grows, see-saw battles there. Russians have begun their long-expected winter 'end-the-war' offensive in southern Poland.... 25 Jap ships were sunk and 13 damaged in a sea and air battle yesterday off the coast of Indo-China. No US ships were damaged.... Japs have begun a full-scale withdrawal from Central Burma and they are leaving Mandalay.

January 15th Monday
Good news comes from all Fronts.

January 16th Tuesday
All Germany is being pounded by a great hour by hour blitz.... Since the 1940–41 blitz here 2,000 pictures from the National Gallery have been stored in caverns in a mountain in this country. Plans had been prepared for their care even before Munich.

January 17th Wednesday
The whole German line in southern Poland has been smashed and 2 vast Russian Armies are coming through the defence wreckage. Marshal Zhukov is the hero and Moscow says the German Army will be destroyed this winter. And Moscow never boasts.... Black market thieves give much trouble still and three more robberies were reported yesterday.

January 18th Thursday
The great news today is the freedom by Russians of Poland and Cracow. One rejoices with Poland and if it had not been such a wet, tempestuous day I would have hung out the Union Jack and the flag of Poland as I have for other freed cities. Better tomorrow perhaps.... It is just 3 months since thousands of Poles lost their lives attempting to free their own capital.... The First Lord of the

Admiralty, Alexander, said yesterday at a lunch to mark the 50th anniversary of the Navy League 'We are sending a fleet to the Pacific whose sinking power will be formidable'.

January 19th Friday
I am flying Poland's white and red flag today in a strong, very cold west wind. Yesterday, Russians with tanks were fighting their first battle inside Germany.... The Premier gave a long speech on the war in the House yesterday and said Germans would be wise to make unconditional surrender now rather than endure what the Allied strength can and will do to Germany in 1945.... Pekinese dog hair combings, sterilised and woven into yarn, are knitted into warm pullovers for sailors. Most in East Sussex are made at WVS headquarters. Pekes' hair makes the warmest, collies and spaniels make a good second.

January 21st Sunday 284th week
Russians go on advancing at an amazing pace.... The coal trouble, especially in London, is acute. There is plenty of coal, but hardly any carters.

January 24th Wednesday
This morning Russians are on the banks of the Oder, last natural defence line before Berlin.

January 28th Sunday 285th week
On the German radio last night Hans Fritsche, correspondent, said 'Now it is our women and children we see fleeing from the War'. Their highways are thronged with a string of refugees. From Poland, Eastern Russia and Silesia they are pouring into Berlin, many sleeping on the icy streets. And Berlin itself is being evacuated. Russians say they will get to Berlin, but that will not end the war as some folks think. Here we are having the coldest winter since 1895.... With electricity and gas frequently cut off house warming is a problem. Even hospitals have to make shift with oil lamps and stoves. There are and will be many burst pipes. Photographic reproductions are given in today's papers of Poland, specially Warsaw now just a ruin. It is described as a modern Pompeii – nothing spared.

January 29th Monday
Preparations are made for the important meeting of the Big Three and Moscow requests that it be held within easy reach of Russia.... Russians are determined to make a clean sweep of the Nazi regime, to deprive Germany of all military power for a long time to come and to make her help repair the damage she has done in Russia.... Owing to lack of fuel and frozen pipes during this bitter weather our Council School is closed. All the radiators in the hall have burst.

January 31st Wednesday
Germans are bringing in their last reserves for the great battle now raging 85 miles from Berlin. The entire Red Army Front from the Baltic to the Danube is on the move.... Last night Hitler celebrated the 12th anniversary of his coming to power with a 15-minute broadcast to the nation, declaring himself the chosen instrument of Providence, and a promise to Germany she will win the war. He appealed to all to make sacrifices. A ghost voice said 'We won't slave for you any longer, you're finished'. When Hitler had recited his achievements the ghost shouted 'You have murdered Germany'.... A message of thanks by Princess Elizabeth to the children of Belgium for the Christmas toys sent to our children was broadcast last night. She spoke in French. More soldiers and lorries are being called up to deliver coal in London.... When Monaco, that tiny principality on the Riviera, was relieved, rich British residents were wearing old clothes held together with safety pins. They still lack food, fuel and clothing, having sold their valuables during the German occupation.

February 3rd Saturday
The International Red Cross says Japan will now allow agents to visit PoW and internee camps in the south.

February 4th Sunday 286th week
Papers say this week is to be a decisive one for the war.... The biggest air raid thus far was made yesterday on Berlin.... The film *Private Life of Henry VIII* has been banned on the French Riviera because it shows too much food and the people are desperately hungry. 'Starvation corner' is the Riviera's new name.

February 5th Monday
I heard yesterday evening that Kenneth Porter is reported missing. He did not come back after that big raid on Friday night. All the same he may be safe. The thaw has hindered advance and the Red Army is slogging through waterlogged rye-fields.... US troops enter Manila, three years and a month after the fall of the city.... The last Germans have been chased out of Belgium for the second time in the war.... The first Burma road convoy to reach China from India for more than 2 years arrived in Kunming at the weekend. The Chinese welcome was tremendous. They let off 'victory salvos' of fire-crackers in true Chinese fashion. The convoy stretched out for 6 miles and took 24 days to complete its 1,040-mile journey.

February 6th Tuesday
Balloon Command ends its separate existence today. Its personnel will be absorbed into other branches of the RAF. Although there were no balloon barrages here,

they were a sight in London and in Kent and their silver floatings in the sky will stay in one's memory.... At Edelsbach was an amazing experience of US precision bombing, the target a ball-bearing factory.[36]

February 8th Thursday
Black marketeers are terrible. Coal trains are diverted to sidings where they get the coal and sell it at anything up to £30 a ton.... Everywhere is corruption.

February 9th Friday
So grave is the bread crisis in Germany, especially in Berlin, that Hitler has ordered peasants to surrender their stocks of grain, even if their cattle die. The reason was 'the grave food and transport situation'. The only food the civilians can get is soup made of millet seeds from street kitchens.

February 10th Saturday
Bert Silen, American radio commentator, was broadcasting an account of a Jap raid on Manila just over 3 years ago, when he suddenly faded off the air. Yesterday he began his first broadcast since his release from a Jap prison with the words 'As I was saying when I was so rudely interrupted'.

February 13th Tuesday
Papers today are full of the conference of the Big Three which is taking place at Livadia Palace, Yalta, a health spa on the south coast of the Crimea. It is known as the Crimean Conference. Defeated Germany is to be divided into 4 Allied occupation zones, her General Staff broken up, military equipment removed or destroyed, and her war industries eliminated.... Although Nazism is to be destroyed it is not the purpose to destroy the people of Germany.

February 14th Wednesday
More planes than ever seemed to pass overhead yesterday evening, taking about 1½ hours.... All countries excepting Germany have welcomed the Crimea Declaration.

February 15th Thursday
Last evening three droves of planes passed over here and in today's paper we read that in the past 36 hours Germany has had the last scourging of the war from the air on her cities, rails, troops and supply lines. 9,000 planes have taken part.... Japs are being cruel in Manila, just a senseless killing spree. Japs chained the door of a building before setting it alight and only 700 of the 2,000 inside are known to be alive.

February 16th Friday
War necessities have made drastic diminution of our forest land and huge quantities of timber have been cut down for use in the war machine, but replanting has been negligible. Today Sir John Anderson announces a scheme for woodlands to be kept up and further land made available for forestation.

February 17th Saturday
Lady Denman, Director of the Women's Land Army for England and Wales, has resigned as a protest against the decision to exclude members of the WLA from Government capital grants to aid in restarting business enterprises, in line with other Services.

February 18th Sunday 288th week
Tokyo bombing grows fiercer.... Both Moscow and Berlin last night forecast that the greatest battle of the war, the final showdown, will start in a few days.

February 20th Tuesday
A plane of ours came down at Rustington on Saturday, killed 5 people and destroyed 4 bungalows just a few yards from the sea. Maybe that was the bang we heard at midday and Horsham was stated in error. There is no mention of a mishap at Horsham.... British, French and US PoWs are on the way to Warsaw and Lublin from German camps over-run by the Red Army and everywhere being helped by Russians and Poles. Some are fighting with Russians.

February 22nd Thursday
The bombing of Germany grows in intensity, night bombers arrive before day bombers have finished work.... Over 11,000 bombers have been used in these attacks. The US Air Force 'finished off' Nuremburg yesterday. They hit the city with 725,000 bombs.... There are to be more hats in the shops because some restrictions have been lifted.

February 23rd Friday
Even Stalin said last night 'complete victory over Germany is near'. Today is the 27th anniversary of the founding of the Red Army.... Part of Brighton beach will be opened in a fortnight, the Marine Parade will be open for traffic tomorrow.

February 24th Saturday
Turkey has declared war on Germany and Japan. She is not likely to fight but wants to be represented at the San Francisco Conference on April 25th for the future of world organization.

February 25th Sunday 289th week
A story is told in today's paper of an Alsatian dog which stopped an escape at a West of England PoW camp. A number of Nazi prisoners had dug for weeks to make a tunnel under barbed wire entanglements into a nearby field. Night after night they worked silently until the tunnel was big enough for them to crawl through. An Alsatian war dog, patrolling outside the barbed wire camp, noticed some loose earth, scratched about, began to dig furiously, dropped into the hole and bounded through the tunnel. He could not get out at the other end, but his barks aroused the guards. Officials were puzzled because no traces of the evacuation work were found. It is supposed the Germans carried the earth in their pockets and scattered it as they returned to their quarters.... General Eisenhower says Germany's strength and morale is lower than ever, but made it clear he had no hope of imminent German collapse, but anticipates a hard fight. 'They are resisting frantically' he said.

March 1st Thursday
Although the security black-out of the US 9th Army is still in force, it was clear from battle front reports last night that the advance goes on in a big way.... Goebbels forecast last night of mass suicides of German people led by their leaders if the war were lost. The people, he said, will be confronted with so much misery and suffering that they must take the obvious course in seeking an honourable death.... He declared Germany would never surrender. Rations are to be further cut. There will be no extra trains for holiday makers this year even if the war does end. Shortage of locomotives, rolling stock and labour are the main reasons.

March 5th Monday
Early yesterday morning, piloted German planes came over to this country, the first time for about nine months and last night more came.... Our windows shook and we heard crashes about 2.30am but we heard nothing last night and we had no alerts either time. Last night the East Anglian coast was crossed, flares and bombs dropped.... The early morning raiders flew high then dived to spray towns, villages, roads and railways from northeast to southern England. Lights were shining from hundreds of windows in one town as high explosive bombs were dropped. Wardens and police shouted to householders to black out, but what is the use of that when the rule was absurdly relaxed as if the war was over and people took down their black-out curtains and replaced them with flimsy muslin or net.... The city of Dresden is completely wiped out, not one house is standing and no remains even are capable of reconstruction.

March 6th Tuesday
G.P.S. Hewitt, a 46-year-old teacher of English in Paris who worked for Germans

as Mr Smith of the Paris radio, was sentenced to 12 years' penal servitude at the Old Bailey yesterday. A light sentence for he sold himself, his country and the country of his adoption to the enemy.

March 8th Thursday
General Patton (Blood and Guts) swam across the 150ft wide icy Sauer River and back again to inspire his men, who were crossing in boats to take Bettendorf. He called them back because they were 'sitting targets' for the enemy. Swimming they would show only the tops of their heads. Thousands of his men then swam to the other side.... Recently dockers have struck and cold storage men have struck in sympathy with them. It affects transport and today I could get only 2lb of potatoes.... The British naval share against Japan is now being built up. In future the strength of the Navy is to be increased. No more risks.

March 10th Saturday
This has been a memorable week, capture of Cologne, and our troops over the Rhine, *and* our wrought iron Lindfield Village sign is put up again on the roadside by the Common.

March 18th Sunday 292nd week
In last Friday's paper an account was given of the new bomb blasting out of existence an island off the British coast. Everything was secret except for the terrific explosion which was talked about for weeks afterwards by people who lived several miles away. When the smooth cloud had rolled away the island had disappeared.[37]

March 20th Tuesday
At midnight came the news that Allied planes had bombed 4,000 vehicles carrying Germans to the Rhine escape bridges.... Men in Stalag Luft III have raised more than £11,000 for the dependents of their 50 comrades who were shot by Germans a year ago after escaping from the camp. Germans would not let certain personal belongings of the shot officers be sent to this country so they were auctioned. Jap suicide troops, under orders 'to die a glorious death' are now fighting their last battle in encircled Mandalay.

March 21st Wednesday
Germans were warned last night that the final battle to end the war is about to burst upon them. Eisenhower told them the Allied armies are advancing east to west across the Rhine and the Oder sweeping across Germany until they meet. This last battle will be one of destruction and certain areas will become danger areas. Inhabitants of 18 named towns were told to go to safety outside the Ruhr.

Montgomery's armies are all up to strength and they are confident, all prepared for R-Day as it is now called, the day when they will swarm across the Rhine. In the meantime terrific bombing continues.... From now onwards two near relatives of soldiers dangerously ill will be able to visit them in W Europe hospitals provided hostels are within reach run by Red Cross and St John.

March 23rd Friday
The mail service to our PoWs in Germany, owing to transport difficulties, is more confused than at any other time in the war. The GPO announced yesterday that next of kin and permit parcel service is suspended.... Tonight the last Fire Guard will go on compulsory 'parade' for the last time. From noon tomorrow, fire guard duties will cease. When Mr Herbert Morrison announced it in the House, he paid a well-deserved tribute to the fire watching service for their constant vigilance. The enemy pockets bypassed after D-Day and still holding out is a remarkable situation and one does not realize that 145,000 Germans are in them as well as 26,000 in the Channel Isles.

March 24th Saturday
The food situation in Holland is very bad, and if relief does not come by June thousands will starve, and unless supplies from Sweden and Switzerland are maintained, cases of typhus, diphtheria and tuberculosis will be worse than they are now.

March 25th Sunday 293rd week
Last night Berlin had its 33rd successive night attack. At the same time in the east, Stalin announced a big new victory SW of Budapest. German cost in killed alone, 70,000 officers and men. Few people will be able to go away for Easter. The few seaside hotels and boarding houses available are booked up and prices up 50 to 200 per cent.

March 26th Monday
Necessary silence is enforced about most of the fighting.

March 27th Tuesday
On Saturday for the first time there were grapefruits in the shops, one for each ration book and another lot of sweet oranges. In April we are promised bananas. About 1,200 toys sent from Australia to children in bombed places are being distributed in East Ham and Wembley.

March 29th Thursday
During Easter recess MPs may be recalled at any moment and consequently are

near at hand.... For Easter, seaside places are packed and although extra food has been sent by the Ministry, bread is usually sold out by 11am. One difficulty is to get staff to cook the food.

March 31st Friday
A security black-out clouds news of our advances.

April 1st Sunday 294th week
Eisenhower told the German Army bluntly last night 'Your Government has ceased to exist'. He told the Wehrmacht how to surrender to save bloodshed now. For the first time German radio faced facts last night and spoke of having to give up.... A great part of the German Army in Holland and NW Germany is flying surrender signs.

April 2nd Monday
Great news came through yesterday as General Eisenhower partially lifted the security black out. Our troops are 100 miles beyond the Rhine and are still going forward.... Paris turned on lights last night for the first time since the war.... 200 Jap civilians committed mass *hara-kiri*...because they had been told they would be tortured if caught alive. When the sole survivor, he had strangled his own daughter, saw the considerate way US troops did treat civilians he wept. The scene was fantastic. US soldiers advancing across the island saw fathers strangling their families and then committing suicide by blowing their heads off with a hand grenade, or hanging themselves from trees. Some of the Americans rushed forward to halt the slaughter, but a Jap machine-gunner mowed the Americans down. After that Japs who wanted to die were allowed to.

April 3rd Tuesday
Seaside places report the best Easter since 1939. For the first time since war broke out a warning of frost was given in SE Scotland and Wales.

April 4th Wednesday
Liberated slave labourers are trekking across Germany and taking revenge on their task-masters. They take what food they need on the journey home, helping themselves to blankets and bedding and if they can find horses and wagons so much the better.... There are thousands let free now, but there will soon be millions for Germany shipped 15,000,000 people from every corner of Europe.

April 6th Friday
More good news came from all sectors of the Western Front last night and

Germans are preparing for a last stand, possibly along the Elbe.... Lighting tests for Victory Day are being practised on Buckingham Palace and other big places are soon to have wiring fixed, National Gallery, the Parks etc.

April 7th Saturday
West End cinemas in London have decided to close on Victory night because of the crowds expected and possibility of danger and damage. Suburban cinemas will use their discretion whether to open or close.

April 10th Tuesday
There is not a unit in all Montgomery's armies which is not reporting advances.... To the memory of Helène Vagliano who gave her life for France there will be erected at Cannes one of the first French memorials of this war. She became the leader of the Maquis at Cannes and worked at the Aid to Prisoners centre in the town. Although flogged and burnt for 18 days she refused to disclose the whereabouts of the resistance leaders. Beaten by clubs, lashed by whips and burnt with red hot irons on face and body, on August 15th she and 20 others were taken to a field and shot. The next day Allied troops arrived, her body was recovered and on October 3rd she was given a public funeral. She has since been accorded the title of 'Heroine of France' and awarded a posthumous Legion of Honour.

April 11th Wednesday
Hanover has fallen.... The race to Berlin is warming up.... A correspondent says no adjective can adequately describe the desolation and destruction of Hanover.... No white flags were flown because people were told they would be shot if they showed them. Instead people threw flowers and presents and shouted in English 'Hello. Good Luck'.

April 13th Friday
We are all saddened today by the news of the sudden death of President Roosevelt.... It is expected organized fighting in Germany will cease in a few days.... The Canadian Government is considering the cases of English brides married to Canadians and deserted since reaching Canada. Although the majority are happily married many are victims of worthless men who gave a big story about their position in Canada.

April 14th Saturday
The 'stand down' for Civil Defence workers is expected next week. Part-time wardens will be released at once, but full timers will be given 2 or 3 months to find other work. Mr Eden is to represent our Government at President Roosevelt's funeral. The House of Commons adjourned yesterday as a mark of esteem. The

Premier feels the world's loss very much, everyone here is sorrowing. Clothes rationing will continue for another two years.

April 15th Sunday 296th week
Our tank spearheads are only 13 miles from Berlin, says Luxemburg radio, but our people are silent on this report. Germans are hitting back in strength before Berlin and Dresden, the 'last ditch' stand has started.... An important announcement giving the date of V–Day is expected soon. It will be given at the same time in London, Washington and Moscow. It will define the date when the Allies will treat Germany as completely defeated, and begin to introduce their civil administration.... Potato rationing may yet be avoided if the public is content to eat about half their usual supply for the next few weeks. Canned carrots are often substituted.

April 16th Monday
Among the 400 Germans captured at Arnhem is one named Walter Sperren who was at German headquarters last September. He said our Airborne Division held out 3 days longer than they, the Germans, thought possible. A General at headquarters called on the phone 'Ain't those English swine wiped out yet?' Our general replied 'Not swine, sir – tigers'.... At Matins yesterday in his sermon Mr Buckingham spoke feelingly of Roosevelt's death.

April 17th Tuesday
The first mutiny on a German warship was confirmed in Stockholm last night.... Eisenhower said yesterday that there will be no announcement of V–Day until all enemy pockets on the Western Front have been wiped out. The war in Europe is not likely to end until Allied troops have occupied Germany completely. 'I do not think there will be a formal German surrender' he said. It was liberation day for PoWs all over the 2nd Army Front yesterday. Great convoys of comforts and foodstuff were going along German roads last night for the 6,500 happy British and American prisoners liberated by the Desert Rats.

April 18th Wednesday
Prisoners say Russians intend at all costs to seize Berlin by April 25th, date of the San Francisco conference. Stalin is silent, but the Red Army is nearer Berlin. In the Ruhr, surrenders go from one end to the other and all roads leading to the American lines were choked with Panzer and Wehrmacht troops yesterday. There were so many, the US troops were clogged and the war in the pocket was brought to a standstill.... 20,000 Allied PoWs were liberated yesterday from camps.... Terrible stories are given of German concentration camps. One is described at Belsen where those of all nationalities were condemned to death by slow

starvation.... A memorial service was held at St Paul's yesterday for President Roosevelt. The King, Queen, Princess Elizabeth and the Premier were there.

April 19th Thursday
At the Village Hall on Tuesday evening a Mr Ottley gave a good lecture, illustrated with slides on D-Day and the Mulberry Ports. Mulberry is a code word and the secret of their making and building at Cherbourg was well kept and the whole affair a surprise to the Germans.

April 20th Friday
Stalin last night broke a 3 day silence on the battle for Berlin, and announced the final drive had opened successfully.... In Holland, Germans have blown the great sea wall and flooded much of the country, creating two big gaps, and the North Sea is over hundreds of square miles of rich country. Scores of towns and villages are in the path of the floods. There was no military reason for the act.... Two Peers and 8 MPs will leave England today to inspect the German prison camp horrors. Their accounts will be published as a White Paper. Eisenhower says atrocities at Weimar surpass anything yet disclosed.

April 21 Saturday
Russians are now only 6 miles from Berlin.

April 23rd Monday
Polish troops with the Canadian 1st Army have captured 5 prison camps where men and women have been living under terrible conditions. More camps lie ahead.... Poles freed 2,000 Polish women who had fought in last year's Warsaw rising.

April 25th Wednesday
The Channel Islands are having fortifications built by forced foreign labour to protect the garrisons, about 30,000 troops. Since the arrival of the weekly food parcels islanders have fared better. Foreign workers are in horrible concentration camps. When they collapse from starvation and die their bodies are thrown in the sea. One camp is at Elizabeth Castle, Jersey; the other at Castle Cornet, Guernsey. The workers are Poles, Russians, and Czechs and are not allowed to talk to islanders.... Sir John Anderson... assures war will be over some time in early summer.

April 26th Thursday
Polish 'Princess Wanda' is to tell her story at the War Office. She fired her Sten gun on German soldiers in Poland and the war made her waitress, factory worker,

1945 261

teacher, seamstress, and a sergeant in the Polish Home Army. Sent to Germany for
forced labour, she jumped from the train.

April 27th Friday
News constantly comes in of mass surrenders by Germans and Fascists.... The
first of the 30,000 timber-framed temporary houses the US is sending for our
bombed places has arrived. Shipments will begin next month of 2-bedroomed
bungalows.

April 28th Saturday
News of advances and captures everywhere are in today's paper.... Dietmar,
German High Command spokesman, told US troops to whom he surrendered at
Magdeburg yesterday that Hitler *is* in Berlin and refuses to leave there. Goering,
he said, had probably been executed already. 'Germany lost the war on July 20th
1944, the day that the plot to assassinate Hiltler did not come off. When Berlin
falls it will be over'. A White Paper is published after the visit to Buchenwald
camp near Weimar. It is terrible reading, an awful truth. The murder camp news
reels will be in cinema programmes on Monday.

April 29th Sunday 298th week
Last night Himmler and the German High Command admitted defeat and offered
terms to Britain and US but not to Russia, a bid to split the Allies. It was rejected.
All agree surrender must be made to *all* the Allies. Hitler is said to be a sick man.
No doubt he is, but there are many reports of him – all different.

April 30th Monday
The Premier will speak in the House tomorrow on the German surrender order.
It is predicted it will not be long before Germany ceases. Their military situation
is hopeless. An announcement of Hitler's death would be no surprise. Mussolini
is dead and those with the 5th Army who entered Milan yesterday saw crowds of
people filing past his bullet-riddled body and those of his henchmen as they lay in
the Piazza Loreto. The feelings of the people as they gazed on the man who ruined
their country were expressed by the woman who drew a pistol and sent 5 more
shots into the body. 'Five shots for my 5 assassinated sons' she screamed.... The
battle for Berlin is drawing to a close, Russians battling for a May Day victory....
On Saturday evening we ended the last of 4 performances of our show 'Victorian
Promenade' produced by Mrs Martin. Proceeds are for the Welcome Home to the
Forces Fund.

May 1st Tuesday
Invitations to Argentina, White Russia and the Ukraine to join the United Nations

Conference were approved in San Francisco yesterday.... 32,000 prisoners were freed from Dachau concentration camp yesterday. Scores of SS guards were taken prisoner and many slain as US troops, enraged by the horrible sights they saw, ranged through the camp. Polish, French and Russian prisoners seized SS weapons and joined their liberators to exact revenge from their tormentors.

May 2nd Wednesday
It is stated in the paper today Hitler is dead, that he was killed in action while fighting at his command post, to the last breath, for Germany. Few believe the statement, it seems too much 'to order'.... The Gestapo are burning documents by the ton.... Borneo held by Japs for 3½ years has been invaded by the Allies.... News that war has ceased in Europe will be announced by the Prime Minister over the wireless and at 9pm on the same day the King will speak to his peoples throughout the world. He wishes the Sunday following VE-Day should be a day of thanksgiving and prayer.

May 3rd Thursday
The war in Italy is over. All German land, sea and air forces there and in W Austria surrendered unconditionally. Berlin has fallen.... Goebbels' right-hand man says both Hitler and Goebbels committed suicide in Berlin.... But even these statements may not be true.... Members of the WVS are to help give London's half million evacuated mothers and children a happy homecoming.... Sir Henry Willink, Minister of Health, thanked on behalf of the Government all the hundreds of thousands of householders who have cared for mothers and children from bombed places. 'They have done one of the finest and hardest jobs of the war on the Home Front, 24 hours a day, seven days a week'. Mr Parsons came round this evening to say our ARP wardenship ceases as from today. This ends our work which we began in 1938.

May 4th Friday
The Wehrmacht is queuing up to surrender.... 'The collapse of the German Army on what was the British 2nd Army Front is too immense to visualise' writes one from inside the lines. The long columns struggling in are 'too big for us to take care of'.... 20 Generals were captured in 36 hours.... Shelterers in London's Tube last night drank their last cup of tea underground, and the Bun Special train has made its last run.

May 5th Saturday
Last night the great news came through that Montgomery gave Germans an ultimatum.... From today Germans will obey orders from the 21st Army Group. Hamburg radio, now under British control, was last night putting out the V signal.

Lord Haw-Haw's place was taken by Vaughan Thomas, who gave Hamburg its orders.... Yesterday evening 340 of our PoWs arrived at Paxhill Camp, one of the 'reception areas'. In the afternoon today, I with many others went there to help sew on the men's badges. Mrs Coxhead drove 6 of us in her car which, as it was a wet day, we appreciated. The mud everywhere at the camp is terrible, no escaping it. Our 'hut' was no.49, warmed with a stove in the middle and a canteen at the end next to the table where I worked. The men all looked well and had happy faces after being prisoners for so long a time. Most of the battledresses we adorned were new and all sorts of regiments – Armoured Corps, Gloucestershire and so forth. Waiting in the rain at the foot of Paxhill, for the bus to take me back in time for the Library, some kind man stopped his car and drove me, with two others also waiting, to the Post Office, for the bus was late if it ever came at all.

May 6th Sunday 299th week
In Copenhagen, Gestapo and Nazi sailors defying the ceasefire were still fighting.... They placed machine guns on the roofs and shot at patriots, wounding civilians. While crowds were celebrating Allied victory in Copenhagen, Danish quisling police fired into the midst of them.... Hitler and Goebbels are said to be buried in Berlin at an undiscoverable place. The last phase of the Burma campaign, mopping up trapped Japs and chasing the rest east into Siam, has begun.... Everyone is awaiting V-Day, bonfires are ready crowned with effigies of Hitler, Goering and Goebbels, shops decorated with red, white and blue.

May 7th Monday
The announcement of V-Day is expected any minute now.... This morning I made a V flag to hang out alongside my Jack when the day is announced, a red V on white.

May 8th Tuesday
Today is V-Day. The news came through yesterday evening and Tuesday and Wednesday are holidays. At 3 o'clock this afternoon an official announcement will be broadcast by the Prime Minister – Victory in Europe Day. The King will broadcast at 9 this evening. All over the world the report of the German surrender... was celebrated yesterday. Londoners could not wait for today, they crowded joyfully Buckingham Palace and Piccadilly Circus and all other big places. The lights made London look as if it were in flames. More than 100 planes roared over London in daylight, every kind from Spitfire to Fortress. Whitehall was in high spirits, but throughout dusk a constant stream of men and women passed round the Cenotaph paying homage to the dead of 30 years ago.... Goebbels, his wife and all his children have been found poisoned in Berlin. Their bodies were recovered by Russians. Neither Hitler's body nor Goering's have been found, maybe they are in hiding.... Boys and girls are happily building a bonfire on the

Common, they began yesterday evening. I went to the Avis' to hear the Premier's speech at 3 o'clock. It lasted for ¼ of an hour and he spoke well as he always does. He said Germans surrendered on Monday the 7th to the Allies at Rheims.

May 9th Wednesday

Yesterday was a tremendous day in London and 8 times during the day the King and Queen appeared on the Palace balcony to acknowledge the cheering crowds. The last time was just before midnight just as searchlights flashed across the sky and bombers dropped flares and coloured lights. About 11 the two Princesses with Guards officers left the Palace quietly and mingled with the crowd when their parents made their last appearance. The King spoke at 9 o'clock in the evening and again I enjoyed listening to him. After thanking God and then everybody, Services personnel and civilians alike for their war-time efforts, he said the years of darkness and danger are now 'please God, over for ever'. On the balcony of the Ministry of Health building in Whitehall the Prime Minister conducted the thousands of people below in singing 'Land of Hope and Glory', a tremendous climax to a day the like of which London has never seen before. He spoke to them as a friend 'This is your victory' and after cheerful speaking and cheering replies, he gave the V sign and the crowd burst into 'For He's a Jolly Good Fellow'. Waving his hat he left the balcony. Another wonderful thing was light everywhere. A procession of flaming torches came along from Pondcroft Road, and the Common to the bonfire, which was lighted about 9.30. A very large swastika and an effigy of Hitler in an old armchair were thrown on to the blaze. It was a perfect night for a bonfire and fireworks, fine and no wind. All the village was about and singing around it went on till midnight. Jose and Bernie Boulger and their friend George saw it from my bedroom window with Jock, but most of the time we watched it from my gate. Earlier in the evening at 7.30 we had a Thanksgiving service in the Church, a special service, details printed on a red leaflet given to all who came. The Church was full. The collection was for the Fund for repairing, in some cases rebuilding, bombed churches. Officially hostilities ended at 1 minute after midnight, but in the interest of saving lives, the ceasefire began yesterday all along the Front. The Channel Islands are also to be freed today. Weather forecasts are given in the papers today for the first time since September 1st 1939. No papers will be published tomorrow. And now the war in Europe is over, this war journal, begun on September 3rd 1939 comes to an end. I have written it every day, excepting of course on those days papers were not published, just for a record to dip into sometimes, to remind me of these 5½ years with its varied work, other than ARP, its anxieties and pleasures. It is impossible to give enough thanks to God for our great deliverance. Not until the war of Japan is over shall we have all our men home again. I pray that will not be a long war.

Helena Hall, Blue Gate, Lindfield. May 9th 1945.

Notes

—᠁—

1. See October 6th 1943.
2. All Saints Church, Lindfield possesses a wealth of fascinating old parish records, many of which were rescued from wartime paper salvage by Miss Hall. They include detailed accounts of the 'Overseers of the Poor' together with records from the Workhouse. The records date back to 1726. These are the papers Miss Hall mentioned.
3. Lord Haw-Haw, real name William Joyce, was a notable Nazi supporter and member of British right wing organizations. Based in Berlin, he broadcast German propaganda to England between 1939 and 1945. He was hanged for treason in 1946.
4. Lady Bagot was well known for her distinguished service to the sick and wounded in the Boer War and the First World War.
5. This refers to her book *Lindfield Past and Present*.
6. Reference to school evacuated to Lindfield.
7. Broadcast from the White Cliffs of Dover.
8. See plate 4.
9. Local auctioneers
10. See plate 8.
11. Typescript recollections of Frank Carey can be found in the Brotherton Library, University of Leeds, reference RAF 021.
12. Every ration card holder had to register with the shops of their choice to obtain food rations.
13. See plate 10.
14. See plate 8.
15. See plate 9.
16. The liner was the *City of Benares*, sunk on 17 September 1940. The event halted overseas evacuation.
17. See plate 1.
18. See plate 7.
19. Extract from a letter received from her brother Graham.
20. Quentin Reynolds was an American journalist who wrote critical articles about the Nazi regime when posted to Germany in 1933. During the war he came to England and broadcast on the BBC.

21. Calling Hitler by this name implied that he had non-Aryan, possibly Jewish blood. The use of this derogatory name by the BBC is an interesting example of the intensity of anti-German feeling prevalent at this time.

22. It is not clear which regiment this refers to as little information is available.

23. The Continental V Army was the creation of Douglas Ritchie, who became known as Colonel Britton. He broadcast over the radio to occupied Europe and was most famous for including the V for Victory in Morse Code in his radio programmes. This was aimed at bolstering morale and spreading passive resistance, which led into the V for Victory campaign.

24. The Zeebrugge raid was carried out in 1918 and was an attempt by the Royal Navy to block the port at Zeebrugge which was used by German U-boats. Although hailed as a success by the Allies, in reality it only blocked the port for a few days.

25. See plate 4.

26. This is an interesting example of how efforts were made to suggest Allied success.

27. Sir William Beveridge's report proposed a system of social security designed to protect the citizen 'from the cradle to the grave'. Published in December 1942, it became the blueprint for the modern British Welfare State.

28. Katin/Katyn. Who committed the murders remained a mystery until 1990 when the Russian authorities admitted that it was the Russian Secret Police (NKVD).

29. The entry refers to the 'Dam Busters' Raid.

30. This was at the Haywards Heath cattle market.

31. The appeal resulted in the 'Bevin Boys' where one tenth of all male conscripts aged 18 to 24 were directed to work in British coal mines.

32. Captain Roger Clutton Mead OBE, DFC, ADC, AFC. His service record can be found online at: http://www.rafweb.org/Biographies/Mead_RC.htm.

33. Refers to Katin/Katyn. See entry for April 27th 1943.

34. The full letter can be found in the journal.

35. See plate 3.

36. Ball bearings were important for the manufacture of armaments.

37. We have been unable to identify the island.

Bibliography

—ᨠᨠ—

Helena Hall's main sources:

BBC Radio News
Daily Sketch
Daily Graphic
Daily Mail
London Gazette
Evening Standard
Sussex County Magazine
Sunday Chronicle
Mid Sussex Times (also referred to as *The Mid, The Middy*)
Letters and ephemera from friends
First-hand experiences

Editors' sources:

Writing Ourselves: Mass-Observation and Literary Practices 2000, by Dorothy Sheridan, Brian Street and David Bloome. Hampton Press, Inc.
'The Liddell Diaries and British Intelligence History' by Eunan O'Halpin. *Intelligence and National Security*, Vol.20, No.4, December 2005, pp670–686.
Mid Sussex Times, Helena Hall's obituary, June 15th 1967.
Lindfield Past and Present by Helena Hall, 1959. 1977 edition published by The Society for the Preservation of Lindfield.
Letter from Val Bassano to East Sussex Record Office, November 16th, 1967. Source, East Sussex Record Office Archives
All Saints' Lindfield A Guide to the History of the Church, 1995 by Brian V. Field, All Saints' Church, Lindfield.
Illustrated Guide to All Saints' Church and the Village of Lindfield, Sussex 1961 by Helena Hall 1968 revised edition by J.H.P.
Lindfield Newsletter Spring 1990 Bulletin Number 54, The Society for the Preservation of Lindfield.

List of Plates

—ᵐ—

NB In the illustration credits, in brackets, the source appears first, followed by the body which granted permission to reproduce the illustration – either Lindfield Parish Council Archives (LPC) or East Sussex Record Office (ESRO). It has not been possible to locate the source of newspaper cuttings; either the source is missing or the relevant newspaper no longer exists.